GENDER AND AESTHETICS

Feminist approaches to art are extremely influential and widely studied across a variety of disciplines, including art theory, cultural and visual studies, and philosophy. *Gender and Aesthetics* carefully introduces and examines the role that gender plays in forming philosophical ideas about art.

The book discusses important topics within feminist aesthetics:

- Why were there so few women artists in the past?
- Art, pleasure, and beauty
- The role of gender in taste and food
- What is art and what makes an artist?
- Disgust, sublimity, and aesthetic values
- The body and the formation of subjectivity

The book introduces in clear language the role gender plays in our understanding of art, creativity, and aesthetic qualities. Philosophies of the past are examined for their influence over gendered ways of conceiving aesthetics; and contemporary theorists such as Arthur Danto and Luce Irigaray are situated in relation to feminist art practices. Each chapter concludes with a summary, and there is an extensive bibliography.

Carolyn Korsmeyer's style is refreshing and accessible, making the book suitable for students of philosophy, gender studies, visual studies, and art theory, as well as anyone interested in the impact of gender on aesthetics.

Carolyn Korsmeyer is Professor of Philosophy at the University at Buffalo, State University of New York. She is author of *Making Sense of Taste: Food and Philosophy* (1999) and the editor of several books on aesthetics, feminism, and literary theory.

UNDERSTANDING FEMINIST PHILOSOPHY
Edited by Linda Martin Alcoff

This major new series is designed for students who have typically completed an introductory course in philosophy and are coming to feminist philosophy for the first time. Each book clearly introduces a core undergraduate subject in philosophy, from a feminist perspective, examining the role gender plays in shaping our understanding of philosophy and related disciplines. Each book offers students an accessible transition to higher-level work on that subject and is clearly written, by an experienced author and teacher, with the beginning student in mind.

GENDER AND AESTHETICS
Carolyn Korsmeyer

FEMINISM AND MODERN PHILOSOPHY
Andrea Nye

FEMINISM AND EPISTEMOLOGY
Phyllis Rooney

FEMINISM AND PHILOSOPHY OF SCIENCE
Elizabeth Potter

GENDER
AND AESTHETICS

An introduction

Carolyn Korsmeyer

Routledge
Taylor & Francis Group

NEW YORK AND LONDON

First published 2004
by Routledge
29 West 35th Street, New York, NY 10001
simultaneously published in the UK
by Routledge
11 New Fetter Lane, London EC4P 4EE

Routledge is an imprint of the Taylor & Francis Group

© 2004 Carolyn Korsmeyer

Library of Congress Cataloging in Publication Data
Korsmeyer, Carolyn.
Gender and Aesthetics : an introduction / Carolyn Korsmeyer.
p. cm (Understanding feminist philosophy)
Includes bibliographical references and index.
1. Feminism and art. 2. Women in art. 3. Feminist theory. 4. Arts—Philosophy.
I. Title. II. Series.
N72.F45K67 2004
700'.1'03082—dc22
2003058656

British Library Cataloguing in Publication Data
A catalogue record for this book is available from the British Library

ISBN 0–415–26658–0 (hbk)
ISBN 0–415–26659–9 (pbk)

This book is dedicated to three girls who grew up together.
One became a dancer, one a writer, and one sang.
For the singer *in memoriam*

CONTENTS

ILLUSTRATIONS

ACKNOWLEDGMENTS

I am fortunate to belong to a dedicated writing group whose members patiently read and commented on earlier drafts of this book. I would like to thank Carrie Tirado Breman, Ann Colley, and Rosemary Feal. Larry Shiner, whose own scholarship has taught me a great deal, generously read the book in draft and offered his thoughtful advice. Andrew Schwartz commented on Chapter 6; Beth Ann Dobie contributed helpful information about the use of food in art; and Peg Brand offered suggestions about the project as it developed. Cynthia Freeland and Rachel Jones, in the guise of anonymous readers for the press, offered attentive and detailed comments that greatly aided the process of revision. I am grateful to all of them for their help.

The Office of the Dean of the College of Arts and Sciences at the University at Buffalo, State University of New York, generously supported the reproduction permissions for the illustrations. Siobhan Pattinson, editor at Routledge, was a great help obtaining permissions and seeing the book through to publication. Finally, I would like to thank Linda Alcoff for putting together the series, Understanding Feminist Philosophy, to which this book belongs.

INTRODUCTION

This book examines the theories and conceptual frameworks that operate in and around art and aesthetics. It addresses these subjects from a feminist perspective, that is, with attention to the roles that gender plays in the formation and application of ideas about artworks, creativity, and aesthetic value. This approach assumes that images, representations, and crafted expression of ideas are important not only for their beauty, virtuosity, or intrinsic value, but also because they are indicators of social position and power. Wherever there is power there are disparities in the ways that it is employed, and art is an enterprise where sex and sexuality, gender and social position, and cultural authority all have formidable roles. Aesthetic power is often hidden or overlooked; when one thinks of aesthetic value, the qualifier "mere" is often implicit, indicating the presumption that practical or moral values not only take precedence over aesthetic value but are cleanly separable from the way something looks, sounds, feels, or communicates emotions and ideas. Arts programs are among the first items to be cut from municipal budgets; they are often classified as contributors to the "enrichment" of public life that may be eliminated without major loss, comparable to skipping dessert with no sacrifice of nutrition. This is a grave error; art and aesthetic taste are powerful framers of self-image, social identity, and public values.

The philosophical discipline of aesthetics is by no means restricted to theories of art or of critical reception and enjoyment. Yet with the exception of artworks, few items of our world are assessed chiefly for their aesthetic qualities. For this reason, philosophy of art occupies center stage in aesthetic theory. "Philosophy of art" is intended to include all of the various arts, although the term "art" is elastic. It has a narrow use in English as well as some other languages insofar as it refers specifically to the graphic arts of painting, drawing, or printmaking, and when one first hears the word "art" a painting probably springs to mind. Much philosophical aesthetics already is predisposed to consider art in terms of the model of painting because of the influence of epistemology, which standardly employs visual examples in the analysis of perception and knowledge. Moreover, there has been an immense amount of feminist research on women in painting and in film. Such factors have tended to produce a skew towards the visual arts in aesthetic theory that this study shall attempt to avoid, though will not escape completely because of the stress on vision that the investigation of perception typically displays. "Art" also designates collectively all of the practices that cluster under the idea of fine art: music, theater, dance, poetry, prose literature, sculpture, architecture, and so on. What is more, sometimes "art" is employed expansively, such that popular movies and television series are included, but other times these media are designated (mere) entertainment rather than real art. Similarly, domestic crafts and artifacts made in non-western societies are sometimes classified as "art" but are often separately labeled "crafts." The theoretical commitments that underlie distinctions drawn between art and entertainment, and between art and craft, are also subjects of this investigation. All of the various forms of art are important for the issues of this book, though not all are treated with equal weight. I have focused on several art forms—chiefly painting, music, literature, performance—to serve as the models for how gender analysis might proceed in the labyrinthine realms of aesthetics.

Although reference to gender is now familiar in feminist discourse, the scope of that term remains a subject of contention. Writers in the early years of contemporary feminism in the 1970s distinguished between "sex" and "gender," where the former term refers to biological differences in the reproductive morphology of males and females, and the latter refers to the many ways that cultures mold their members into different social roles. But it has never been easy to spot the zone where biology leaves off and culture takes over. Indeed, some feminists are inclined to believe that even sex itself is a category whose identification is socially constructed rather than a natural given.[1] What is more, even if we acknowledge a biological foundation for sex identification, the term "gender" does not simply refer to the social roles assigned males and females. Often we find terms such as "masculine" and "feminine" assigned to systems of evaluation quite detached from real persons; "masculinity" and "femininity," as well as other gender-related terms, are not regularly exchangeable with "male" and "female." This means that a study of gender in aesthetics extends far beyond a study of women artists and demands an analysis of oppositional concepts and schemes of value whose meanings fluctuate in different historical and cultural contexts.

Gender analysis in philosophy proceeds on a number of different levels. Some of them pursue relatively obvious references that theorists make to males and females, though most require some probing beneath the veil of philosophical neutrality that theoretical language typically employs. The relevance of gender in theories is obvious when one considers concepts of femininity and masculinity as they directly pertain to the lives (upbringing, social position, education) of men and women. Examples of such overt gender abound, such as the numerous comments one can find in the history of philosophy about women's supposed creative limitations. Schopenhauer's remark that women are incapable of important artistic creativity, for example, is quite obviously about gender; its relevance is at the explicit surface of the text. Less noticeable, more covert gender is present in theories that are related to ideas of masculinity and femininity but presented in less direct terms. As we shall see, concepts such as beauty, taste, and genius possess this dimension. At the deepest level of gender significance lie entire conceptual frameworks that are founded on presumptions whose connection with gendered ways of thinking is by no means immediately evident. Here gender resonance is slant and opaque, and explicit references to masculinity and femininity are likely to be altogether absent. Consider an observation such as "Eating is a matter of bodily necessity but the subject has little to no philosophical relevance." On the surface this statement appears to be innocent and neutral; but as we shall see, it is a symptom of gendered thinking operating at its most tenacious and subterranean level. We might call this "deep gender." All of these levels are important for investigating the conceptual frameworks that guide philosophy—including aesthetics and philosophy of art.

From time to time throughout this study I shall make the claim that a concept is "gendered." By this I mean that some basic term used in philosophy and art theory appears to be generic or neutral; that is, it appears to refer to general human nature or to artists without regard to whether they are male or female. However, a gendered concept is one where there is a hidden skew in connotation or import, such that the idea in question pertains most centrally to males, or in certain cases to females. I consider hidden gender a particularly interesting force over thinking because it can be so insidious. Most of the time it is either nearly invisible or apparently trivial; and yet careful scrutiny reveals systematic meanings that exercise considerable influence on the framing of ideas. There are several modes of "gendering" to be found in concepts in aesthetics, including a practical mode that is evident when there are actual barriers erected, as was the case in periods of the past for women who wished to study painting or sculpture but were barred for reasons of assumed ability and propriety from studio settings. There is a conceptual mode that frames the very way we think; this is the one that most occupies this study. And there is a mode that exerts power over desire and fantasy that probably is most evident in fashion and personal choice—the roles one imagines oneself adopting, for example—none of which can be completely severed from traditional aesthetic norms. The multiple levels at which gender functions in and around concepts of art and aesthetics illuminate how central feminist analysis is to understanding culture in general.[2]

My investigation will center on fundamental concepts in aesthetic theory, such as art, artist, aesthetic, taste, beauty, and sublimity. These are components of the machinery of philosophical aesthetics that operate whenever artists create, critics criticize, and audiences appreciate. At the same time, this field has never proceeded from within one disciplinary perspective alone, and much of my line of thought owes a great deal to the efforts over the last several decades of scholars in different disciplines who have examined the practices that have excluded or otherwise negatively affected women's participation or recognition in various artistic fields. I have referred to only a fraction of this scholarship, and the notes and bibliography indicate to the reader paths into this vast literature. Many of these researchers have rummaged through archives seeking lost manuscripts and scores, revisited the collections of museums, drawn attention to the artistry of domestic artifacts, and criticized established thinking in literature, dance, theater, music, architecture, art history, film, photography. Scholars from these disciplines have also discovered a good deal about how gender itself is constructed in artistic milieus. Cultural studies has drawn attention to the potency of popular culture, which reminds us that we must not forget television and movies, popular music and advertising and fashion, nor should we ignore the perpetuation of aesthetic norms in other aspects of life, such as the stealthy power of cultural icons: singers and actors, for instance. Such performers often link artistic production with public longing and fantasy, and they exert more persuasion over us than we might want to admit—another facet of aesthetic authority.

One might anticipate that a study such as this would analyze the art that women produce in the hopes of discovering some kind of "feminine aesthetic" that has been operating in women's creative work as a kind of underground counter-tradition to a dominant "masculine" cultural norm. Sometimes scholars do locate female perspectives in opposition to their dominant culture within particular artistic movements, though attempts to generalize more broadly about the work of women have been sharply debated among feminist scholars.[3] Not only does the diversity of art produced by women defy stylistic generalization, but so does the diversity of women themselves. Women do not constitute a discrete class or a culture separable from larger social groups—no more than men do. The complexities of individual and group identities always include historical position and social factors such as class, religion, nationality, race, and ethnicity; these mingle with gender and sexual identity to make generalizations about all women's creative activity difficult.

Not only art but feminism itself demands the same caution. The term "feminist," whether it modifies a political movement, a perspective in academia, theorists, or artists, describes an orientation and a set of shared questions, but not conclusions, products, or strategies. More particularly, "feminist philosophy" does not comprise a group of theories that agree on every point, so looking for the feminist perspective on anything is always wrongheaded.

These cautions, however, do not restrict the relevance of gender analysis throughout culture; rather, they alert one to the complexities of gender and the fact that it is interpretable from many critical perspectives—as is the case with all philosophical subjects. Although as a theoretical category "feminism" does not define a uniform political or philosophical stance, there are common assumptions that inform the pursuit of feminist perspectives in aesthetics and art theory. Performance theorist Peggy Phelan puts it this way: "Feminism is the conviction that gender has been, and continues to be, a fundamental category for the organization of culture. Moreover, the pattern of that organization usually favours men over women."[4] This analytical common denominator does not presume that all feminist theory looks the same, nor that all feminist arts look the same, nor all work by women.

The scope of this study lies within what is broadly designated "western philosophy," which comprises theoretical traditions that trace their origins to theories born and bred in Europe. (This is a term more conceptual than geographical, since philosophical traditions that claim those roots extend from east Africa to Australia.) The first three chapters are historical and focus upon a critique of theoretical concepts and a discovery of the masculine bias they often manifest. These sections introduce a number of ways that gendered ideas operate in ideas about artists, fine art, craft, and aesthetic value. The argumentative procedure I follow relies on analysis of the system of binary opposites that organizes thinking about numerous philosophical topics. As feminists have long argued, gender asymmetries in theory as well as in practice are underwritten by venerable dualisms that pair mind and body, form and matter, intellect and sense, culture and nature, as well as other binary combinations. All of these are loosely aligned with distinctions between male and female and between masculine and feminine, usually to the detriment of the "feminine" term of a pair.

We start by investigating the traditional concept of the artist and by analyzing how the notion of the creator of art is heavily gendered as a masculine ideal. By this I mean that, in spite of the fact that there have always been women practitioners of the arts, the paradigm or model of the artist conjures up the image of a male creator—one who works alone or directs a crew of underlings, and who, at his very best, possesses the distinctly male trait of "genius." These are not timeless concepts but begin to develop in the European Renaissance, achieving their full range in the Romantic period, and they still hold considerable sway over our ways of thinking today.

What we now think of generically as art is usually fine art, a narrower designation that traditionally includes at its core architecture, sculpture, painting, poetry, and music. As the concept of fine art gradually developed from the Renaissance through the seventeenth century, some types of creativity, such as needlework, dropped out of consideration as "art" and become designated "craft." Those items now in the craft tradition include a good many of the domestic products made by women of all classes to beautify the home and make it function comfortably. The narrowing of the idea of art to fine art had notable consequences for the products that many women made, because theories of fine art began to demarcate art from all other products, including things made for daily use. Fine art at its most important is supposedly the product of genius, not just skill. It has its own, self-contained meaning and is valued in and of itself for its intrinsic properties. As the idea of fine art crystalized, it effectively eclipsed the many household artifacts produced by women which, however beautiful, had undeniable practical function.

The idea of fine art is connected to concepts of how that art is to be appreciated and what kinds of value it possesses. Chapter 2 takes us to the idea of "the aesthetic" itself, a term of value that encompasses art, natural beauty, and the ability to judge aesthetic quality by means of discriminating taste. The notion of good and bad taste can be a powerful framer of behavior, intimately connected to standards of beauty both artistic and personal. It is also a norm where factors such as social position, class, and leisure are especially pertinent. Taste was a concept that framed early modern aesthetic theory itself, so this section will review the history of aesthetics and the ideas at its core, such as beauty and sublimity, that themselves possess gender connotations. "Beauty" is a term that is associated with femininity both as it applies to the physical appearance of persons and to the qualities of certain kinds of artworks. By comparison, "sublimity" connotes both the unruly power of nature and the breadth of vision of the artistic genius. In these concepts of aesthetic value we find further elements that influence the ways that women and men, and women's and men's artistic activities, are assessed.

These opening chapters chiefly concern the ways in which theory produces and perpetuates gender bias in concepts of art, creativity, and aesthetic dispositions. Chapter 3 extends and amplifies this analysis by considering the practical implications carried in theory. While philosophy tends to stress conceptual frameworks above all else, we should also take note of the effects these frameworks have on the lives of real people: their possibilities and the ways they shape and perceive their worlds. Contemporary feminist scholars in the critical disciplines have spent considerable effort exhuming the lost women artists of history and bringing them to light so that we don't permit their individual efforts to be obscured by the far greater numbers of their male counterparts.[5] The barriers they faced are discussed here in terms of the discrepant opportunities for the (female) amateur in comparison with the (male) professional, especially in the eighteenth and nineteenth centuries when the concept of fine art was in ascendence among the middle- and upper-class arbiters of taste, and ideals of womanhood and propriety were particularly restrictive.

The fourth chapter interrupts the historical narrative and adjusts the focus of analysis to a deeper level in order to pose a background inquiry about aesthetics: what factors go into determining whether a topic is considered worthy of philosophical interest at all? Artworks have traditionally been a subject for philosophical discussion, as has discerning taste on aesthetic matters, but on what grounds? Literal taste, for example, has never secured a foothold in philosophy, nor have eating, food, and drink (except in some moral discussions where moderation is advised). These objects and activities are clearly important for life, but they have rarely if ever figured as topics for serious philosophical discussion; indeed, they have usually been regarded as beneath consideration. The reasons that account for this are gendered at the "deep level" outlined above, and reflection on food and eating illuminates from a distance the elements that frame concepts of art and aesthetic traditions. This chapter is a bridge of sorts: it looks back to the first three by situating philosophy of art in the context of questions about how philosophical issues are traditionally formulated. And it looks towards the discussion of contemporary theories of art in Chapters 5 and 6 and the deliberate violation of traditional aesthetic norms on the part of many artists practicing today. Because one of the many means by which artists have challenged art traditions is by employing food in their work, Chapter 4 serves as a connector to recent reversals of the aesthetic values of the past promoted by the anti-patriarchal artistic works that feminists have pioneered.

The final two chapters consider feminist artists who self-consciously reflect upon the legacy of the past and use it to make statements about the present and the future. Their efforts are situated in the context of two very different philosophical approaches: the formulation of general concepts of art within the analytic tradition that describes much Anglo-American philosophy, and the excavation of subjectivity and gender within psychoanalytically influenced movements incorporated in some influential European theories. Attempts to define art are discussed in Chapter 5, which pays particular attention to the violation of traditional concepts of art by means of anti-art and philosophical responses to these historical changes. Feminist contributions to the revision of thinking about art are placed in relation to earlier anti-art movements and to contemporary philosophical reflections on the nature of art. Chapter 6 considers the deliberate feminist appropriation of philosophical theory in the making of art, paying special attention to the employment of hypotheses about the construction of gender and sexual desire on the part of feminist and postfeminist artists.

These chapters discuss contemporary theories from two schools of thought that are often considered rivals: the analytic and postanalytic approaches that largely characterize philosophy practiced in the English-speaking world, which has produced some major literature on general theories of art; and postmodern continental European approaches that make use of deconstruction and psychoanalysis, which have influenced large numbers of feminist art theorists as well as practicing artists.[6] Although these different schools of thought sometimes seem to have little in common, I believe their rivalries are often exaggerated. Here I have emphasized their similarities by pointing out their shared roots and by stressing historical continuities of the questions they pursue. The themes I select to illuminate their common tradition concern some of the most challenging aesthetic values that art can present: the classic sublime with its foundation in terror, and the contemporary evocation of disgust as an aesthetic effect in some of the most confrontational and difficult feminist art.

Much feminist art repudiates the aesthetic values of femininity extolled in earlier times, including the very basic notion of beauty. Indeed, many feminist artists have turned the idea of beauty inside out and experimented with arousing disgust and other disturbing emotions in the process of disclosing, questioning, or debunking myths of female identity. But the prevalence of disgust in art of today is more than a critique of traditional ideals of beauty. It also signals a turn of emphasis in philosophy generally to matters of "the body," so long the subordinate counterpart to "the mind." Philosophy has traditionally privileged mind—abstract, nonphysical, intellectual—over the body—concrete, material, sensuous. This ancient value structure, however, has been eroded in much recent philosophical thinking, and one of the multiple influences leading in that direction has been feminist critiques of the tenability of the mind–body distinction. That challenge as it appears in aesthetics is one of the subjects charted by this book, which proceeds from critiques of aesthetic theories of the past to construction of new speculations about creativity and art based upon the body, its desires, and its social and historical positions. With the concluding consideration of the body and its physicality, we can see feminist endeavors advancing ideas about art and aesthetics in both theory and artistic practice.

1

ARTISTS AND ART

A brief history of concepts

What is art? What is an artist? Each concept is defined in terms of the other: who counts as an artist partly depends on what is produced, and whether a product is a work of art partly depends on who produced it. Let us begin by considering the concept of the creator: the person who makes art, whether that art be poetry or painting or music, architecture or sculpture or dance. Of course, by listing these particular arts, I have already importantly prejudged the terms of discussion, for the answers would be different had I included the person who makes quilts or jigsaw puzzles or wedding cakes; or the person who spins, weaves, or throws pottery; or who blows glass or manufactures furniture or binds books. As we shall see in the course of this chapter, the identification of certain persons as artists changes through history with shifting categories of things that are considered works of art.

The contemporary notion of an artist is inseparable from ideas about self-expression, imagination, and creativity, all of which suggest a particular kind of freedom that artists are accorded. Today an artist is often considered to be a breed of free spirit, a nonconformist unbound by social convention or pedestrian rules. At best, this freedom may indicate genius, even though the originality of genius is often misunderstood until the passage of time delivers a verdict. Thus this vision of artists often pictures them as romantically isolated and lonely figures. This chapter will question the origin and conceptual framework that supports this popular image of the artist in order to determine why there are so few women in the lists of recognized artistic geniuses. Indeed, especially at certain periods of history, it has been difficult even to conceive of women fitting into the image of a fully autonomous artist who creates for the sake of creation alone. Why is this, and what does it indicate about the role of gender distinctions in concepts of creativity?

Historians have produced considerable scholarship about the patterns of exclusion that, at significant periods of the past, have all but barred women from entering fields such as painting or sculpture or musical composition, and that have hampered their advancement and recognition in other fields such as literature.[1] Our focus now, however, is not chiefly on the history of exclusionary education or social barriers; these are contingent practices that change with the passage of time and the exigencies of situation. Rather, we are interested in the nature of the very concepts that shape philosophy of art and aesthetic norms, the theoretical frameworks that influence social practice. Here we also find gender distinctions and tenacious concepts of "femininity" and "masculinity" in play.

Conceptual foundations

This investigation of the way that gender operates in aesthetics requires a preface: a review of foundational assumptions about human nature and of what makes possible the achievements of culture and civilization. Art is a phenomenon comprising significant components of culture, and the best of it is taken to present reflection and insight into human life and its meaning. Those people who produce art of profundity and lasting value, whether satirical, taxing, tragic, comic, uplifting, or beautiful, are accorded special honor and considered to embody a lofty and difficult level of human achievement. The concept of the artist-creator is founded on beliefs about what qualities of human beings give them the capacities for the highest levels of cultural accomplishment; according to venerable tradition, *rationality* is the essential mental capability that grounds human achievement in general. Feminist perspectives on reason and rationality are directed at all areas of philosophy, though they are cited in aesthetics less often than they might be, probably because art and aesthetic values are frequently and facilely associated with "non-rational" areas of endeavor, with intuition and imagination and feeling. But at the same time the governance of these mental activities, which separates inspiration from nonsense and aesthetic insight from mere eccentricity, requires a disciplined and tough mentality that is traditionally considered to be rooted in rational capabilities.

The concept of an independent rational faculty that separates man from beast and thereby describes essential human nature dominates western theories of knowledge, of morals, of politics, of human nature, of culture; indeed, there is no area of philosophy not under its long influence. It is also one of the most complexly marked of theoretical concepts, operating in different forms in various contexts, modifying not only gender but also the position of subordinated social groups in general. Though often not explicit, rationality has significance for the idea of creativity and the ability to be trained in artistic skills, as well as for the autonomy of mind that is requisite for inventiveness and originality.

First, some general observations: reason is traditionally designated the faculty of the mind that distinguishes human from nonhuman activity. This is both a descriptive and a normative generalization, for it is believed to be a fact that only human beings exercise rationality. To some extent they thereby escape the laws of nature and are capable of building cultures and civilizations, exercising a degree of choice over how they live that is not possible for other animals. Therefore reason also has a value-laden meaning: it is not only an essential human trait that virtually defines what it means to be a human being, but it is also our best quality, the one that permits artistic achievement, moral choice, scientific knowledge. These general claims about rationality pertain to all human beings—male, female, past, present, familiar, foreign.

And yet: different degrees of reason are frequently invoked to account for social difference and for what, in certain periods of history, is considered to be a "natural" superiority of some people over others, a superiority of mind and temperament that validates hierarchies of power, education, and rank. It is by no means restricted to the superiority of male over female; one can find such reasoning at work in accounts that try to justify slavery, for example, or in speculations about the persistence of class and economic differences in societies. Such rationales are consistently and systematically invoked to describe gender difference in social roles and abilities; for in numerous theoretical contexts reason is considered the chief trait that elevates male over female within our species. That is to say, while females possess reason, they exercise it less adeptly than do males, thus making them, in the opinion of many influential philosophical and religious systems, less capable of self-governance and therefore the natural subordinates of men in all circumstances from domestic life to politics.[2] The dual role of reason—not only to mark the difference between human and nonhuman but also to distinguish among members of the human species—has resulted in a tangled set of conceptual counterparts that connect reason with "masculine" activities and traits, and nonreason with "feminine" correlates. Insofar as women are human, they are rational. Insofar as they are feminine, they are drawn into a system of symbols that represent the nonrational regions of mind and uncontrolled and inchoate nature. Note that this division of abilities and traits does not really separate males from females. It is more apt to separate what are extolled as human/male traits from symbols and concepts that are contrastingly labeled "feminine." Further complicating the situation, in some circumstances characteristics that fall on the "feminine" side are appropriated by male subjects; this happens with values associated with artistic creativity and discerning taste, as we shall soon discover. Because both the sense and the reference of gendered terms can be ambiguous, understanding their import always requires careful attention to historical and social context.

While our focus is on aesthetics, it is worth bearing in mind the widespread influence of these ideas in virtually all fields of philosophy, and relatedly in those areas of science, politics, psychology, and religion that historically justify their scope and methods by reference to philosophical foundations. All of these areas are tied together, so constraints in one field reverberate in others.[3] In brief: in epistemology—the study of the nature of perception and the formation of knowledge—the paradigmatic knower is modeled on a concept of male nature which is capable of exercising reasoning abilities to their fullest extent, while to female nature is ascribed a contrasting emotional and intuitive temperament. Because emotions are standardly regarded as unreliable and idiosyncratic, this description has both theoretical and practical consequences not only for female educational and scientific achievement, but also for the idea of female moral reliability. In ethics and moral philosophy, the model of the person who exercises responsibility, possesses just principles, and executes free choice and clear decision-making is the male agent. By comparison, the image of femininity is merciful and kind but also vacillating, swayed by particular circumstances and practical exigencies, and apt therefore to be inconsistent and irresponsible. This female moral sensibility may be seen in wicked or good lights. Hamlet railed, "Frailty, thy name is woman!" when he worried that his mother had succumbed to sinful sexual desire; but the Victorian sentimental image of the "angel in the house" pictured the chaste mother of the home as imbued with natural kindness and goodness, the all-forgiving source of love. Neither the flattering nor the unflattering characterization, however, equips women to exercise public power. The public sphere of policy and law-giving is conceived as both masculine and the purview of males, for political life requires that one be capable of formulating dispassionate general laws to govern society with disinterested justice. The domestic sphere is conceived as a female domain, where matters of particular concern and quotidian remedies for the ups and downs of personal life are addressed.

Generally speaking, the world of male values is abstract and associated with the "mind," that of the female, concrete and particular and associated with the "body." It has seemed to follow in philosophies from Aristotle onward that cognitive abilities and natural proclivities have been unequally distributed in males and females.[4] In what has become a rather infamous series of binary oppositions often analyzed from feminist perspectives, human traits and activities are paired in conceptual hierarchies that systematically place women and "feminine" traits and activities in subordinate positions. Reason and the mind, justice, activity, and public responsibility are all identified as masculine domains where males best function, while emotion and the body, whim, passivity, and domesticity are assigned to the feminine realm.[5] In short, no matter what activity we examine, the conceptual framework that organizes ideas about who is best equipped to do what, tends to place the male function as the most important for all but domestic roles (and even here, it is the male head who is supposed to govern the household).

As we shall see, this hierarchy has deep implications for notions of creativity and the idea of the artist. Even though the image of the artist changes and develops in different historical contexts, one detects in both theoretical and practical dimensions assumptions about the differential capacities of male and female artists. Notably, this occurs in spite of the fact that when theorists investigate the creative power of the artist, reason often does not take center stage but gives way to imagination, inspiration, intuition, or emotion. If these are contrasted with the rational faculties, and if the rational faculties are gendered as masculine, then why do we not see female characteristics clustering around ideas of artistic creativity? This question will be addressed in more detail later, where we shall see how the split between femaleness and the exercise of the highest, most strenuous, and difficult human capabilities promotes an image of women as closer to nature and more distant from the construction of civilized achievement. Although metaphors of labor, midwifery, and birth are prevalent in discourse about artistic creativity, women are associated with procreativity—a natural function that ties them to their bodies and to "animal" reproduction; it is men who are assigned the role of artistic creativity free from biological destiny. All of this has a very long history, and a review of this history can help us see the depth and extent of the gendering of the concept of the artist.

This chapter will lead up to some modern concepts regarding the artist that are the immediate precursors to our own times. These include ideas about creativity, imagination, and skill that have gradually emerged since the Renaissance, attaining systematic theoretical justification in the eighteenth century. Not only is this period formative of the ideas about creative artists that, by and large, still hold sway today (despite the fact that they were shaped some time ago), but also the ideas developing in this era combine with reigning concepts of human nature and womanhood to imbue the idea of the artist with an especially virulent gender prejudice. But before tackling these more recent influences over our concept of the artist, it will be useful to consider the older historical backdrop against which modern concepts of the arts emerged.

The idea of the artist: ancient predecessors

When we discuss the classical Greek and Roman roots of concepts of art and art-making, we also have to be specific about which art forms are to be considered, reminding us once again that the notion of "artist" is inseparable from ideas about what counts as "art." Today the general term "art" chiefly refers to the fine arts, such as painting or literature or music or theater. But this itself is a modern development, one that, as we shall see, had especially important consequences for the idea of the gender of the artist. However, no generic term that encompasses all of the genres of art was in use at the time that early philosophers such as Plato and Aristotle wrote about the subject we now designate "philosophy of art." When ancient writers discuss artists, they distinguish among sculptors, painters, poets, musicians, orators, and so on. The Greek term that is often translated "art" in English is *techne*, which is better translated as "skill in making or doing" and can be applied to any kind of purposeful human activity. Although we now use the term "art" in contrast with non-artistic artifacts such as manufactured objects, older senses of this term employed it in general contrast with nature—i.e. to that which is not a product of human endeavor.[6]

While there is continuity between ancient theories of art and our own, the concepts employed have a history of development; we cannot simply match term for term and obtain an accurate picture. One important thing that the absence of a generic term "art" signals is that the distinction between fine and applied arts was not yet in use. So rather than singling out artists from (say) engineers or craftspeople, the term we translate "art" denoted particular activities of doing or making something which contributed to the welfare of society, including not only what we now call the arts but also what we would designate sciences and crafts.[7] Because we often read the history of philosophy for clues about our own intellectual heritage, we tend to select comments about painting or sculpture or poetry or music, of which there are many in the ancient texts. In so doing we ignore oratory and recitation, not to mention metallurgy, shipbuilding, and other activities that the Greeks would have considered "arts" as well. Our modern distinction between fine art and craft or applied art is also culture-specific. It is not found in traditions such as those that arose in Japan, China, or India, for example, although those civilizations produced huge numbers of finely-wrought artifacts that now reside in art museums, as well as a large literature on art and standards for aesthetic evaluation.[8] This is yet another indication that the products that count as art also have a history that shifts in tandem alongside the changing idea of the artist.

In the first century AD the Roman historian Pliny the Elder wrote his encyclopedic *Natural History*, which includes many chapters on artists of the ancient world. Pliny is our chief source of information about these ancient artists because he compiled his work by consulting the earlier literature that was still extant in his time but which has since been lost or destroyed; by his own reckoning he used over 2,000 sources.[9] (He died at Pompeii during the most famous and destructive eruption of Vesuvius in the year 79.) Today we have editions of his work that select the portions on art and group them together, but Pliny's own organization proceeds differently. He deals with bronze sculpture in the context of discussing metals, with painting as a subdivision of the manufacture of pigments, and with clay modeling and marble carving in the treatment of those natural elements and the way they are shaped and used. Not all of his approach is unfamiliar, however. Although he organizes his discussion of sculptors, painters, and architects by medium, at the same time it is clear that he also believes they represent shared concerns, such as rendering nature accurately, commemorating important personages, and making objects of skill and beauty. In other words, despite a method of grouping these arts that we would not replicate today, Pliny singles out the artists of his own past with familiar admiration as he notes the esteem in which they were held, the innovations they introduced, and sometimes quite precisely the monetary value their works were assigned. (In a criticism of what he considered the degenerate work of his own time, he extolls the artists of the past, "when the noblest of their nation thought art one of the paths to glory, and ascribed it even to the gods."[10])

Pliny makes several observations about women and the arts that prefigure patterns of thought that we shall see repeated in later times. First of all, because his goal is completeness, he notes the several women artists, particularly painters, for whom there is an ancient record. It doesn't take very long: "Women too have been painters," he notes, and goes on to name seven. He seems to consider it unusual but not outlandish that women should paint and engage in other mimetic arts; indeed, he records an ancient story according to which the first portrait modeler was a girl who drew the shadow of her lover's profile on the wall:

> The maiden invented the art of modelling figures in relief. She was in love with a youth, and while he lay asleep she sketched the outline of his shadow on the wall. Delighted with the perfection of the likeness, her father, who was a potter, cut out the shape and filled in the outline with clay; the figure is still preserved at Corinth.[11]

From such accounts alone one might conclude that women artists were simply in the minority in the ancient Mediterranean world. But other observations complicate the picture considerably. Pliny describes the erection of statues in cities, a practice that was chiefly for the purpose of commemorating and honoring the deed of some citizen. A few were erected to women, but the Roman senator Cato objected to the practice of setting up statues to honor Roman women. Apparently the presentation of female images in public, standing in for their real counterparts, represented something less than appropriate to conservative Romans.

Mimesis: illusion and reality

This is the heyday of the mimetic or "imitation" theory of art, which regarded many types of "making," including painting, sculpture, poetry, and music, as essentially representations or imitations of reality. What counts as an "imitation" is loosely construed and does not mean slavish copying. The mimetic relationship between art and reality varies with medium: painting and sculpture reproduce the look of persons and objects; music can represent not only sounds of nature and voices, but also moods and feelings; the plots of tragic poetry (as Aristotle maintains) imitate action and life. Imitation theory judges art not only for beauty and virtuosity, but also for insightful representation which enlightens audiences about complicated or painful themes. The Roman poet Horace (65–8 BC) summed up the combination of aesthetic and cognitive value credited to mimetic art when he asserted that the best poetry instructs while pleasing. The mimetic theory of art received its first theoretical examination several centuries before Pliny with Plato's highly critical analysis in the *Republic*. Skillfully mimetic visual products such as sculptures and paintings are capable of such realistic renderings that they can actually fool the eye of the beholder. The artist who could make something visually indistinguishable from nature—or even superior to nature—was held in especially high esteem by most Greeks, though not by Plato, who mistrusted such tricks played on the senses and feared their effects on the intellect, for by deceiving vision they replace truth with illusion. In contrast, Aristotle considered poetic mimesis to be an important means by which one can come to understand difficult truths of living.[12] Aristotle considered poetry to be more philosophical than history because its rendering of what could happen to a person has more universal resonance than a chronicle of particular facts that actually did happen.

Pliny himself praises artistic visual illusion and the skill of painters who could actually deceive viewers into believing that painted objects were real. The most well-known of his tales features a contest between Zeuxis and Parrhasios over who could paint most realistically. Zeuxis drew a picture of grapes so lifelike that the birds flew down to peck them. When Parrhasios presented his painting, Zeuxis reached to remove the cloth that covered it and discovered that his fingers touched only the painted surface. He conceded that Parrhasios had won the contest, for while Zeuxis had fooled birds, Parrhasios had deceived another man. More intriguing illusions for considering gender are recounted in the several tales of artists and patrons becoming enamored of the images of women they created. When paintings depicted human beings, one of the pitfalls of wonderful mimesis was that the image was so lovely and lifelike that it actually inspired desire—a longing to possess the painted image that was as strong as if the subject were alive. The story of Pygmalion is the most famous of these: the sculptor Pygmalion carved a statue of a woman so beautiful that he fell hopelessly in love; in pity, the gods granted her life. In the absence of divine intervention, artists have to settle for the original model, but even in these cases the role of woman is regarded as both object of desire and work of art. Here is an anecdote from Pliny about the painter Apelles, so praised for his skill that Alexander the Great permitted no one else to render his likeness in paint.

Alexander gave him a signal mark of his regard: he commissioned Apelles to paint a nude figure of his favourite mistress Pankaspe, so much did he admire her wondrous form, but perceiving that Apelles had fallen in love with her, with great magnanimity and still greater self-control he gave her to him as a present, winning by the action as great a glory as by any of his victories. He conquered himself and sacrificed to the artist not only his mistress but his love, and was not even restrained by consideration for the woman he loved, who, once a king's mistress, was now a painter's.[13]

The conflation between the painted image of Pankaspe and the actual woman (or at least the body of the actual woman, for Pankaspe's own point of view is quite absent in this story) is profound—not to mention the fact that she was treated as chattel, however dear chattel, and given away in the manner in which her painting might be passed from hand to hand. In one form or another this switch between being an active subject and being a painted and admired image reappears throughout the history of representational art, well into our own times. It is a role that especially afflicts women, more particularly, women of a certain type—young, beautiful, possessible, sometimes exotic. Look for it in future stories.

Musing on creativity

It is in the theories of antiquity that we discover the germs of ideas about genius and artistic inspiration that have had profoundly different import for male and female creators. For it is also an ancient idea that the creative power of poets and musicians comes from a divine source, the poet himself being a conduit between external inspiration and artistic product. In myth the sources of inspiration are personified in the figures of the Muses. The number of Muses and the arts with which they were associated vary with time and place and were not fixed until relatively late antiquity, though today we picture them as nine female figures who embody the spirit of some art form and figuratively inspire a (male) human creator. Considering the Muses shifts focus away from graphic and sculptural arts, for they are the founts of poetry and music. The Greek cultures that engendered the myth of the Muse held poetry in all its forms in especially high esteem and considered this form of artistic creativity the one most likely to be divinely inspired.

Calliope, often considered the chief among the Muses, presided over epic poetry and eloquence. Erato's domain was love poetry, Euterpe's was music, Melpomene's, tragedy; Thalia: comedy; Polyhymnia: sacred and heroic songs; Terpsichore: dance and lyric poetry. Two of the Muses oversaw areas we would not classify today as arts: Clio was the Muse of history, Urania of astronomy. (This is a reminder that poetry was long considered a source of historical record, and that astronomy—and mathematics—were and still are associated with music.) The Muses are represented as young, lovely women, associated with the musician god Apollo. They initiate what becomes a long tradition of attributing to some feminine force the inspiration a man needs to create. Their original role as figures for music and poetry suggests that they take the form of voices whispering in the ear, perhaps even maddening the poet into flights of creativity that ordinary mental capacities such as reason cannot accomplish. Indeed, this picture of the inspired creator led Plato in the Ion to discount poets as sources of wisdom, for they create when out of their heads rather than with the guidance of the intellect. While most of the recorded poets of ancient times are men, Sappho of Lesbos (c. 620– c. 565 BC) was extolled in her own time and for centuries to come as the most brilliant of lyric poets. For the most part, however, the personification of creative impulses in a feminine form does not record or honor actual female creativity. Quite the contrary, mythologizing feminine creativity by ascribing it to nonhuman beings pushes actual women to the margins of artistic activity—in deceptively complimentary terms—and assigns to men the social role of actually creating art.[14] Because of the long influence of classical and classicist ideals over European traditions, such images have persisted well into modern times. For example, Auguste Rodin suggests the auxiliary role of women to male artists in his eroticized portrayal of The Poet and the Muse (c. 1905), a composition repeated in The Eternal Idol.

We can find an extremely subtle and complicated gendering of a theory of creativity in Plato's Symposium, which is a dialogue dedicated to speeches about love that is set during a drinking party celebrating the winner of Athens' annual prize for tragic poetry. It features Diotima, the one and only female speaker in all of Plato's work, though she "speaks" by means of an account related by Socrates, and she is not literally present since he is telling a story of her tutelage when he was a young man. Socrates relates how this wise priestess demonstrated to him the true nature of love and the objects of love. All of us seek immortality, argues Diotima, both the prolongation of ourselves that children represent, and the more abstract, lasting creations of our minds that artistic or intellectual work produces. The true lover pursues

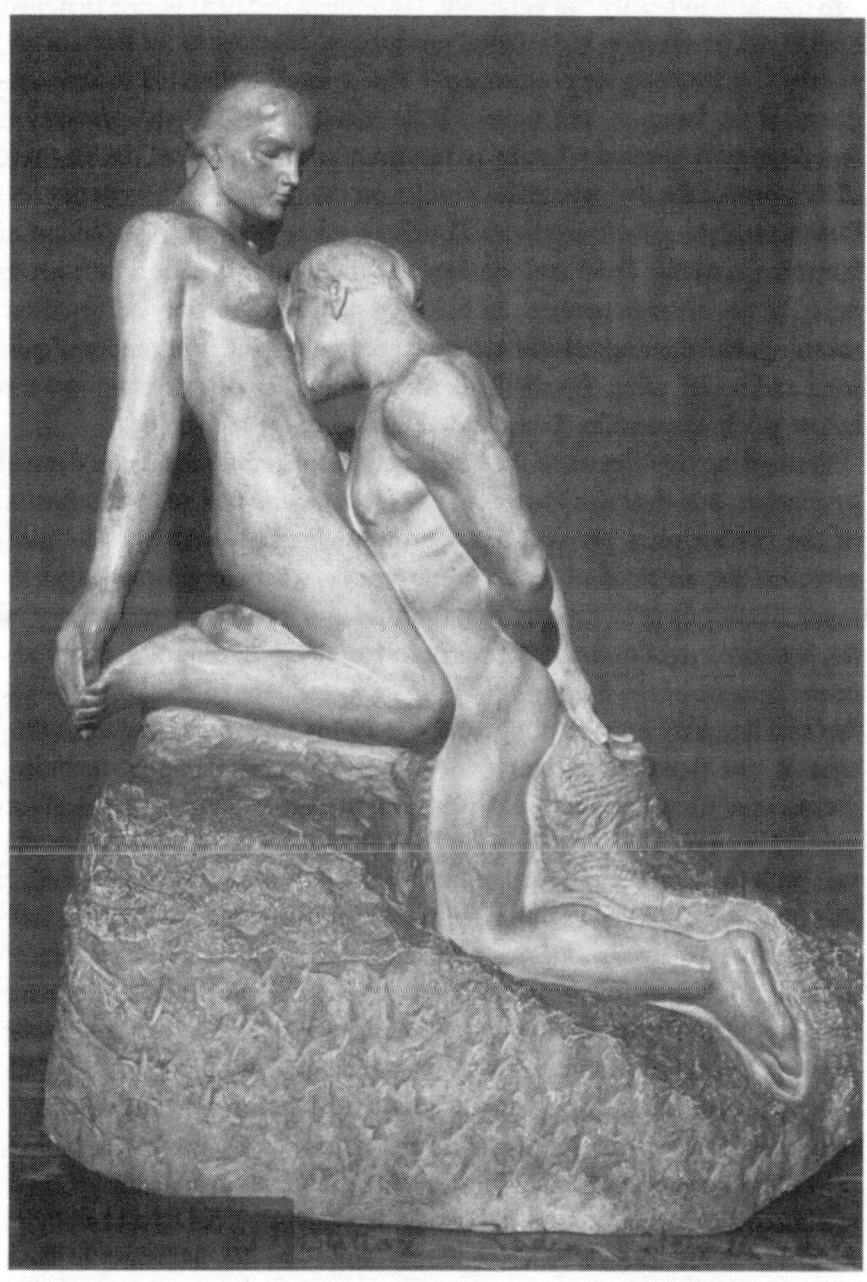

Figure 1 Auguste Rodin, *The Eternal Idol*, c. 1905. Réunion des Musées Nationaux/Art Resources, New York.

"giving birth in beauty," an enigmatic (and much debated) phrase that links both actual procreation and cultural production, whether in the form of art, poetry, law, learning, or philosophy.[15] This speech is directed to the male guests at the banquet, and there is little reason to think that Socrates has female creators in mind when he relates the story. Nonetheless, the language of this part of the dialogue relies heavily on the imagery of pregnancy and birth to analyze artistic creativity. This is an example of the detachment of feminine concepts from real women and their appropriation by men to describe the creative process, an instance of the complexity of gendered meanings and their mixed and complex correlation with the gender of persons and social roles. We shall see more examples of this phenomenon below when we consider the extended history of artistic genius.

Though the significance of the birth-metaphors in the *Symposium* is debated by scholars, it is clear that Plato does not place procreation and reproduction of the species on a par with artistic or intellectual creativity. His most extended discussion of art occurs in the *Republic*, where he acknowledges the tremendous power of the arts over the soul and the polis, concluding that the just state ought to control or outright ban the most beautiful poetry and music because of the dangers they pose to society. The mimesis of art—the fact that it merely imitates things and events—is a barrier to understanding what is true about reality. Moreover, it gives us many pleasures, including pleasures of the senses, and such pleasures are apt to numb the critical faculties. Mimesis substitutes illusion for truth, and it arouses emotions that war with the intellect and further hinder the philosophic quest for truth.[16] The importance of Plato's philosophy for gendered ideas about art is indirect, for he mistrusts mimesis generally, no matter who its maker. But his influential metaphysical distinction between the eternal, abstract, intellectual world of ideal Forms—the truly *real* world—and the transient, particular, sensuous world of physical objects feeds the dualism between mind and body that has such disparate significance for both male and female and for masculine and feminine concepts. In the course of this study we shall see how the deep gender of mind–body dualism plays out in aesthetic concepts, including the distinction between beauty and sublimity, the disparity of evaluation of women's and men's products, and even the exclusion of foods from among objects counted as art.

Art-making: individuals and groups

In this sampling of comments from ancient sources I have selected those that describe the individual maker of art, for example the single poet infused with inspiration from the presiding Muse. However, this model is not appropriate for all art forms. Many of the artifacts that we value for their aesthetic quality and their artistry are not the products of a single artist to whom any special creative vision could be ascribed. For much of recorded history, objects for various purposes were produced in workshops where numerous skilled artisans were trained to execute commissions for the noble and the wealthy, and for secular, religious, or private ends, and there are numerous examples of arts where teams of people contribute to producing either an extensive body of work or works of particular size or complexity. This is true of some art forms at any period of history, such as architecture and theater production; and it was notably the case with the arts with which medieval Europe is most associated, such as the giant gothic cathedrals whose construction spanned many years and required the talents and efforts of several generations, or the illuminated manuscripts and tapestries which were produced in monasteries. Some of the latter were enormous (the Bayeux Tapestry, which is actually an immense embroidery, is over 200 feet long) and were not the projects of one individual. It was the job of monasteries, the repositories of scholarship, to preserve learning by copying important texts both scriptural and philosophical, many of which were beautified with margin drawings and elaborate lettering. This shared creative work was conceived as a service to God. This kind of artistic production, no matter how wonderful the product, simply does not lend itself to inspired diversion or expressions of individual imagination. Teams of women and men together may have produced some of these works, and we have only a few records of their identities. They were not always anonymous, however; indeed one Claricia included not only her signature but her self-portrait in the tail of a "Q" in a twelfth-century psalter. It would be unfounded, however, to conclude that some universal drive for individual artistic self-expression burst forth in this letter, as enthusiasts of the expression theory of art might venture to claim. In fact, Claricia may have just been a bit bored at the time, indulging in a piece of doodling that turned out well. While we do have some records of those who worked on them, manuscript illuminations by and large are not the kind of works that invite individual signature. They are produced in a context that does not single out the artist for particular honor,

Figure 2 Illuminated letter Q, signed Claricia. German psalter from Augsberg, late twelfth century. The Walters Art Museum, Baltimore.

even though the great illuminations manifest obvious skill, care, and inventiveness. But the point is that the concept of the artist as a lone individual genius expressing his ideas in the free exercise of imagination is appropriate for only a limited sort of art-making. If we restrict our concept of the artist to this figure alone, then not only will we overlook a good deal of work by women but the efforts of lots of men as well. And although it is getting ahead of the game to mention film in this historical review, the problem of fitting "teamwork" creativity into the concept of "the" artist continues with many arts today, including the complex endeavors of film-making and television production.

There are also entire bodies of cultural products that are made within societies where this concept of the artist does not obtain, including the arts of many tribal and traditional cultures, the products of which are variously classified "art" or "craft," and the makers of which can rarely be identified as specific individuals.[17] Both philosophers of art and museum curators confront similar difficulties in deciding how to present objects of different cultures in the frameworks of our contemporary art theories and institutions. The distinction drawn between art and craft leads us to the modern idea of the artist, which focuses almost exclusively on the maker of what we now call "fine art," a concept to which we now turn.

Fine art and the modern concept of the artist

As we can already see with this brief review of ideas concerning the arts in earlier times, up until recently there was no commonly utilized category that unified all of the different genres of art. Artifacts were more often classified according to their media or even their functions, though the media themselves were sometimes hierarchically ranked. The material manipulations of sculpture and painting placed these arts in a lower, more physically-bound category than the inspired works of the poets, for example. Works in all media were admired if they performed their assigned functions with grace and elegance, and those who made them were praised for their skill and artistry. The categories of art have always been, and no doubt always will be, somewhat fluid.

However, in the early modern period of the seventeenth and eighteenth centuries, there arose a conceptual and practical division that exerted particular power over the idea of the artist and brought into sharp relief presumptions about his gender: the concept of fine art. Fine art is contrasted with practical or applied arts, crafts, and popular entertainment. It singles out works that are produced for their *aesthetic* value alone, in contrast to works that are made also for some practical function (such as eating utensils, clothing, and cushions). With this distinction, the term "artist" came properly to apply to the creator of one of the fine arts, whereas "craftsman" or "artisan" designated the maker of a functional object designed not only for beauty but for use.

The emergence of a fine-art tradition has a long, complex, and somewhat debatable history. Some theorists place the development of a "modern system of the arts" as late as the eighteenth century.[18] Others consider it more or less in place by the end of the Renaissance. While perhaps it was not until the modern period that the idea of fine art was fully framed, certainly during the Renaissance, especially in Italy, there was a self-conscious and concerted effort on the part of workers in certain media to raise the status of their efforts by means of reconceptualizing their products. Those who worked with materials that demand a degree of manual labor—painters and sculptors and architects—desired to raise their social station, and this required a revision of the category designating their specialized art forms. They sought to be recognized as contributors to the liberal rather than to the mechanical arts, that is, to the arts that further human understanding. The early Renaissance followed a late classical categorization of "liberal" arts (including rhetoric, poetry, mathematics, among other disciplines) and the "servile" or "vulgar" arts that involve physical labor or entertainment and are produced for some utilitarian end.[19] Painting, carving, casting, and hewing involve physical effort and a degree of dirt and messiness, and for some time the physicality of these activities was considered a barrier to classifying them as liberal, free, "intellectual" endeavors serving the higher calling of the mind. Artists in these media strove to be considered creators along the lines of the cleaner disciplines of music and poetry, where little physical effort is required. Advocates on behalf of architecture separated the intellectual demands of the engineering and design of complex structures from their actual physical building, which involves the undeniably physical labor of carpentry, masonry, and so on. The talent and skill required of the designer, it was argued, elevates this utilitarian art form above mere physical labor. Relatedly, the art of painting was linked by figures such as Leon Battista Alberti and Leonardo da Vinci with the kind of learning obtained through the sense of vision and with the science of optics, especially as techniques of rendering space by means of linear perspective developed.[20] Thus one element in separating what would eventually become known as *beaux arts* or fine arts from labor and craft involved a deliberate reconceptualization of the efforts of painters, sculptors, and architects. This they accomplished not only by the magnificence of their products during this impressively productive period of art history, but also by arguing on behalf of the cognitive, scientific achievement represented by such accomplishments. The more an art form requires the intellectual arts of mathematics and science, they maintained, the greater its claim to be a liberal—a "free"– endeavor.

The changes to the concept of art and of the artist that went into the separation of decorative craft or utilitarian artisanship from fine art were gradual and uneven, and they took several centuries to accomplish. By the eighteenth century, it was generally agreed that there are five major fine arts: music, poetry, painting, sculpture, and architecture. This period saw a burgeoning critical literature on the nature of the arts, comparing them to one another according to common principles. Other arts such as gardening, prose literature, dance, or theater were sometimes added to the list, but these five make up an established core. The identification of specific forms of creativity as fine arts is one prominent example of how theory and practice go hand in hand, in this case arguably with practice actually trailing theory.

One of the most important factors that eventually sealed the separation of fine art, or art proper, from other kinds of making, concerns the kind of value assigned to works of art, for to fine art came to be ascribed values that are chiefly aesthetic rather than functional or utilitarian. Since many of the arts that women typically produced include artifacts such as needlework made for decoration and domestic uses, the division between art and craft had the effect of eliminating from the concept of art proper a number of genres where women had a prominent presence.[21] As the idea of fine art gradually developed in the modern period, the arts came to be considered products produced chiefly for their beauty or sublimity or other aesthetic virtue; and relatedly, the role of the true artist was seen as producing works for aesthetic appreciation independent of any particular practical function. This is what chiefly distinguishes the work of fine art from craft. A craft object, which may be finely made and beautiful, is not a proper artwork because it is made to serve some function, a function which limits the free creativity of the artist-maker. As Victor Cousin asserted in his 1818 lectures at the Sorbonne, "utility has nothing to do with beauty."[22] The end of art is beauty, though in Cousin's formulation this aesthetic value still connotes the indirect presence of moral and spiritual value in art as well.

The artist is before all things an artist; what animates him is the sentiment of the beautiful; what he wishes to make pass into the soul of the spectator is the same sentiment that fills his own . . . This pure and disinterested sentiment is a noble ally of the moral and religious sentiments; it awakens, preserves, and develops them, but it is a distinct and special sentiment. So art, which is founded on this sentiment, which is inspired by it, which expands it, is in its turn an independent power. It is naturally associated with all that ennobles the soul, with morals and religion; but it springs only from itself.[23]

By these standards, crafts would be doubly disqualified from these aesthetic concepts, both because of their utility and because they lack the spiritual and moral dimension that true beauty possesses.

The concept of the aesthetic will be treated at greater length in the next chapter, but it is important to note at this point how the idea of the aesthetic entered into the shaping of a tradition of fine art. The notion of aesthetic value emerged from new approaches to pleasure and to the receptivity and appreciation that were summed up in the idea of "taste." Purely aesthetic pleasure was singled out for its contrast with other sources of pleasure, such as practical use, economic value, social meaning, or the satisfaction of sexual desire (though this latter separation is especially complex and arguably compromised when one considers the gendered meaning of aesthetic pleasure. This will be discussed at a later point.) As the notion of fine art, in contrast with utilitarian arts, began to develop, more and more theorists maintained that the true value of art is purely aesthetic, that art is for beauty and for the aesthetic pleasure it furnishes. Reinforcing these values, certain artistic institutions arose in the modern period that provided venues for pure aesthetic enjoyment, most particularly concert halls for listening to music and art museums where paintings were made available to the public to appreciate the efforts of artists past and present, who were now conceived to be persons who create for beauty and aesthetic insight. In the eighteenth century and into the nineteenth, beauty and moral value were still closely linked, a connection evident in Cousin's statement above. As more and more attention was directed to articulating what is distinctive about beauty and other aesthetic qualities, moral philosophy and aesthetics parted company. In its most extreme form this separation engendered an "art for art's sake" mentality popular in the nineteenth and early twentieth centuries that justified artistic expression purely on aesthetic grounds, sometimes even flouting moral standards. (The separation of beauty and moral goodness is a theme of some of the works of the poet Charles Baudelaire and the novelist and playwright Oscar Wilde, for example.) But even in less pure versions the idea of art created just for the consideration and enjoyment of its aesthetic value widened the gulf between fine art and those artifacts made for use, no matter now elegant or beautiful they might be. This gulf is also evident in theories about the artist, especially the idea that the best creator is an artistic *genius*.

Genius

While the concept of genius has classical origins, it has undergone many twists and turns in the history of art and philosophy. The eighteenth century and the Romantic movement promoted a particularly powerful role for genius and fostered the cult of the individual man of exceptional capacities who gives less gifted artists the tools to create. In Kant's famous words: "Genius is the talent that gives the rule to art."[24] During this period, moreover, genius was ferociously guarded as a male preserve.[25]

Genius does not describe males in general contrast to females, because the world produces few geniuses at all. This term is reserved for the select number of creators who have not only produced superior artworks, but whose vision has altered the direction of the field altogether. As Kant put it, the genius opens paths for artists of lesser accomplishment to follow, whether they be male or female. The gender of genius is founded on special capacities of these few extraordinary persons, capacities that are grounded in overall differences in the abilities of men and women. While artistic creativity is not merely a function of superior reason, it is a feature of a superior mind; and the model superior mind is a male mind: one that is strong and capable of independence from tradition and social norms, and that rises above the quotidian concerns that shape ordinary activities. In the latter feature alone, we can see that any person who is largely defined by domestic roles will be precluded from the concept of a genius.

Social role is but one impediment to female genius; anatomy can be another, especially in the earlier versions of the theory. Renaissance notions of genius pictured a great artist as one who can create by a controlled kind of madness (the madness of the Muse, for example, harkening back to the classical image of inspiration). Such flights of creativity break away temporarily from ordinary human limitations, transcending even reason. According to prevalent conceptions of the human constitution, females could not participate in this rare event. The theory of humors that governed understanding of character for centuries characterized males as "hot and dry" but females as "cold and moist," and the vapors that arise from the uterus, it was held, cloud the mind and dim the ability to apprehend Truth, thus restraining the female artist from ascending to the insight of genius.[26]

By the time that Kant wrote about genius in the powerfully influential *Critique of Judgment* (1790), the semi-divine connotations associated with genius, signaled for example in the ancient idea that the poet is a conduit for divinely inspired lyric, had receded. In their place was the artist himself: the genius who creates from the reserves of his own imagination. Genius signals a powerfully original mind that vaults over tradition and rules of art to discover entirely new ways of conceiving and enacting creativity. Kant himself carefully restricted the innovations of art to safeguard the work of genius from the perhaps equally unprecedented work of the lunatic: even nonsense may be original, he noted; the genius who masters an art form must be thoroughly schooled in that form in order to shape his inspirations.

Speculations about artistic imagination that flourished in nineteenth-century Europe could reach some extremes, sometimes extolling the inspirational value of anti-social and amoral behavior, and even insanity—all rumored to cling to such darkly glamorous figures as the popular English poet Lord Byron. This approach to genius bordered on a (highly romantic) view of madness that dovetails with ideas about inspiration and persists well into our own times.[27] The value placed on dangerously fanciful imaginative activity pushed ideas about creative methods to a limit, as many contended that true artistic imagination stems from an inborn spark that is antithetical to the plodding rules of reason, a position that represents a brand of resistance to the dominion of rationality so prevalent in philosophy. However, none of this was especially welcoming to female creativity, and not because women were always considered sane. But the version of madness that was most ascribed to women was the type named "hysteria," a label that derives from the Greek word for "uterus." Hysterics represent a kind of biological disturbance rendered in psychological form, not the profound depth of spirit that artistic madness supposedly taps in the course of artistic creation. Although this version of the imaginative genius is founded on an understanding of creativity that is anti-rationalist, it still describes a male domain.

As Christine Battersby has argued, we can see in the Romantic idea of genius a dramatic instance of how traditionally "feminine" traits involving emotion and other "nonrational" mental characteristics are appropriated for male creators and actually removed from females. Metaphors of labor and birth popularly describe artistic inspiration and creation, for example. Both masculine traits (toughness, courage) and feminine ones (emotional sensitivity) are interpreted as having special creative powers and are assigned to the best minds of an age, minds with virtually exclusively male exemplars. Kant grumped that a woman who even attempts profound learning or creativity might as well wear a beard, and when Balzac praised the novelist George Sand (the pen name of the prolific writer Aurore Dupin [1804–76]), he credited her with the character of a man.[28] Gender presumptions are less explicit in Friedrich Schiller's On the Aesthetic Education of Man (1793). Schiller advocates the cultivation of sensibility and feeling, which he argues are necessary to complete the rational individual. The balance Schiller champions seems at first to invite a unity of "feminine" and "masculine" traits in the notion of the aesthetic. However, the point of view throughout his work is uniformly male, an impression made explicit when he refers to "woman" as an object of beauty, whether real or painted, and when he discusses family life.[29] This influential writer, who sincerely endorsed aspects of mind that are sometimes taken to be "subjective" and "feminine," is not thereby acknowledging the sensibilities of actual women. He is rather recommending an amplified description of a complete man.

Expression theories of art

The eighteenth century saw so much writing on the subject of art and beauty that in retrospect contemporary scholars tend to date the beginning of the separate discipline of aesthetics at this time. Among the many ideas about art and creativity that emerged from these debates was a particularly enduring one that extolled the role of the artist for creating from his unique imagination through an act of "expression." The distinction between fine art and other kinds of making achieves particular theoretical rigor in expression theory, one of the most influential and popular movements in the history of aesthetics. Indeed, the idea that the purpose of art is expression is still widely taken for granted.

"Expression theory" does not denote one particular view of art but a robust and varied approach to the nature of art, of creativity, and of artists; it has enjoyed advocates for more than two centuries.[30] Concepts of expression are quite various, and many proponents of this notion do not even share basic definitions of what it means to express. Some theorists focus on the controlled display of individual thoughts and feelings that the disciplined imagination is able to externalize in a work of art, such that others gain an understanding of the artist's unique insights. Other versions of the theory permit "expression" to refer broadly to the manifestation of style and values of a historical period—a fallback position that is more elastic than the former, since one often does not know the identity of an artist to whom thoughts and intentions can be ascribed.

Nothing explicitly precludes women artists from inclusion in concepts of artistic expression. With this set of theories, it is the range that expression is apt to exhibit that betrays a gender skew. In order to plumb their creative imaginations, artists require considerable freedom—freedom from tradition, from the fetters of social expectation and constraint, perhaps even from family and other responsibilities. Quite apart from the fact that in many social regions women are accorded less freedom than are men, especially if that freedom includes unfettered movement in public places, this requirement deepens the divide between fine art and crafts. If fine art is regarded as an intrinsically valuable product that expresses an artistic vision, then arts that have an inescapable practical dimension are poorly accommodated. Craft, for example, whether it be needlework, carpentry, potting, sewing, or whatever, is always subject to the requirements of what is being made. A blanket is no good unless it is warm and large enough for a bed; a cup is useless if it doesn't hold liquid. These are not merely incidental necessities; according to some dedicated expression theorists, they are impediments that prevent such products from ever achieving the status of art.

This is especially clear in the work of an influential twentieth-century expression theorist, R. G. Collingwood. Considering art of modern times in particular, Collingwood distinguishes several types of products that he believes are often confused with art proper, including entertainment and craft.[31] Craft is not the product of expression, he argues, because its ends are known before the maker begins. That is to say, if one sets out to make a basket, one knows in advance what the basket should do and how its design can satisfy its purpose. The design is in service to that practical end. By comparison, true artistic expression is the very act of becoming clear about some idea that begins as an inchoate restlessness in the mind of the artist. With art proper, no foreordained purpose—whether utilitarian, religious, or civic—interferes with free, creative expression. This stipulation is not intended to discriminate by type of artifact, for Collingwood recognizes art by the mental activity of the artist rather than by the medium he or she employs.

Nonetheless, his focus on a special act of expression precludes from the concept of the true artist anyone whose primary ends, by necessity or interest, are practical. Real artistic creativity simply cannot be conducted in the process of working with objects or activities that are chiefly made to serve another goal. Another class of products he distinguishes from art proper includes events or artifacts that are produced for amusement, for their goal is the arousal of enjoyment or emotive states in the audience rather than the expression of an idea.

These restrictions also eliminate from the concept of art proper traditional community arts, such as stories and songs, and the entertainment that affords diversion from the rigors of labor or servitude. They probably rule out the products of many traditional non-European cultures, collections of which move unstably between art museums and museums of natural history. In other words, the distinction that separates fine art from craft or entertainment has as many implications for the class, social position, or even nationality of the maker as it does for his or her gender.[32] What is noteworthy about the implications for the presumed gender of the artist, is that everything that is included in the elevated category of fine art has a typical maker who is masculine, to the point that for some art forms women were actually considered unfit to participate fully, and were diverted to lesser, adjunct roles. (Some examples of this will be discussed in Chapter 3.) And the things that have come to be designated "women's work," such as domestic decorations and needlework, are all included under the craft label.

To be sure, there were a number of influential writers who resisted the distinction between fine art and craft or applied art, both in theory and in practice. In the nineteenth and early twentieth centuries on both sides of the Atlantic there were vigorous arts and crafts movements that produced carefully wrought, hand-made objects both for use and for aesthetic delight. (The most famous of these was led by the English artist and theorist William Morris.) Both the objects produced and the writings that articulated the philosophy behind this movement sought to close the divide between art and craft, as well as to combat the disappearance of hand-made artifacts, which were being replaced by products of factory manufacture. An even more extreme critique from the point of view of an expression theorist was articulated by Leo Tolstoy, who became disgusted with the nineteenth-century European cult of beauty and fine art and promoted the arts of Russian peasant culture, which he considered the purest, least corrupted form of artistic communication.[33] This sort of opposition notwithstanding, the divide between fine art and craft and between true artists and artisans by and large became firmly fixed in modern aesthetics and philosophy of art.

Summary

In sum, the concept of the artist is a combination of theoretical movements and historical practice, both partly a consequence of the way that artists are conceptualized in the discourse of western culture. In this context the term "discourse" sums up the complex and deep system of thought that surrounds paradigms of artists and their endeavors. These elements are evident in philosophical disquisitions, critical commentary, and historical writings, all of which both inform our understanding of the past and are adopted in current conceptual maps. Although there are women artists in the historical record, not only are they a small minority but, more importantly, their presence has little effect on discourse about the artist. As one commentator puts it, "the artist is always gendered male unless called 'the woman artist'."[34] The traditional roles of women, who are more confined by social restrictions than are men in all social classes, do not suit the image of the artist as a free and independent creative spirit—neither conceptually nor, for most of history, empirically.

A survey of historical attitudes may seem simply a collection of empirical facts about times gone by that were brought about by social conditions that have since changed so radically that the past tells us little about the present state of culture. I have been arguing for a deeper cause and a more extensive set of consequences for gendered meanings within which ideas about art and aesthetics are framed: for the hypothesis that gender is a systematic and occasionally insidious phenomenon that can impart to concepts considerable power to shape the ways we think and see the world. Subsequent chapters will bring the ideas surrounding art and artists into our own times; I shall argue that despite radical changes both in the worlds of art and in the status of women in society in general, the conceptual foundations framed in centuries past possess vigorous tenacity. It is true that ideas about men and women and the organization of social relations have changed dramatically, and we should not exaggerate the power of older ideas. At the same time, gendered expectations about what qualifies as art and who qualifies as an artist often persist well beyond our self-conscious reflection and expectations, and this can mean that the weight even of remote historical periods may be heavier than we anticipate.

Figure 3 Judith Leyster, *Serenade*, 1629. © Rijksmuseum-Stichting, Amsterdam.

Perhaps I can illustrate what I mean with an anecdote: when I was a college student, more or less oblivious to feminist matters, I took my first trip to Europe. In Amsterdam, at the Rijksmuseum, I admired the paintings from the period of Dutch baroque art, lingering especially over a small picture of a lute player. The lighting was warm and intense, the face of the musician wore a provocative smile, his hands were finely drawn . . . I peered more closely at the caption to find out who painted the canvas: it said *Judith Leyster: 1609–1660*. "Oh that's interesting," I thought. "In Dutch 'Judith' must be a man's name."

2

AESTHETIC PLEASURES

Philosophies that developed ideas about fine art and a distinctive realm of aesthetic value in the early modern period became foundational texts for contemporary aesthetic theory, and this chapter examines a few of the most influential. We shall see that insofar as they imported gender distinctions into the concepts of beauty, sublimity, pleasure, and the aesthetic itself, these theories helped to intensify the idea that both artists and the best critical judges of art are ideally male. Later, in Chapter 3, we shall also see that all of these factors had considerable significance for the practice of women artists, for within the relatively abstract discourses of philosophical aesthetics there are networks of concepts that describe and prescribe the boundaries of how women should act, how they should think and feel, and the qualities they ought to cultivate in art and in life. In other words, there is an oscillation between the abstract dimension of discourse and its implicit, and sometimes immediately practical, ramifications. Let us begin with some general background regarding the philosophical climate in which the central modern concepts in aesthetics were articulated.

The aesthetic

"Aesthetic" is a term coined by philosophers to denote a type of experience for which there was no adequate vernacular term.[1] When the term "aesthetic" was first employed in German philosophy in the eighteenth century, it referred to what was regarded as a level of cognition that one receives from immediate sense experience prior to the intellectual abstraction which organizes general knowledge. But it was soon revised to refer more broadly to the particular insight that a strong experience of *beauty* imparts. The immediacy, singularity, and intimacy of both sense experience and beauty indicate particular intuition rather than general knowledge. As theories were formulated to explain the idea of a special domain of aesthetic pleasure, the term eventually became (in the nineteenth century) the label for a discrete area of philosophical study: aesthetics. This coincidence of labeling and theory development has led some scholars to declare that aesthetics originates in the eighteenth century, which would be an exaggeration. However, this period witnessed profound discussions of pleasure and of the objects of pleasure that ground many of the modern approaches to critical appreciation and to art.

The central role of pleasure in aesthetic theory is easily understood if one examines the classic term of aesthetic approbation: beauty. What is beauty? When one calls an object beautiful, to what does one refer? This has always posed something of a puzzle, because objects of beauty are so various that it is hard to locate any single quality that they share. A poem is beautiful, a swan is beautiful, as are a song, a gesture, a person. Some philosophers, notably Plato, have maintained that "beauty" names the quality possessed by all such objects and in virtue of which they are beautiful.[2] According to such analysis this quality, though mysterious and hard to pinpoint with accuracy, is objective, meaning that it resides in the object itself and is not dependent on the response of a perceiver for its existence. Other philosophers have been more skeptical about the presence of an objective quality in beautiful things, surmising that what they share is not a specific property but the capacity to evoke a response in a subject—the person who finds them beautiful.

For a variety of reasons, this latter, more "subjective" approach to beauty gained momentum in the late seventeenth century and persisted as a topic of intense debate throughout the eighteenth. The general catalyst for this was the rise of empiricism, a philosophy that argues that all our ideas are ultimately traceable to sense experience. Since there is no simple sensible quality of beauty, empiricists claim, this value is best understood as an idea compounded from the perception of various sensible qualities of objects plus the feeling of pleasure.[3] For example, finding a sunset beautiful involves perceiving its intense redness, the radiating beams of the sun on a dark horizon, and so on—along with the feeling of pleasure that they arouse. There are no empirical, scientific grounds for thinking that "beautiful" is the name of a quality of such objects themselves; it is a subjective effect involving the arousal of feeling.

The emphasis on pleasure raises some problems because pleasure seems to be keyed to individual, even idiosyncratic responses, but beauty seems to be more than a matter of purely subjective whim. Moreover, it was widely pre-sumed in the early modern period that pleasure comes about when some desire is satisfied, and that desires tend to be selfish and self-interested. Gen-erally speaking, they sustain and promote one's own personal situation, whether physical or social. The simplest example of pleasure by this model would be the bodily pleasure of eating; eating is delightful when one is hungry and the desire to eat is acute. Even more pertinent for consideration of gender is the aptness of sexual desire for this model: pleasure comes about when desire is aroused, then satisfied. Not only was beauty implicated in the linkage of pleasure and desire, but so were other value qualities such as goodness and moral virtues, for they also involve some sort of pleasure responses rather than reference to objective qualities such as goodness. While some philosophers (notably Thomas Hobbes) endorsed the idea that human activity is powered by egocentric drives, and that all value qualities indicate the direct or indirect satisfaction of selfish desires, most considered this both a dangerous and an inaccurate description of human character and activity. They endeavored to furnish shared standards for pleasure responses that circumvent the idiosyncratic selfishness of personal desire. In aesthetics, this task concerned how to establish a "standard of taste."[4] Although there were many different theories addressed to these issues, most shared a ten-dency to detach pleasure of an aesthetic sort from other kinds of evaluations, whether sensual, practical, or eventually even moral.[5] (As we saw in the last chapter, the association of beauty with virtue remained strong, and moral qualities were the last of the other values to separate from the aesthetic.)

The term "taste" is central in these debates about aesthetic response to art and to nature. The literal, gustatory sense of taste has never been considered an "aesthetic sense," that is, a sense that delivers aesthetic pleasures or that takes as its object a work of art. (The reasons for this exclusion, which them-selves are riddled with gendered significance, are explored in Chapter 4.) However, the language of taste does provide the chief metaphor for under-standing aesthetic apprehension and appreciation. Several features of the gustatory sense dispose it for this usage. The idea of a distinctive region of aesthetic experience originates in recognition that there are immediate, sin-gular encounters that bring insight and pleasure. The sense of taste also requires intimate, immediate experience; what is more, taste rarely occurs without a pleasure—displeasure component to the sensation. Moreover, like the appreciation of poetry or music or other arts, one can develop the taste of the palate so that food preferences become more refined and sophisticated and one takes pleasure in subtlety and complexity of flavor. These are among the features of the gustatory sense that suit it for use in aesthetic contexts.

Taste is also undeniably "subjective," so much so that it is the target of the old expression, "there's no accounting for taste." This maxim indicates the tendency to conflate a subjective experience with one that is also *relative* to different individuals, that is, one that has no shared standards of appropriateness or accuracy. The so-called problem of taste that occupied writers in the eighteenth century was how to acknowledge the subjectivity of taste yet retain a foundation for standards of taste when discussing art. For no matter how centrally pleasure is involved in appreciation and aesthetic judgment, some art is better than other art, and therefore some taste is better than other taste. How does this work?

Taste and beauty

Beauty is not the only quality discussed in these theories, for critical language usually refers more precisely to harmony, balance, wit, and even more exact descriptors of individual works of art. But beauty is the most general term of aesthetic approbation as well as one that manifests marked gender complexity, and so it will be the center of this discussion. Analysis of beauty goes hand in hand with surmises about the facility to discern or feel beauty, that is, with taste. Sometimes thinkers speculated about common qualities in the objects of beauty, but without recourse to an objective quality indisputably identifiable as beauty, many philosophers tended to appeal to common human nature to locate a standard of taste.

One of the most famous writers who analyzed human nature in order to understand taste preferences and their foundations was the empiricist David Hume. In his essay "Of the Standard of Taste" (1757) Hume was cautious in his approach to locating a standard, for unlike many of his contemporaries he was reluctant to name the properties in objects that cause the pleasure of taste. That there are such properties seems obvious; but Hume refrained from identifying them as did, for example, Edmund Burke, Francis Hutcheson, or William Hogarth. Hutcheson argued that beauty is caused by the perception of a compositional quality he called "uniformity amidst variety"; Hogarth, a painter and engraver as well as a theorist, zeroed in on the "line of grace," a smooth, S-shaped curve of certain mathematical proportions.[6] All instances of beauty, whether in nature, persons, or artifacts, display curved lines in some degree, Hogarth claimed.

Figure 4 William Hogarth, "The Line of Grace". Detail after Plate I, *The Analysis of Beauty*, 1753.

As Hume no doubt recognized, such objective correlates to the feeling of what we now call aesthetic pleasure (the term "aesthetic" was not used in English until the early nineteenth century) only describe a certain range of pleasing forms and therefore have limited use in resolving the problem of taste. They are inadequate to account for all visual beauties, let alone for the enjoyments of music or poetry. Therefore Hume concentrated on the common proclivities that he believed were embedded in human nature to explain tendencies among people of education and training to agree about matters of taste over time. He described in detail the qualities of the human constitution that make possible the education and development of discerning judgments about objects of evaluation, including what he called "delicate" (or sensitive) taste. Hume's is one of the theories of this period where the presence of gender is rather subtle and low-keyed.[7] We detect it mainly in incidental remarks that suggest that he pictures the model judge as male, an indication that he has imported into his notion of taste some of the gender skews already present in concepts of human nature. We shall see how gendered taste operates in more detail shortly, but first let us add to our considerations some more explicit evidence of the gender valence of aesthetic values.

There are theories in which we find not only gender but outright sex at play in the analysis of beauty, including one that appeared in the same year as Hume's essay, Burke's *A Philosophical Enquiry into the Origin of our Ideas of the Sublime and Beautiful* (1757). Burke was not the most influential writer on the burgeoning field of aesthetics, a laurel that must go (as do so many) to Kant. But there is something to be said for not always discussing modern philosophy in terms of Kant, and Burke has another advantage: the gendered basis for beauty is not in the least hidden in his theory. Indeed he locates the causal trigger for beauty in an erotic origin.

Burke on beauty

In contrast to Hume, who focuses almost exclusively on human nature, Burke spends a lot of time examining the objects of taste, analyzing the root cause that triggers the pleasure of beauty. Much of his Enquiry is devoted to discovering which features of the world affect the body and mind in regular and predictable ways, exciting the passions and their attendant pleasures and pains. He shares with other writers of his time the presumption that affective responses are similar among people and differences are relatively minor deviations from a norm. "There is in all men a sufficient remembrance of the original natural causes of pleasure, to enable them to bring all things offered to their senses to that standard, and to regulate their feelings and opinions by it."[8] According to Burke, basic affective responses are virtually automatic reactions to external stimuli.

Like many of his contemporaries, Burke divides the major aesthetic responses into two sorts: the beautiful and the sublime. (We shall learn more about the sublime in Chapter 6; here it is introduced as a point of comparison for beauty.) Beauty is a species of pleasure; the more difficult response of the sublime is actually founded on pain, especially the profound emotional pain of terror, which under certain conditions can be converted into "delight." These responses may be categorized further according to their concern with society or self-preservation. Society is the realm of beauty and concerns life and health; self-preservation (or threats to self-preservation) provide the realm of the sublime. The taxonomy continues with the subdivision of "society" into the society between the sexes and general society. The heteroerotic connotations implicit from the start emerge explicitly in the discussion of relations between the sexes, where Burke finds the fundamental source of beauty.

Animals, Burke asserts, experience only the passion of lust. But man mixes this with social qualities, "which direct and heighten the appetite which he has in common with all other animals." Sensible qualities determine what he finds beautiful.[9] This primitive aesthetic response is below reason and rational control. Some things—and personal beauty is just one of several (including mimesis)—simply please because of the way we are made

> without any intervention of the reasoning faculty, but solely from
> our natural constitution, which providence has framed in such a

manner as to find either pleasure or delight according to the nature
of the object, in whatever regards the purposes of our being.[10]

And like theorists since Plato, Burke believes that beauty arouses not just
pleasure but love.

The kinds of objects we find beautiful, says Burke, are small, bounded,
curved, soft, gentle in contour, and delicately colored. This is true of a flower
or an abstract shape or a human body. By contrast, sublime objects are
rough, jagged, unbounded, powerful, fearsome, and dark; they threaten life
rather than suggest its perpetuation. The general, abstract characteristics of
any beautiful object are extrapolated from the beauty of the female body.
Burke gushes over this beauty as it is manifest in a woman's neck and
breasts: "The smoothness; the softness; the easy and insensible swell; the
variety of the surface, which is never for the smallest space the same; the
deceitful maze, through which the unsteady eye slides giddily . . ."[11] As if to
cool his ardor as well as his prose, he invokes Hogarth's formal line of grace
as confirmation, but this can be read equally well as implicating gender in
the mathematical serpentine line itself.

The connection of aesthetic pleasure with erotic desire and the obvious
gender basis of Burke's presentation of beauty (not to mention its presump-
tive race and cultural bias, for he rules out dusky skin as beautiful) is
sufficiently obvious that feminist critique is perhaps almost beside the point.
But his theory is so central an exemplar of modern aesthetics that we can also
view it as a paradigm of ways of thinking that appear throughout the field in
subtler forms, where masculinist and Eurocentric attitudes are more covert.
Such has been the argument of those who claim that even Kant's pure, disinterested beauty should be understood as a veil for heteroerotic well-springs
operating underground. Burke's analysis also indicates why feminist theory
has frequently had an adversarial relationship with the concept of beauty,
namely because of the tendency to focus on the objectification of the appearance of women.[12]

If aesthetic theories all resembled Burke's, then there would be little controversy about the gender valence of the basic aesthetic value of beauty. But
theories differ considerably from one another even when they are products
of the same cultural era, and in many the erotic possibilities for pleasure
were actually ruled out from the category of genuine aesthetic responses. It
is these that are the most influential progenitors of the ideals of aesthetic
contemplation which were widely espoused later in the nineteenth and

twentieth centuries. Arguably, the most influential theorist of the eighteenth-century Enlightenment was Immanuel Kant.

Kant on judgments of taste

As a matter of fact, Kant also speculated that the origin of aesthetic pleasure lay in erotic attraction, but that this original source is discarded early in human history as civilization develops more sophisticated and distanced aesthetic pleasures. As though anticipating Freud, Kant remarks that the fig leaf was a manifestation of reason that began the control of the senses that makes pure aesthetic pleasure possible.[13] This whimsical remark occurs in an essay not considered among Kant's most significant, and the analysis of beauty in his more important Critique of Judgment (1790) is considerably more neutral.

Kant had particular influence over the adoption of a modifier that came to describe aesthetic pleasure, disinterested. Unlike Hume, who was chiefly concerned with standards of taste for literature and art, Kant entered the discussion of aesthetic pleasure with objects of nature and abstract forms as his paradigm objects of beauty—specifically of what he called "absolute" beauty, which is the object of the "pure" judgment of taste. His approach to locating a standard for taste was to disqualify from purely aesthetic experience any pleasure that referred to the satisfaction of desire or the accomplishment of a goal. As a consequence, the old link between the values of beauty and goodness was loosened considerably, for his analysis distinguishes aesthetic pleasures from moral approval in stronger terms than had hitherto been articulated. Although Kant somewhat opaquely calls beauty the "symbol of morality," in the Critique of Judgment the pleasure that constitutes beauty is distinct and sui generis.[14] (For the realm of moral judgments Kant formulated a strenuous universal moral law that quashes any impulse toward subjective relativism in ethics.)[15]

In addition, he explicitly separated aesthetic pleasure from the pleasures of sense, thus widening the divide (present since antiquity) between the pleasures of the bodily senses and aesthetic pleasures.[16] Pleasures of sense include erotic enjoyments, which are clearly the product of the satisfaction—real or imagined—of sexual desire. They also include gustatory pleasures. Literal taste for food and drink, he noted, is merely sensuous; these enjoyments are the result of the satisfaction of some bodily need. But aesthetic pleasures have nothing to do with the body, nor indeed with the satisfaction of any personal interest at all. Aesthetic judgments are free from interest, or, to use what is now the more common idiom, they are "disinterested."[17] "Disinterested" does not mean that we care nothing for them; it means that our pleasure is not rooted in personal advancement or gratification—in the satisfaction of one of our desires. In Kant's account of the pure judgment of taste, this term also means that no concept of the object is in use when we judge it beautiful; that is, we are not assessing it as an excellent example of its kind but are appreciating its singular form as it stimulates harmony between the imagination and the understanding.[18] (One reason that most artworks have "dependent" or "adherent" beauty rather than "free" or "absolute" beauty, according to Kant, is that one must employ determinate concepts in the assessment of art. That is, one must employ ideas about how an object, event, or person should be represented.)

Kant is not merely stipulating a difference between "higher" and "lower" pleasures when he distinguishes between aesthetic and sensuous pleasures, though that is an additional outcome of his analysis. Rather, his reasoning is driven by his endeavor to resolve the problem of taste. Kant sought to discover for beauty and the feeling of aesthetic pleasure grounds for a kind of universality and necessity parallel to the foundations that he had previously established for empirical knowledge and moral directives. His is the strongest and most rigorous standard of taste, much stronger than Hume's, for the latter was content with finding the general principles that by and large indicate a tendency to agree on matters of taste. Kant wanted to discover the grounds for genuine universality of aesthetic response. This is one reason he rules out bodily pleasures; he believes that they are too idiosyncratic and personal to command agreement.

At least to some extent Kant's description of pleasure as a means to identify aesthetic quality seems to conform with familiar experience. One may recognize that someone else's performance of a piano piece is more beautiful than one's own, for example, even if the other person won a coveted recital prize. If that beauty is recognized through pleasure, then this instance of pleasure clearly has nothing to do with the satisfaction of one's desires. Setting aside one's interest in winning the prize makes available the aesthetic pleasure of the other contestant's performance. I am only reviewing a small portion of Kant's theory here, but we can see even with this much of his position that with all personal desires and interests cleared away, what remains to account for aesthetic pleasures are the elements of the mind that we all possess. A *subjective* pleasure is made *universally* available.

If we go along with Kant's purification of aesthetic pleasure and judg-ments of taste, stipulating that they be free from desire, then it may appear as if gender has disappeared from this debate, for all traces of the erotic roots for beauty seem to have been expunged. We might therefore feel confident that claims about universality of the capacity for judgments of taste are truly gender neutral, at least by the terms of this brand of philosophy. But as one probably anticipates, gender is not so easily left behind. To address this issue let us consider the concept of taste in broader context.

Whose taste?

Ideal standards for taste are personified in a common eighteenth-century figure of speech: the man of taste or *homme de goût*, the idiom popular in France. One may wonder just how literal "man" or "*homme*" was supposed to be; was taste considered to be an achievement of males only? Not really, for taste was extolled and exercised across genteel society, including in the salons of France which were hosted and superintended by women, and it spread as a popular ideal with the growth and social ascendence of the middle-class. What is more, taste implies refinement, and the development of sensitivities of the man of taste was understood to soften his rough edges and make his temperament more consonant with "feminine" qualities. The concept of taste or aesthetic discernment was perhaps even more overtly attuned to differences of social position, class, and education than to gender. And although writers usually confined their remarks to fellow Europeans, there is also an implicit and very deep race presumption about the scope of the term.[19] One finds the occasional dismissal of the "Negro" or the "Indian" or the "Oriental" as unlikely to participate in the refinements of aesthetic judgments, though there was some internecine rivalry as well; one early British writer criticized the "Goth" (German) for his mistaken taste in architecture.[20]

On the other hand, although women were considered capable of devel-oping fine taste, arguably the model of the ideal aesthetic judge, the arbiter of taste, was implicitly male, for men's minds and sentiments were consid-ered to be more broadly capable than women's. Here we find once more the combination of theoretical assumptions and social norms that produces the opinion that higher mental powers are asymmetrically exercised in males and females. The greater mental facility of males supposedly renders them more capable of judgments of taste for complicated subjects, according to philosophical tradition; and the socially-grounded assumption that women's experience is appropriately narrower than is men's means that they are unlikely to have the breadth of expertise to render their taste on tougher subjects as insightful as men's is likely to be. The distinction between a "feminine" taste for things that are pretty and charming, and a "masculine" taste for art that is more profound and difficult, was often noted in the literature of this period. Burke's distinction between the small, curvy, feminine charms of beauty and the rugged, masculine proclivities for demanding subjects and for sublimity reflected popular thinking. As Kant put it in his early work, *Observations on the Feeling of the Beautiful and Sublime* (1763), the narrow scope of the beautiful characterizes a woman's sensibility, whereas a man should strive for the deeper understanding of the sublime.[21] Both are positive capacities, but it is the latter that accomplishes the more profound and commanding scope—aesthetically, artistically, epistemically, and morally.

There is an obverse to the idea of masculine and feminine taste that further reveals the lesser standing of the latter. Among the terms of criticism that were commonly used in assessing works of art, one of the most opprobrious was "effeminate." Male artists were the ones to whom this negative term would be applied, for a work of similar quality by a woman would simply be feminine and thereby charming and minor. There is no equivalent negative variation on "masculine" to serve as the counterpart of "effeminate," which is a derogatory term employed with sufficient onus that one realizes just how unlike women male creators apparently were supposed to be. (Alan Sinfield goes so far as to call effeminacy a "misogynist construct" that is designed to patrol the borders of masculinity.)[22] Labels such as "virile" were terms of praise and did not connote exaggerated masculinity. We shall see in the next chapter how the polarities between feminine and masculine tastes were to serve not only to demote women as taste-setters, but also to criticize and truncate women's opportunities to participate in the arts.

The cluster of concepts involving taste, standards, and disinterested pleasure has been the subject of much critical analysis in recent years. Shared, even universal, standards of taste were conceived at the time of their formulation to be grounded in common human nature; narrowing the focus of aesthetic pleasure to a zone free from personal desire was advanced as a way to get rid of the differences among people so that their common pleasures might be exercised. In this respect Enlightenment aesthetics may be considered a rather democratic philosophy, for by definition human nature must be the same in us all. And yet clearly not everyone was considered a candidate to be an arbiter of taste or a participant in the highest aesthetic pleasures. The common capacities resident in human nature need to be developed and refined in order to be sensitive to the best products of culture, and this requires a degree of good fortune, education, and privilege. Those happy attributes have never been equally distributed in societies, and in eighteenth-century Europe, despite the popularity of democratic political ideals, there were marked discrepancies of availability of the kind of education and economic mobility that were recognized as fundamental for the development of refined taste. As some critics have pointed out, seeking to establish standards for artistic enjoyment can be seen as an attempt to regulate and homogenize pleasures according to a gauge that reflects distinct class bias, not to mention national and racial preferences.[23] In promulgating the existence of standards for subjective pleasures, the preferences of people who were already culturally accredited, as it were, became the standard to be emulated. Ideas about taste and beauty, no matter how assiduous the attempt to universalize standards and to "purify" them of bias and prejudice, seem ineluctably to absorb reigning social values.

Aesthetic attitude theories

While establishment of a foundation for universal taste must face the criticism that such quests impose rather than discover standards, other aspects of these attempts expand the range of objects that may be considered to have aesthetic merit. Post-Kantian approaches, sometimes called "aesthetic attitude" theories, extended Kant's prescription for disinterested pleasure beyond the pure regions for which he devised it, and prescribed an attitude from which all and only aesthetic qualities, whether from art or nature, may be apprehended. Aesthetic attitude theories recommend that the best way to achieve aesthetic enjoyment is to assume a disinterested, contemplative stance intended to clear one's mind of prejudice and personal preoccupations, opening one's sensibilities to the aesthetic qualities—formal, expressive, imaginative—that are available to the attentive spectator, reader, or listener. While educated familiarity with the arts provides a fund of knowledge that makes sophisticated appreciation possible, the immediate prerequisite for appreciation is the distanced, quiescent, reflective stance.

The nineteenth-century philosopher Arthur Schopenhauer, whose theory was a precursor to aesthetic attitude approaches, went so far as to regard aesthetic contemplation as a rare source of relief from the pressures of the individual will; he considered experiences of beauty to lighten conscious-ness of existence with all its problems. Pure aesthetic contemplation removes its object from history and from all the relations it has with anything outside it. The ideal aesthetic experience, according to Schopenhauer, is one in which consciousness even of one's individual identity recedes in the act of aesthetic absorption. (His affinity with classical Indian and Buddhist philoso-phies is evident in this idea.) The disappearance of awareness of one's individual self represents about as extreme a version of the generic, disin-terested perceiver that one can imagine. Schopenhauer describes this state:

> Therefore if, for example, I contemplate a tree aesthetically, i.e., with artistic eyes, and thus recognize not it but its Idea, it is immediately of no importance whether it is this tree or its ancestor that flour-ished a thousand years ago, and whether the contemplator is this individual, or any other living anywhere and at any time.[24]

Schopenhauer is explicit that sexual interest is among the attitudes that inter-rupt contemplation and intrude the restless will into an experience, so for him at least there is a clear gap between aesthetic pleasure and the pleasures where desire operates. (Schopenhauer's misogyny is also in play in some of his comments. He refers to women as the "unaesthetic" sex.)[25]

In less extreme (and less metaphysically encumbered) terms, this approach to aesthetic value was promoted for well over a century. For some philoso-phers, the "aesthetic attitude" was the crucial factor in being able to discern the unique, intrinsic properties of art and to separate them from the confus-ing influence of other interests and values. In an influential text of the mid-twentieth century, Jerome Stolnitz asserts that only by ridding ourselves of practical, sociological, or historical interests can we appreciate anything—including art—for its intrinsic value. He defines the aesthetic attitude as "disinterested and sympathetic attention to and contemplation of any object of awareness whatever, for its own sake alone."[26]

The recommended attitude permits reception of difficult art by inducing one to overlook discomfort or moral disapproval in order to appreciate what an artist has accomplished. In this way it also acknowledges the expectation that an artist might have expressed something unique that necessitates an open mind and heart to discover and appreciate. This approach can defend a zone of experience by elevating aesthetic value to the same or even higher standing than social mores. In the mid-nineteenth century, for example,

Charles Baudelaire set out to write poetry (*Les Fleurs du Mal*) that was beautiful but violated familiar moral expectations, pressing the distinction between moral and aesthetic norms. And as we shall see in Chapter 5, the notion of pure aesthetic value independent of the content of art also contributed to formalist defenses of non-representational styles when they were among the controversial leading innovations in painting and sculpture. In more recent times we have seen extreme transgressions of moral codes in works of art that yet are defended because of their beauty, beauty that can only be appreciated if one adopts a disinterested aesthetic attitude. (This was a common—and successful—defense of the much-debated homoerotic photographs of Robert Mapplethorpe during the legal controversies around exhibitions of his work in 1990.)[27] In other words, the formal dexterity and beauty of art can supply an aesthetic value that overrides the moral disvalue of its content, and appeal to this distinction has at times been critical for the social and even legal justification of outlaw artworks. But this strategic virtue also has a problematic obverse, one that is germane to feminist critiques of the idea of disinterested contemplation.

When Stolnitz defines an aesthetic attitude, he stipulates that "perception is directed to the object in its own right and that the spectator is not concerned to analyze it or to ask questions about it."[28] However, it is precisely the prohibition on asking questions that has prompted many feminist critics to reject this tradition in aesthetics. Not only does it render the perceiver peculiarly quiescent, it places in a category of nonaesthetic properties many of the aspects of art that furnish its meaning. When the artwork at issue has a sexual charge, as is the case with the representation of nudes, the division between aesthetic and nonaesthetic properties stifles questions about social roles, power, and sexual control, as we shall see shortly. Moreover, critical approaches that emphasize the value of form (line, composition, combination of elements) over content (the subject matter of art) have pervaded many artistic disciplines, especially in the twentieth century. As musicologist Susan McClary observes of her discipline, "musicology fastidiously declares issues of musical signification to be off-limits to those engaged in legitimate scholarship. It has seized disciplinary control over the study of music and has prohibited the asking of even the most fundamental questions concerning meaning."[29] Construing the aesthetic in these isolating terms ignores its social significance and its power, including its power to hold the representation of the female in thrall to what Cornelia Klinger calls an "aesthetic ideology" consonant with the social subordination and exploitation of women.[30] Both artworks and the individuals who appreciate them must be considered in all of their specifically historical relations in order best to understand how works of art achieve meaning. While reinstating this broader base for understanding art risks diminishing both the disinterestedness and the universality of aesthetic appreciation, it also re-establishes an aspect of art that sometimes becomes muted in the aesthetic tradition but that certain theorists since Plato have addressed: its power.

Feminist critiques of aesthetic perception

Perhaps nowhere is the ideology of extreme disinterested contemplation more questionable than when applied to paintings of female nudes, which one feminist scholar argues virtually define the modern fine art of painting.[31] Aesthetic ideologies that would remove art from its relations with the world disguise its ability to inscribe and to reinforce power relations. With visual art, those relations are manifest in vision itself: the way it is depicted in a work and the way it is induced and directed in the observer outside the work.

Consider for example Jean-Léon Gérôme's painting entitled *A Roman Slave Market* (c.1884). This subject, which features both vulnerable female flesh and an exotic setting, was a popular one for painters of this time; Gérôme himself painted six versions of this theme.[32] The painting depicts a young slave girl on auction before a group of scrutinizing male potential buyers. Viewers of this work may have different reactions; they might be scandalized, outraged, embarrassed, or titillated by the subject, and at the same time they might find it beautifully proportioned and finely painted. At least some of those responses issue from what Stolnitz would consider an inappropriate moral attitude that interferes with aesthetic perception. The proper aesthetic attitude permits one to transcend one's moral discomfort and appreciate such formal qualities as the sensuous curves of the woman's body against the dark background of the market. But even if we grant that such a distanced appreciation may somewhat suppress discomforting awareness of the scrutiny of the male buyers of female flesh, it would require an act of mind-numbing blindness altogether to extinguish critical consideration of gender and eroticism in this work. That is, disinterestedness may rule out prejudice and interfering moralizing, but it does not and should not make one overlook what is obviously going on in the painting, nor would the painter (or the philosopher himself, for that matter) likely approve of such willful ignorance of what he was probably at pains to depict. Consider just

Figure 5 Jean-Léon Gérôme, *A Roman Slave Market*, c. 1884. The Walters Art Museum, Baltimore 37.885.

how complex is the phenomenon of "looking" as it operates in a picture like this—not only how we the spectators regard it but also how viewing perspectives are represented within the painting.

Direction of the eyes of the depicted figures bidding on the girl up for auction are particularly unsubtle examples of rapacious scrutiny. The hoard of staring men see the girl in her most exposed state, for we only see her back. Part of the experience of this painting involves realizing that we cannot see what they do, and that the girl is painfully posed not just as salable property but also for the titillating pleasure of all who regard her. One senses that she feels herself being seen. She shields her face, unable to return their gaze. Her vulnerable pale skin stands out against the shadowed crowd, which in contrast appears dark and predatory. For some viewers this painting may be far too uncomfortable to be pleasurable at all; in aesthetic attitude terms, they are unable to achieve the requisite moral detachment to appreciate its artistic qualities. Or possibly the pleasure a viewer finds in the unprotected beauty of the girl and her distressing state may be furtive, reluctant, even slightly shameful, its erotic valence hard to suppress. In any event, a full consideration of the operation of vision must consider its connection with desire, and some of that connection is noticed by one's own response to the eroticism and edgy sadism of the image. While a wholly political or moral attitude towards this painting indeed might blunt one's appreciation of its artistry, the idea of a completely "disinterested" attention for this type of artwork sounds either pretty difficult to maintain or a bit of a hoax, since interest is present in a sort of displaced and abstract—yet still erotic—savoring of beauty. The painted figures and the spectator are all in dynamic relations, and it is these that illustrate a dimension of the authority of vision itself. In this case, the overt power is the rather conventional dominance of male viewers over a vulnerable female. The experience of beauty is supposedly disinterested, although representations of female nudes often stress their sexual desirability, and sexual desire is an obvious "interest." One might therefore suspect that the recommended disinterested attitude serves as a safeguard against desire, specifically heterosexual male desire, in order to keep women proper objects of aesthetic judgment along with painting, sculptures, and scenery.

Analysis of vision and of what has become known as "the male gaze" presume that the ability to look at others is an indication of sexual and social power.[33] Theories of the gaze stress the activity of vision, its mastery and control of the aesthetic object. These theories reject the separation of desire from pleasure, reinstating the erotic, covetous gaze into the core of beauty. The imaginative viewing position prescribed by the spectator of a painting like Gérôme's is arguably both masculine and heterosexual. As Laura Mulvey puts it, women are assigned the passive status of being-looked-at, whereas men are the active subjects who look.[34] Insofar as it covertly persuades viewers to assume the requisite viewing attitudes, art exerts authority and has sway over the way we think about ourselves and the world through the presentation of subject matter. As Naomi Scheman states:

Vision is the sense best adapted to express . . . dehumanization: it works at a distance and need not be reciprocal, it provides a great deal of easily categorized information, it enables the perceiver accurately to locate (pin down) the object, and it provides the gaze, a way of making the visual object aware that she is a visual object. Vision is political, as is visual art, whatever (else) it may be about.[35]

Nowhere is the power of vision more sharply illustrated than in a painting with a theme that might stand as a critical emblem of the male gaze, Artemisia Gentileschi's portrayal of *Susanna and the Elders* (1610). The story of Susanna is taken from the Old Testament Apocrypha and tells of a beautiful woman who, while bathing, was watched by two of the powerful male Elders of the community. They demanded sexual favors and threatened to tell her husband the king that she was an adulteress if she did not comply. She did not and was saved by Daniel. However, it is not her rescue but the moment of being spied upon in her bath that became a favorite theme of Renaissance and Baroque painting. This point in the story not only is dramatic in the narrative, but also it is ready-made to permit the spectator of the painting to gaze along with the Elders at Susanna innocently bathing. Unlike many other versions of this theme in which Susanna is painted before she discovers her privacy has been violated, Gentileschi's rendering of this theme dramatically portrays Susanna's virtual helplessness and horror at her exposure. Her nakedness is awkward and painful rather than titillating. (I leave the reader to speculate about the relevance of the gender of the artist to the way that the power of looking is pictured in and prompted by this painting.)

Theories of the gaze also challenge the presumption that the model audience for art is a universal, generic spectator, noting the potential disruption of appreciation at those times when the point of view prescribed by the object does not conform with the subject position of the viewer. To say that an "imaginative position" is prescribed means that the artwork directs the viewer to regard the work in a particular way, that is, specifically in a way that privileges a masculine spectator as the authoritative viewer of art and judge of its quality.[36] Paying attention to the complexities of depiction is more than social criticism; it enhances our appreciation of artworks, for only by taking notice of the power of vision is one likely to discover the possibilities for different vantages of "looking." Indeed, awareness that a masculine viewpoint is more or less standard for the genre of the nude makes one alert

Figure 6 Artemisia Gentileschi, *Susanna and the Elders*, 1610. Schonborn Collection, Schloss Weissenstein, Pommersfelden, Germany (Foto Marburg/Art Resource, NY).

to the difference in the way that Gentileschi has represented Susanna's moment of discovery, for this picture is less evidently addressed to the male voyeur than is the case with Gérôme's painting. It also alerts one to the presence of other modes of looking, such as the possibility of homoerotic desire in the works of Michelangelo, Caravaggio, and others who pose the male body for visual pleasure.

Acknowledging all of this does not necessarily require complete rejection of the older aesthetic tradition. Even a successfully disinterested stance, if that means that one does not prematurely condemn art because of its content, does not necessarily cancel out discrepancies of perspective that different perceivers take to an artwork. That is, there may be a variety of perspectives on a work, all of which qualify as disinterested in that they suspend practical involvement and moral assessment in order to appreciate a work's intrinsic presentational qualities. The alert viewer is aware of how a work invites appreciative points of view, but that point of view is not necessarily adopted.[37] This is an important qualification to any premature presumption that there might be a single "male gaze" that is prescribed for art. But becoming aware of how "looking" operates in visual art dramatizes the fact that active viewers come in many varieties and interpret art and its values from a multiplicity of perspectives.

The reinstatement of desire in theories of aesthetic pleasure now probably dominates critical discourse. Among the charges directed against the legacies of the Enlightenment, the anti-universalist conclusion is also strong. Many agree that to understand how art is regarded one must attend to more specific social positions and not just posit an "ideal viewer." This assumption describes much recent critical work in the humanities and social sciences among scholars who have concluded not only that a neutral, universal point of view is impossible, but that any attempt to formulate it will be distorted by the class, gender, national, and historical perspective of the formulator. Universalist ideals have been replaced by the value of the *particular* perspective mindful of its situation in society and history, without pretense to universality.[38]

What has been articulated about vision and the gaze is suggestive about the structure of aesthetic appreciation itself, or certainly about the structure of these theories of appreciation. Aesthetic objects are assigned the passive role of being-looked-at rather than active looking; they are objects presented for the tasteful scrutiny of the perceiver. On a more abstract level, one can posit that structurally gender is at work in the difference between the passive object of perception and the active perceiver. Combined with the gendered thinking that pervades eighteenth-century accounts of beauty, this structural relationship can take on what we might call the form of gender in the relationship between subject and object, a structure that possesses traits parallel to those obtaining between masculine and feminine positions more literally described.[39]

To be sure, the structure of aesthetic appreciation understood in these terms is far more suitable for certain kinds of art than for others. It posits a spectator–art disjunction that will not serve, for example, for participatory arts in which groups dance or sing together. The fine-art tradition and the aesthetic theories that underwrite it did not utterly ignore these kinds of arts, but theories of taste are theories of connoisseurship rather than of participation, and so we see here a perpetuation of assumptions about what kinds of arts are central models for aesthetic theory.

Summary

The legacy of the eighteenth-century Enlightenment has been powerful and tenacious, formulating a number of developments in aesthetics that are still in use today, including the contentious idea that aesthetic value is independent of and sometimes outweighs moral assessment. At the same time, we can find gender and cultural biases operating in the quest for universal aesthetic norms, and with these biases there are good grounds to suspect that "universal" taste necessitates imposing some sets of cultural norms and suppressing others. This is an obvious way of interpreting the distinction between "high" and "popular" culture.

Enlightenment thinkers had some good reasons for rejecting desire as the foundation for all pleasures and for safeguarding a zone of distinctively aesthetic values. The isolation of aesthetic qualities from their social dimensions, however, which became a tendency among later theorists, blunts the power of art. As feminist critics have observed, ideas about disinterested perception tend to elevate formal qualities above content and social meaning. Criticisms of purely aesthetic perception and speculations about the "gaze" reinstate not only desire and satisfaction in the function of perception but also acknowledge the cultural authority of art to perpetuate power relations.

While the uses of feminist insights in contemporary art and theory will be taken up again in Chapters 5 and 6, in the next chapter we need to recall the highly gendered atmosphere of aesthetics in the eighteenth and nineteenth centuries, a situation in which the passive, beautiful object stands as a feminine counterpart to the activity of the male artist. As we shall see, this description does not remain safely within the zone of theory but exerts practical influence over what women could actually do. Combined with the rising ideas about fine art that were discussed in Chapter 1, the aesthetic ideals of the modern period contributed to a climate in which women's participation in the arts was fraught and difficult. We shall now turn to consideration of how aesthetic theory underwrites artistic practice.

3

AMATEURS AND PROFESSIONALS

The first two chapters presented the philosophical roots of gendered concepts surrounding the notions of artist, art, and aesthetic response; this one takes a look at how some of those concepts have influenced the opportunities for women practitioners in several arts. Because we are continuing an analysis of the fine-art tradition, the historical location of this discussion will be the eighteenth through the early twentieth centuries. This focus will lead us to examine a significant factor that often separates female from male practitioners in the fine arts as they develop in modern times: the identification of an artist as an "amateur" or as a "professional." The status of professional or amateur, as we shall see, is not a matter of merely personal choice or convenience. It has substantial consequences for the contributions that artists are able to make to their arts, for amateurs are satellite figures marginal to the formation of the artistic canons that furnish paradigms of art.

Education and training: who learns?

The concept of genius, as we have seen, is a contested category constructed to glorify the talents of especially gifted people and to elevate them above those destined for ordinary occupations. Feminist scholars have skeptically observed that social factors play as influential a role as inborn talent in selecting mostly male artists to stand in the ranks of geniuses. This is not a new idea; Virginia Woolf noted in 1929 that historically women have not been in positions where their talents could be tried and developed.[1] No matter what gifts nature may bestow on artists, they must be trained; without education genius is merely a potential. Certain art forms present formidable barriers, not only to opportunities for recognition but also to the fundamental training required to discover talent and produce art.

The intellectual and philosophical ideas about the individual genius whose work is the unique product of his creative efforts developed in the particular social and economic context of modern Europe, and changes in art practice and consumption further contributed to the gendering of the idea of the artist. But the participation or exclusion of women in the arts has not been by any means uniform. It varies considerably depending on which art form one selects for attention. This chapter will review briefly three genres of art—music, literature, and painting—as samples of the ways that women have been permitted or hindered from full participation in the arts. I have selected these three in particular because each genre illuminates different features of conceptual frameworks governing art and the idea of the artist. Music, which has presented some of the most tenacious barriers to women participants, elucidates subtleties about concepts of artistic sensibility, emotion, and subjectivity. It is also a venue for discussing restrictions surrounding performance and the public presence of the artist. Prose literature, specifically the novel, represents the other end of the spectrum of opportunities, for novel-writing virtually began as a women's genre, and women have always been major participants in this art form, although the critical reception of their novels indicates some panic regarding the prominence and popularity of female artistic sensibilities. Even though women still faced certain barriers that men did not, the history of novel-writing is not a history of exclusion. Indeed, one could surmise that successful women artists breached some well-protected precincts of creativity. Painting illuminates theories about the mentality of the creator of visual art, focusing on the scope and power of vision and its ties with the intellect. Theories about what is required to paint the world with accuracy are explicitly rooted in venerable philosophical ideas about human nature, knowledge, and achievement that were discussed in the first chapter.

To understand thoroughly the resonance of gender in the fundamental concepts and practices of any given field would require considerably more detail and depth of research than can be presented here. Once again, the purpose of this study is not to review the critical history of painting or music, architecture or dance or literature, but rather to sketch gendered patterns of thinking about aesthetic matters and how art practice manifests the tenacity of certain fundamental philosophical frameworks.

The general thesis that I shall advance is that the idea of women's participation in art centrally relates both to concepts of feminine disposition and capacity and to ideas about what constitutes a person's descriptive identity.

When placed into the social milieus that prevailed at formative points in the history of the arts, expectations about women's identity and the terms in which they defined themselves especially hampered their entering the fine-art professions. Several touchpoints of analysis are useful to consider: (1) Whether an art form demands the public presence of the artist, such that she would be on display to an audience. In social classes and milieus especially sensitive to matters of propriety, whether or how a woman appears in public can be more or less crippling for the female performer, whether musician, dancer, or actor. (2) Whether it requires a skill commonly considered diminished in the female creative mind, such as mathematics. If it does, then education and training in that art are apt to be foreclosed or truncated. (3) Or whether it requires a breadth of experience that is considered inappropriate for a female to obtain. This issue often limits the reception rather than the production of women's work, such as their writings, which are often enjoyed but criticized for restricted scope and narrow vision, insuring that women's efforts will be counted as minor, manifesting "feminine taste." Not all art forms make the same demands on their practitioners, and so we find that patterns of inclusion and exclusion vary with genre, time, and place.

Music

Making music is a common pastime that pervades many aspects of life: domestic, public, religious, ceremonial. Work songs divert the mind from hard labor and provide rhythm for physical tasks; lullabies croon babies to sleep; aimless humming passes the time. Virtually all cultures make music, and the ways that women and men sing, dance, or play instruments vary in many of them.[2] Most traditional music has both aesthetic and utilitarian functions; that is, music is enjoyed for its own sake as well as for the diversion, amusement, or civic or religious ends it accomplishes. At certain times and places in history, women have been important participants in the performance and even the composition of music. This was the case, for example, in the courts of Europe in the Middle Ages and in religious establishments such as nunneries.[3] From the Renaissance through the modern period that has produced most of our canonical art music pieces, however, women's access to music education and opportunities to perform have been quite restricted.

The kind of music that became identified with the fine-art tradition eventually became the work of professionals. Their job was to perform with dexterity for audiences which sought aesthetic pleasure and expansion of their cultural understanding through the work of the best composers. Some of the compositions of the western tradition that are admired as the pinnacle of musical achievement were written not as art music but for religious ceremonies and liturgies, but the paradigm of the musical composition in the fine-art system is a work that is just to be listened to for its beauty, intricacy, novelty, or complexity—in short, for its aesthetic qualities alone. What in the visual arts is labeled the distinction between craft and art, in the music world appears as the difference between music that serves a further purpose (accompanying a civic ceremony, religious worship, and entertainment) and "art music" that is created for aesthetic enjoyment.[4] It is a tradition that is especially reflective of upper- and middle-class tastes, and the ideas of womanhood that circumscribed women's musical activities were similarly situated in these classes.

Performance

Young ladies of the modern period were encouraged to develop a certain range of artistic talents, including painting and drawing, and skills of singing and playing a musical instrument such as a piano, harpsichord, or harp. They sometimes became quite accomplished, and the musical daughter could be a considerable asset to a household for the entertainment and sociable diversion she provided. (Readers of the novels of Jane Austen will recall how many times female characters are called upon to sing or play for company.) Certainly in domestic settings, performance of music was encouraged by families, educational practices, and the many books of manners, deportment, and household management that were published.

Public performance is another matter. For centuries, women's appearance on stage in any role at all was not only frowned upon but banned by law in many communities. Equally strong was the social sanction of making a display of oneself in public, which violated norms of propriety and modesty. (The impropriety of positioning oneself to be regarded in this way indicates sensitivity to the power of vision discussed in the last chapter.) Indeed, when female performers did become more common on stage, they were often from the lower classes of society.[5] As a rule, musical accomplishments were conceived as a domestic revenue which would not lead to anything like a professional commitment. The restrictions of propriety extended beyond musical performance to publishing one's compositions, a circumstance that also obtained with literature. Some of Fanny Mendelssohn Hensel's work apparently was published under her brother Felix Mendelssohn's name for this reason.[6]

Although we now think of professional musicians as persons of accomplishment and relatively high social standing, at earlier periods of time, "professional musician" was not necessarily a label of highest compliment, for it indicated someone who needed to earn a living through his or her art (in contrast to the musical members of the nobility). But more importantly it also indicates a person who is formally trained in an art form. It is the professional aspect of art that has been most widely inaccessible to women. In the Middle Ages, for example, complicated forms of polyphonic music were taught in cathedral schools, and while women often performed the music they rarely learned how to compose it, for the schools were open only to male clerics. A similar situation obtains in numerous other traditions: the participation of women is so much narrower than that of men that despite their encouragement to develop some talents, they were rarely able to pursue them to the same degree as men of their own station. As the modern period saw the growth of a middle-class art-consuming public and a market for art that beckoned artists to make their living through music (or painting or writing), the absence of professional opportunities for women usually kept them in amateur status both as performers and composers.

Reigning concepts of femininity posed further difficulties with performance in public, some of which now appear quaint or almost comical. At least since the Renaissance, women were directed towards "feminine" instruments, meaning those that could be played without making faces or assuming indecorous postures. The playing of the bass viol or the cello, which are held between the knees of the performer, was considered by many to require an indiscreet pose. Although the sweetness of the flute disposed it for female players, many wind instruments distort the cheeks and redden the face. Several types of horns induce an unbecoming deluge of saliva. Early in the twentieth century, one music director lamented that the affiliation of musicians with labor unions was forcing orchestras to accept female performers, to the detriment of both the orchestra and the women on stage:

> Women harpists are admitted to be more desirable than men, the harp being essentially a woman's instrument. It requires such delicate fingering, you will find everywhere women are in demand for this work. But . . . nature never intended the fair sex to become

cornetists, trombonists, and players of wind instruments. In the first place they are not strong enough to play them as well as men . . . Another point against them is that women cannot possibly play brass instruments and look pretty, and why should they spoil their good looks?[7]

It seems that the female artist cannot escape being regarded as an aesthetic object, even while she is actively engaged in producing other aesthetic objects.

The idea that women harpists would be welcomed because the delicacy of the instrument matched the delicacy of the player was regarded in a somewhat jaded light by one of the pioneers of women's orchestral playing, Ethel Smyth, who considered the association of the harp with femininity a dubious benefit:

> The harp being a cumbrous and rather unlucrative instrument, woman has been permitted by ancient tradition to play it. Indeed I think her colleagues rather cherish this solitary white-armed presence in their midst, much as the men in the Welsh regiment cherish the regimental goat.[8]

Perhaps the dismay that originally greeted the idea that women musicians should play alongside men in symphony orchestras now appears curiously old-fashioned, but one should note that many conventions barring women from such activities were abandoned only recently. The distinguished Vienna Philharmonic Orchestra, for example, opened its ranks to women only in 1997.[9]

Despite the inhibitions imposed by propriety, there were some spectacularly accomplished female musicians in eighteenth- and nineteenth-century Europe. Often when women did enter the ranks of professionals, they were members of musical families whose parents promoted their talents and afforded them training far beyond that which was readily available to others, as was the case with the famous pianists Clara Schumann (1819–96) and Fanny Mendelssohn Hensel (1805–47). Both were members of families with even more famous male members who were composers and performers (Clara married Robert Schumann; Fanny's brother was Felix Mendelssohn.) But in their cases, as with Mozart's sister the century before, the pressure to marry and to meet the demands of family eventually overshadowed their

careers (though Schumann managed to maintain a remarkable public repu-
tation and presence). This is not to say that they were forced into domestic
obligations against their wills, but that those roles exerted formative influences over their own expectations and desires. If their first identity as
women, defined in relation to a man and a family, threatened to eclipse their
identification as professional musicians in the cases of these talented and
well-positioned women, one can only surmise how many others never made
it out of the parlor.

Composition

The relegation of women musicians to largely amateur status naturally
affected their work as composers as well as performers. And most signifi-
cantly for the idea of the *great* artist, amateur standing affects to profound
detriment the ability to compose music of historical significance. As one
music historian observes:

> Musicologists have emphasized the development of musical style
> through the most progressive works and genres of a period, whereas
> most women composers were not leaders in style change, in part, at
> least, because they were excluded from the professional positions
> that engendered new developments.[10]

Inaccessibility of professional training has direct consequences for the
gender of the idea of "genius," a label that by now one ought to regard with
considerable suspicion. Doubtless some people are more talented than
others, and some are prodigiously gifted. But no talent accomplishes anything by itself without the discipline of training, familiarity with tradition,
and license to experiment with the boundaries of accepted style. Amateur
status disposes one to participate in tradition without making major changes
to it; therefore, amateurs are unlikely to introduce the innovations in a genre
that are recorded in history as pathbreaking and canonical of a form. Marcia
Citron makes this point with regard to professionalism in the formation of
the musical canon, that is to say, an agreed-upon body of work that represents the most important products of an artistic tradition.

> Professionalism . . . involves having one's music published, per-
> formed, and written about. These are obvious ways to bring

compositions to the attention of the public. Such practicalities might suggest that professionalism is at odds with the ideology of canonicity. For canonicity implies high-minded characteristics like transcendence, disinterestedness, and aesthetic distance. But these describe an ideology and not the realities of canonicity.[11]

Popular distinctions between feminine and masculine artistic qualities, discussed in terms of taste and the gendered distinction between beauty and sublimity in the last chapter, further served to circumscribe the kinds of music in which women were comfortably engaged. Music historian Carol Neuls-Bates observes that

> Critics of the late nineteenth century developed a system of sexual aesthetics that analyzed music in terms of feminine and masculine traits. Feminine music, which women were expected to cultivate exclusively, was by definition graceful and delicate, full of melody, and restricted to the small forms of songs and piano music. Masculine music, by contrast, was powerful in effect and intellectually rigorous in harmony, counterpoint, and other structural logic.[12]

Thus the huge symphonies such as those of Beethoven and Brahms stand as pinnacles of musical accomplishment. When women composed, their efforts were directed more towards smaller-scale (and less remunerative) parlor music.

Genius and subjectivity

The paucity of women who had as many artistic credits on their records as men reinforced the presumption that the female mind is incapable of genius. The antifeminist—one could say misogynist—philosopher Jean-Jacques Rousseau declared that women possess no artistic sensibility and are incapable of genius.[13] He tied this incapacity with the need to educate women as satellites to men, approving of their domestic artistic accomplishments so long as they are sufficiently curbed that the comfort of the male companion is not compromised. In the next century Schopenhauer quoted Rousseau with approval and added his own extended opinion about women's systematic inferiority to men:

The most distinguished intellects among the whole sex have never managed to produce a single achievement in the fine arts that is really great, genuine, and original; or given to the world any work of permanent value in any sphere . . . when Nature made two divisions of the human race, she did not draw the line exactly through the middle. These divisions are polar and opposed to each other, it is true; but the difference between them is not qualitative merely, it is also quantitative.[14]

Although the attitudes of Rousseau and Schopenhauer were expressed with particular vitriol, they were by no means uncommon. Even advocates for women's education cautioned that their accomplishments needed to be moderated so as not to interfere with their chief roles as wives and mothers. And this attitude was expressed by women as well as men, for at the time few truly believed that the sexes were equally endowed with the same range of talents and capabilities or that women could successfully compete with men in the most difficult artistic endeavors.

At the outset of this study we raised the question of why art, which is so tied to emotions and their expression, should be considered as male an enterprise as science. In theories about the absence of genius and artistic creativity in women we can see part of the answer: women's emotional expression is too much a part of their *nature*. When they have and display emotions, their feelings are manifestations of something they are fashioned to do, not an accomplishment that extends beyond what nature dictates. In an influential nineteenth-century treatise, music critic George Upton asserted that "woman" is emotional by nature. However:

The emotion is a part of herself, and is as natural to her as breathing. She lives in emotion, and acts from emotion. She feels its influences, its control, and its power, but she does not see these results as man looks at them. He sees them in their full play, and can reproduce them in musical notation as a painter imitates the landscape before him . . . To treat emotions as if they were mathematics, to bind and measure and limit them within the rigid laws of harmony and counterpoint, and to express them with arbitrary signs, is a cold-blooded operation, possible only to the sterner and more obdurate nature of man.[15]

These links between rational discipline, mathematical facility, and aesthetic distance that are required to channel emotion into musical creativity effectively make the artistic exploitation of even the "feminine" trait of emotions a male prerogative. In these distinctions one perhaps detects some anxiety at play among male artists who desired to keep their artistic sensitivity intact without being described with the dreaded critical term "effeminate" that was discussed in Chapter 2. Susan McClary notes that music, an art sometimes suspected of feminine tendencies, was carefully defended by means of its connections with mathematics.[16]

Undoubtedly the prevalent caution regarding women's talents had psychologically inhibiting effects on the progress of those who desired to try (as we sometimes can know from their own letters and diaries). With messages about a circumscribed feminine ambit of taste and ability so pervasive, it would be nearly impossible not to internalize at least some of these values for oneself. Ideology, expectation, and education have influence not only over the opportunities of people to create but over their subjective preferences, their tastes.[17] As McClary states, "The codes marking gender difference in music . . . themselves participate in social formation, inasmuch as individuals learn how to be gendered beings through their interactions with cultural discourses such as music."[18] The implications of the limits on artistic scope and the ability to express a range of feelings and ideas may be extended even further into the development of personality. Sue Campbell links expression with the reserves of mental life itself: "If what we feel is, by and large, what we express, then people can control our feelings by controlling our modes of expression. There is no such thing as a protected private life of feeling."[19]

There is more than education and psychology, attitude and self-confidence at work here. The very concept of the type of person who is being given such admonitions indicates that the identity of a woman is conceived in relation to family in contrast to the more autonomous identity of a man. As we have already seen, gendered ideas perform in pairs: masculine–feminine; public–private; mind–body; reason–emotion, and so on. While the professional–amateur duality is a social and historical phenomenon, its meanings are fastened firmly into this venerable system of opposites. The amateur artist is a person who performs and creates in a private, often domestic environment and earns little or nothing in recompense. No matter how accomplished, an amateur performance is for a relatively small audience of intimates; its purpose is diversion and entertainment, the musical

version of decoration. There is nothing to prevent males from being amateurs, and many are. But amateur status is linked to the activities of private
life, as are women themselves. The practical effects of the professional–
amateur duality complicate ideas about genius, artistic standing, and assessments of women's contribution to culture.[20]

Literature

We can see another twist on female professionalism when we turn our attention to prose literature and the rise of the novel as a popular art form. Here
women participated in large numbers, sometimes to the dismay of those
interested in the status of the fine arts. The concerns of the latter were
directed not only to the suspicion that women were unlikely to write prose
that was elevating and profound, but also to the genre itself. The novel is a
relatively new art form that developed in Europe in the eighteenth century,
and in the early years it seemed to represent a long step down from the
more important form of poetry. Novel reading was regarded as risky entertainment that was apt to corrupt the mind with romantic and adventure-
some ideas and with flights of imagination that diverted attention from
practical duties and the demands of real life.[21] But novels were very popular,
and in many areas of Europe and America which saw the growth of a large
middle-class in the eighteenth and nineteenth centuries, there emerged a
readership eager for the diversions of literature.[22] Expansion of education
resulted in widespread literacy, and the growth of lending libraries, popular
periodicals, and inexpensive book publication enhanced the size and diversity of the reading public. Large numbers of women were eager readers,
occupying a substantial portion of the market for literature. All of this
aroused certain concerns about the "feminization" of taste, by which was
meant sentimental and romantic indulgence in imagination and enjoyment
of formless, emotive writing.[23] Over time, as the novel settled into its own
traditions and its popularity became secure, its prestige also rose.[24]

Literary opportunities were open for women partly because the novel
was a new and popular art form that was written in vernacular language.
Higher learning was still available only to a narrow sector of society, chiefly
male, often clerical; and study of scholarly languages such as Latin, Greek,
and Hebrew was a largely male endeavor. In earlier times, when the written
tongue was likely to be Latin, women wrote less, though they appear to
have been among the earliest contributors to vernacular poetic arts.[25] But

by and large poetry, especially during the time when the prose novel became popular, was rooted firmly in the classical tradition, both in its forms and in the themes and literary tropes in which poets were expected to be fluent.[26]

Their lack of education in learned languages has had some ironic benefits for women in the history of literature, and not only in Europe. Consider the case of the Japanese prose novel. The novel is a considerably earlier art form in Japan than in Europe, having first appeared in the eleventh century. The initial and paradigm example is the mammoth *Tale of Genji*, written by a lady-in-waiting at the imperial court, Murasaki Shikibu. Lady Murasaki, like nearly all the women of Japan in that period, had only limited access to formal education. She was not taught the language of culture and learning, Chinese, which was reserved for privileged men (though like many quick-minded sisters she evidently picked up some knowledge of the language from the lessons her brother received). So when she wrote her tales for entertainment, she naturally wrote in the language she knew: vernacular Japanese. In this case, far from being a disadvantage, her lack of learning placed her squarely at the birth of prose literature in Japanese.

Of course, waiting for conventions of written language to change does not afford the kind of opportunity for fame that one can count on. However, despite a sometimes oppressive history of the exclusion of groups from education or opportunities, human beings are rarely just the passive victims of circumstance. They create what they can within the space available and by whatever means they have at their disposal. Sometimes in so doing they produce fine work in established traditions; other times they create new genres. As with any endeavor, the judgment that history eventually bestows is fickle and unpredictable.

In short, the novel represents an art form that, unlike painting or music, architecture or poetry, had no male-dominated tradition into which women writers had to insert themselves, for the genre began with little precedent and less prestige. As Virginia Woolf observed:

> There is no reason to think that the form of the epic or of the poetic play suits a woman any more than the sentence suits her. But all the older forms of literature were hardened and set by the time she became a writer. The novel alone is young enough to be soft in her hands.[27]

The advantage of this situation was that women were not competing in a male-dominated tradition or market. The disadvantage was that the entire genre was considered inferior to the more austere, demanding, and profound genre of poetry, as well as to other prose forms such as essays on political economy, religion, and science. Moreover, female authors tended to be evaluated as "women" writers in their own special, demoted category.

Despite the fact that women faced barriers and discouragements in their pursuit of writing careers, the means necessary to write are not so restricted to professional forms of learning as is the case with music or painting. Reading, writing, and story-telling can be successfully accomplished in private. Emily Dickinson and Jane Austen are but two famous examples of women who created from within domestic, even isolated households. They were prompted to write from a variety of motives. For example, Austen's father encouraged her writing for enjoyment and family entertainment, but as she grew older she also needed the money that her works eventually earned. A number of women began writing in order to support their families, as was the case for Frances Trollope (mother of the more famous Anthony Trollope), widowed with young children, for, difficult as it is to find the time and space for concentration, writing can be done at home before and after attending to domestic duties.

Women writers experienced a version of the divided mind that beset musicians, for while their literary accomplishments were often praised, at the same time publishing entailed declaring oneself in public, and to many that was an improper act of exposure. This was one reason why so many women, especially in the mid-nineteenth century, chose to publish under masculine pseudonyms or insisted on a degree of anonymity. However, women accommodated these conditions with very different approaches, from the flamboyant French writer George Sand (1804–76), who assumed male dress as well as a man's name, to the domestic Elizabeth Gaskell (1810–65), who used her own name only after the success of her first novel, which was published anonymously. Mary Ann Evans (1819–80), who wrote under the pseudonym George Eliot, lived a public life until her relationship with a married man made it prudent that she more or less withdraw from society out of deference for the sensibilities of their friends. The social pressure for propriety and discretion competed with the desire for fame that many possessed, as well as with a whole-hearted embrace of a professional identity.

Writing and selling

The market demand for literature and the increasing numbers of writers who endeavored to make a living by selling their work led to some paradoxical changes in ideas about the fine art of writing. In the eighteenth century and before, those who sought to make their living by their pens were not protected by anything like copyright regulations, so pirated reprints deprived them of the fruits of their labors. To address this problem, writers began to demand recognition of the ownership of their work, to be considered the "authors" of works that are their creations, the revenues from which ought to belong to them as well. A legal concept such as copyright may seem remote from the idea of artistic genius, but Martha Woodmansee argues that the regulations that were put in place to insure payment also contributed to the development of certain concepts of the artist and especially of the author—the authoritative creator of a work that belongs to him and him alone.[28] We saw that earlier concepts of genius often pictured the creator as a conduit of ideas from some semi-divine source; the image of the Muse pictures a mysterious voice that takes over the mind of the poet and infuses it with inspiration. But in the modern period, when authors were struggling to be recognized as such, the source of artistic inspiration was removed from divine precincts and internalized. The creative artist himself is the origin of ideas expressed, and the product of his pen belongs to him alone. With the rise of such values, copyright laws came to recognize writings as property and the profits from sales as owed to the author. Authorship and earnings converge in the idea of the professional writer.

Market considerations and establishment of property in writing were one factor in the evolving concept of the literary artist. Secondly, and not entirely consistently, the mass, popular art produced at this time appeared to many writers and critics to be diluting and corrupting the ideals of genuine art, not least because of its perceived "feminine" qualities of emotional flabbiness and slipshod form. To combat this problem, many theorists began to distinguish True Art from mere mass entertainment, and here again the ideal of pure aesthetic enjoyment was invoked. The work of the true artist is available to the few, those with "taste" who are capable of purely aesthetic enjoyment, and therefore popularity is a suspect trait.[29] Only real art yields the sort of appreciation available from the disinterested contemplation that was so promoted by modern aesthetic theory. This high-minded aesthetic consideration was somewhat at odds with efforts to gain authorial compensation, for the true artist should be wholly satisfied with the successful completion of his work and should need no further approval; he does not, in other words, seek to please or amuse the majority of his audience. He creates only for himself and the connoisseur, the "man of taste." This concept of the true artist is developed hand in hand in the practice of the arts and in the philosophies of the arts of this period. And the theory and practice contributed to what remains a strong distinction between "high" art—for the few who are able to appreciate it—and "low" or "popular" art for the masses.[30]

These values influenced the concept of art and of the artist, even though they did not necessarily describe the actual art market, particularly for prose literature. Popular novelists, including a mass of female authors known collectively and derogatorily (in Nathaniel Hawthorne's phrase) as "scribbling women," sold well, but most were not considered true artists. Thus it came to pass that some very successful women writers have receded from the record of modern literature. But even in their own time there were quite a few acclaimed women novelists who were recognized as accomplished artists. In fact some of them, such as George Eliot and Charlotte Brontë, were admired in their own time for their brilliance, even for—to invoke that contested term—genius.

Subjectivity again

As we saw with the case of music, it was widely believed that subjectivity often makes women sensitive performers but prevents them from being great composers. A variation on this theme appears in the critical commentary regarding novel-writing. The romantic and intimate plots of many popular novels written by women, which abound with sentimentalized descriptions of relationships, domestic life, spiritual struggles, and effusions over picturesque vistas, were understood to be as much an outpouring of the feminine mind as the product of artistic discipline. Such writing was often seen as evincing women's subjective nature, hence less art than display of temperament. This is a version of the idea that women's natural subjectivity abets their artistic creativity at the same time as it circumscribes its quality.

The objective–subjective distinction is one of the pairs of opposites with explicitly acknowledged gendered meaning, for the capacity for objective, dispassionate judgment has a venerable history of ascription to males.

Because artistic preferences and matters of taste seem rather "subjective" themselves, dependent as they are on appreciative assessments based upon pleasure responses, one might not think that subjectivity is a particular liability in the aesthetic domain. But as we are beginning to see, this is emphatically not the case. The sense of "subjectivity" that was ascribed to women creators refers to a tendency to write (or compose or paint) on the basis of feeling rather than discipline and disinterested assessment. The products of such creativity may be personally meaningful but idiosyncratic, unable to pass the test of more rigorous critical comparative assessments. This criticism of women's alleged subjectivity is a symptom of the theme we have already seen present in ideas about genius, namely that when emotions, feelings, and sensibilities are endorsed, they are considered mostly insofar as male artists embody them.

Painting

In the history of painting the distinction between amateur and professional status is also part of the network of factors that influenced, and often inhibited, women's accomplishments. The absence of professional standing can be seen as part of the answer to art historian Linda Nochlin's famous question: Why have there been no great women artists?[31]

The making of painted images occurs in numerous contexts, including domestic. Decorative wall borders, embroidered cushions, silhouettes of children, are but a few of the sorts of images that commonly are made for the home, whether that setting be poor or wealthy. In most cases in the past as well as the present, such decorative tasks have been the work of women and girls (though the larger and messier art of mural or wall painting was more often the project of men), so painting or decorative design in general is certainly not a process that has been closed to women. But once again those endeavors are not only domestic—and therefore more or less private—they are chiefly amateur. They represent what one does for fun or to make one's surroundings more pleasant. But these products are not what makes for a life's work, a profession or career or calling. That kind of dedication signals a life path wholly different from the amateur, and at important periods in the evolution of modern painting the distinction was critical.

To achieve professional standing in the graphic arts, one needs the expertise provided by extensive education and training. These opportunities present themselves to persons who are relatively independent and free to move about, and also who have economic means provided or earned. These restrictions have usually meant that it is men who are able to avail themselves of the opportunities to learn certain art forms. Of course, opportunities may be snatched or wrenched against the odds, so women have been painters too. But we are not just calculating the odds of learning the refined and difficult techniques of one particular art form. Of greater importance is the fact that throughout much of the history of western art, women were stubbornly denied access to teaching studios for two types of reasons: One has to do with notions about what they may *see*, and the other with what they can know.

Seeing

Painting is an especially dramatic genre to investigate the gendering of the concept of the artist and of vision in action, for as a depictive art it engages both the idea of the artist who *sees* and depicts what he sees, but also the object that is *seen*. In the western tradition, the kinds of paintings—traditionally called "history paintings" because they tackle important narratives as well as Biblical stories and classical myth—that have been credited with the most profound subject matter require depicting the human form. And from the Renaissance onward, often that form is unclothed. Even when it is covered, arranging clothes and draperies so that they fall properly is aided by an intimate knowledge of human anatomy. To learn to draw with accuracy typically requires access to a teaching studio where nude models are employed.

As late as the nineteenth century, studios were considered improper places for women, partly because the model employed there might be nude. The fact that some of these nude models were female didn't violate this dictum, since their role was considered more object than subject and they were more like props in the studio than observing, active subjects. (Until the late eighteenth century, most studio models were male, but thereafter female models assumed the role of ideal objects of beauty and subjects for art.)[32] The American painter Thomas Eakins (1844–1916), who taught at the Philadelphia Academy of Fine arts and believed in the extension of art education to women, was forced to resign his post in 1886 because of his practice of employing nude models in mixed classes. The role of model is a peculiarly passive one. A model—with or without clothes—poses at the bidding of the artist and must hold uncomfortably still for long periods of time, turning him or herself into a fixed object to be studied in the process of being painted. The model might even be metaphorically dissected, with one person's hand serving as the better model, another's arm, another's face. (Since classical times this was recommended as the way to put together the most beautiful image of a person, for actual living people rarely embody beauty in all their parts.) Sometimes we know the identity of models, especially if they appear repeatedly in the work of an artist.[33] But often they are as anonymous as the other objects of a scene. Attentive looking is active, and it renders the body which is seen an object of lingering scrutiny. Under circumstances where artists were male (and virtually all studio teachers were male as well), even though models were both male and female, we can see how the seer–seen distinction shapes itself to the old masculine–feminine duality, a practical version of what has been theorized in terms of the male gaze.

Models were (and are) important aspects of the painting enterprise, and sometimes the interior of a studio itself was the subject of painting, indicating art-making in progress. Awareness of the impropriety of women in the studio culminated in a remarkable contrivance by the painter Johann Zoffany in his work commemorating the founding of the British Royal Academy of Art in 1768. In his painting, The Academicians of the Royal Academy, Zoffany depicted all of the members of the Academy in an artist's studio, complete with one male model posing nude at the center of attention and another in the process of removing his clothes. But Zoffany faced a delicate problem: two of the charter members of the Royal Academy were women: Angelica Kauffmann (1741–1807) a distinguished history painter in the classicist "grand" manner, and Mary Moser (1744–1819), a flower painter.[34] For the sake of completeness he had to include them in the picture, but their presence among the other artists of the studio would violate norms of propriety. To solve this difficulty he painted them as portraits on the wall, portraits whose eyes discreetly avoid engagement with anything that is going on in the room. Kauffmann and Moser are doubly framed, fenced away from the studio itself.

This oddity of depiction reveals the anomalous nature of the idea of the "woman artist." Clearly there were women painters, and equally clearly some, such as Kauffmann, earned considerable influence and renown. So it would not be accurate to proclaim that the male gender of the concept of the artist prevented women from becoming painters and achieving success in that endeavor. And yet the literal marginalization of Kauffmann and Moser on the walls of the painted studio—pictures within a picture—calls attention

Figure 7 Johann Zoffany, *The Academicians of the Royal Academy*, 1771–2. The Royal Collection © HM Queen Elizabeth II.

to the fact that their participation in art is aberrant and had to be managed carefully in order not to upset the deeper social order. Although this is an interesting case of representation possessing the power to embarrass and offend as if it were reality, Zoffany's solution does more than preserve propriety. It represents the gender not only of actual artists but also of the very idea of the artist, for the commemorative painting was as much homage to the foundation of the Academy and to the discipline of painting itself as to its present members.

Linear perspective

Another dimension of gender asymmetry may be found in discourse surrounding one of the central techniques of painting and drawing, linear perspective, expertise in which permits one to render three-dimensional space on a two-dimensional picture plane. The development of linear perspective in Europe began in Italy in the fourteenth or fifteenth century. Over time the basics of drawing in perspective were disseminated in many parts of Europe, and books were published that explained how to locate vanishing points and how to arrange parallel lines so that they appear to converge in the distance. The mathematical rigor of perspective permitted a scientific rendering of the look of objects as well as their proportionate size in relation to one another. Not only geometry but the science of optics came into play, for perspective was widely held to render a painting, in Alberti's image, a window to the world, as if the viewer were actually looking out on a scene in nature. For centuries, perspective was touted as a revelation of the operation of the eye, and because vision is the highest cognitive sense, of the mind as well. Through the intricacies of perspective the arts of painting and drawing drew abreast with science as a means to discover truths of nature. Indeed, a staple tenet of treatises on drawing from the Renaissance through the early twentieth century was the claim that the intellect and the cognitive sense of vision are stimulated and developed by drawing in a way that no other activity approximates.

Because there is nothing fleshly, improper, or socially dubious about mathematics or optics, it might seem as if training in perspective should not present any barriers to women who desired to learn this art. (And indeed if they wanted to succeed, at a certain point they simply had to learn this technique. Before the deliberate distortions of post-Impressionism, paintings rendered without perspective were considered amateurish and badly done;

in our day they are usually relegated to a category of "folk art.") However, here we encounter once more the role of rationality in theories of human nature, for mathematics is among the most cerebral of human accomplishments. Women were afforded fewer opportunities for training in painting, partly because their schooling was limited, but also because they were often not considered intellectually capable of learning sophisticated techniques, such as the mathematically-based linear perspective.[35]

Discourse surrounding this claim contains intriguing conundrums, for it was argued that women: (1) didn't have sufficiently mathematical brains to be able to learn linear perspective; and (2) didn't need to learn techniques like perspective, because their natural good taste meant that they could create beautiful pictures without rules. Now if women really could not manage the calculations necessary to learn perspective, it was hardly necessary to bar them from trying. But of course they could and did; those women who were trained (often in the studios of artist-fathers) have left a visible record of complete adeptness at perspective and other sophisticated academic techniques.[36]

Odder still is the idea that women do not need lessons in a technical skill such as perspective, because by nature they create beautiful things and don't require the tedious distraction of rules. This position can be found in writings influenced by European art theory, such as the drawing manuals of the nineteenth century that circulated in North America. These popular books instructed rural and frontier women how to beautify their homes and elevate the taste of their communities by emulating the styles of European forebears. To address this large audience many authors of drawing books distilled the complexities of art instruction in manuals designed for amateurs, often even for schoolchildren. They disseminated traditions of European aesthetic theory by this means, hoping to improve the taste and artistic standards of the new American nation. The amateur painters eager for such instruction are rather similar to the large audience of women readers anxious for popular literature and, like the latter, they worried certain critics and art professionals because of concern that American taste would become diluted and feminized by an influx of amateur female painters. (One artist-author of a popular nineteenth-century drawing manual prefaced his book with an appeal to men to join the ranks of painters. He estimated that the women in his classes outnumbered men twenty to one.)[37]

Some of the manuals aimed at this audience taught the rudiments of perspective.[38] Others proposed shortcuts that bypassed the mathematics of this technique, and still others declared that the lady painter did not require the strategies of her male counterpart: "The profound ploddings necessary for him are not required of the *female learner*—Her quick intuitive apprehensions may well dispense with such a prop," declared one drawing-book author.[39] But praise of a painter on the grounds that her work doesn't require education or effort is faint indeed, and other instructors insisted that women needed as firm a grasp of the mathematics of perspective as men.[40]

We have already seen how the idea that an accomplishment is an outgrowth of a person's basic nature actually diminishes that achievement, interpreting it more as an extension of innate disposition than an accomplishment. (A similar phenomenon can sometimes be seen in descriptions of the technologies of so-called primitive peoples, such as designs for streamlined boats, weaponry, medicines, pottery, and so on; these developments, rather than being attributed to the innovations of far-sighted individuals, are frequently treated as intuitive or evolutionary developments of the group.) When a "natural" ability is attributed to a group of people who are assumed to need no real training to hone that ability, then the compliment is withdrawn, for their products are not even in competition with those of trained professionals, where critical evaluation is at its most rigorous and personal tastes are put to the test to see if they measure up to the highest standards.

Assessment according to reigning critical standards is available only if one enters an art field as a professional. And despite all the factors that encouraged women to remain amateurs in the graphic arts, some made the transition successfully. The painter Berthe Morisot, for example, had to make some tough decisions to move from the standard drawing lessons approved for middle-class girls of nineteenth-century France into the professional training that she undertook on the way to becoming a major figure in the Impressionist movement.[41] (One reason that Morisot succeeded in the professional world of painting was that the Impressionists rejected the traditions of history painting and focused on everyday modern life, where paintings were more likely to feature clothed figures.)

The public exposure granted the professional painter raises yet another sense of "subjective" to add to our list of meanings to analyze, for removing artistic products from the intimate appreciation of family and friends offers them for public scrutiny alongside the work of others of professional standing. Consider this remark about the development of Berthe Morisot's career from art historian Anne Higgonet:

It would be hard to overestimate the importance of Morisot's exhibitions in her transition from amateur to professional painter. To exhibit was to seek public exposure, to court professional comparison or judgment, and to suggest that she could be paid for her work. No matter how much time she had devoted to painting, no matter how great her native talent or her commitment, if Morisot's work had never faced public scrutiny it would always have remained amateur. It wasn't so much a question of profit or critical consensus as of detachment. Professional means in part impersonal—that is, what goes beyond the subjectively satisfying.[42]

This discussion of amateur status has raised the idea of subjectivity in several contexts, all to the detriment of women artists. What was seen as their relatively more emotional temperament seemed to suit them for certain types of artistic participation, but hindered them from the best accomplishment, if one follows this rather condescending attitude towards both emotions and subjectivity. This needs to be measured alongside movements in the history of aesthetics that promote emotion and feeling over or alongside reason, for attention to the gender implications of claims about creativity indicates how tempered and cautious that promotion really was.

Reassessing the past

This chapter has stressed the ways that reigning aesthetic concepts circumscribed the opportunities for women in the modern period; this is a way to chart the practical influence of philosophies of art and creativity. But the story doesn't end here, and despite the traditional judgments of their works, there is no need to conclude that women actually produced little art of merit. It is equally important to take note of what they did accomplish within their constrained circumstances, for artists are always active agents, no matter what the odds are of their being successful or recognized. Though there is no space here to review the discoveries of feminist scholars, a good deal of contemporary research has been devoted to uncovering the work of neglected or forgotten artists and writers of the past and reassessing their legacies.

For example, the restrictions on the scope of experience that women usually could draw upon for resources in their narratives, combined with assumptions about their relatively fluffy mental capacities, fed the presumption noted in the previous chapter: that women were not capable of creating the profound arts that are described as "sublime." Even granting the limits that social norms permitted women, this critical judgment is disputable, as some contemporary scholars have pointed out. Feminist revisions of the critical assessments of past times include arguments for a "female sublime" present in the literary record in the works of authors as diverse as Charlotte Brontë and Emily Dickinson.[43] This has entailed not only re-evaluating the works of women, but also critical revision of the very concept of sublimity.[44]

Equally, art historians have discovered and resurrected forgotten women painters, correcting and enriching our understanding of art of earlier times. Art historian Mary Garrard, for example, has brought the work of painter Artemisia Gentileschi from neglect into prominence.[45] To counterbalance the fact that women's presence in the arts has often been eclipsed by men, researchers have begun to spotlight the work of many women closer to our own times whose work has been overshadowed by better-known male colleagues. Thus now there is more interest in the work of the artist-wives of famous painters, such as Elaine De Kooning, Lee Krasner (wife of Jackson Pollock), Sonia Delaunay, and Frida Kahlo (wife of Diego Rivera). Feminist attention foregrounds congenial elements of the works of artists who created without the sustaining context of a political movement,[46] and this has brought about a body of research reassessing female artistic practices and speculating about the possible existence of female artistic styles and traditions.[47] In short, the historical record of creative production is never quite closed but continues to invite re-evaluation and interpretation.

Summary

Snapshots of certain periods in the development of three art forms are hardly sufficient to present the range of participation and exclusion women have historically faced regarding training and opportunities in the arts. They are indicative, however, of some patterns of thinking that permeate discourse and practice in aesthetics and the fine arts. The actual social conditions of men and women in different classes, historical periods, and cultures situate these patterns and lend them variety and change, but we can see in virtually all venues asymmetrical conceptions of female capacities, which are paired and contrasted with dominant male counterparts. In the modern period, the idea of the professional artist adds but one more layer to these venerable frames of thought.

Things have changed over the last century, of course, and few prospective artists today find themselves confronting the constraints of propriety that plagued the nineteenth-century woman, nor are women barred from the same sort of study as men. Does this mean that the old conceptual frameworks that have been in place for centuries have at last disappeared from consciousness? This is most unlikely, though they are certainly not functioning as they used to. Chapter 5 will speculate about the concept of art and artists today and bring the operation of gender in aesthetics into our own times. Before we move to that topic, however, let us take a short detour to consider an area at the outer margins of aesthetic theory, one that has many traditional associations with women: food and eating. Here we shall see subjectivity at work in another aesthetic form and broaden our appreciation of the resonance of gender in systems of evaluation.

4

DEEP GENDER

Taste and food

Now I introduce a subject that will (eventually) act as a transition between the traditional concepts of fine art and aesthetic value and the alterations to that tradition that mark recent trends in aesthetics and art practice. This transition is approached from a somewhat oblique angle, for we are not at this point adding to the chronology of development of art from modern to postmodern times. Rather, we shall undertake an investigation of the value structure that continues to inform concepts of creativity, aesthetic value, and the nature of art. But the overt subject appears at first to be at the sidelines of all of that: *food*. The ostensible marginality of this topic is only apparent, however, for its thorough analysis requires probing into the fundamental machinery of philosophy. It may seem improbable to make such a grand claim in relation to the humble subject of food, which at first glance doesn't seem to have a lot to do with philosophy at all. But it is precisely to discover *why* food and eating do not fall within the standard purview of philosophy that a gender analysis is useful.

This examination retraces some of the material presented earlier, this time in order to ask questions concerning a deeper level of gender analysis. Previously we investigated how gendered thinking colors aesthetics. Now it is time to inquire about how it underwrites assumptions about what counts as a "philosophical" subject. As we have seen throughout this study, the reliance on conceptual frameworks using now-familiar binary opposites has fostered a preference for reason over emotion, mind over body, abstraction over particularity, and so on, systematically linking the "superior" term (mind, reason, abstraction) over its supposedly subordinate counterpart (body, emotional sensibility, particularity). Because of the widespread association of gendered meanings with binary concepts, even epistemic and metaphysical categories, such as objective–subjective and universal–particular, are aligned with the masculine–feminine duality. Therefore, thinking in terms of these kinds of pairs very quickly leads to the assignment of gender to phenomena that are quite remote from actual males and females. Most importantly for our investigation of the philosophical neglect of food and eating, these pairs of opposites are ranked in a basic and crude way not only as "masculine" and "feminine" but also as "important" and "not so important." Thus finding the marks of gender in the concepts that frame philosophical debate is a way of discovering how philosophy distinguishes issues worthy of investigation from other sorts of matters that have been considered unworthy of interest— and therefore "unphilosophical." Gender can be the lens through which we discover basic aspects of philosophy itself at its very roots, as well as the common frameworks of thinking that it supports.

We can see the covert operation of gendered values at work in philosophical analysis of the senses, and this will be our entry point for considering food. While not all the arts rely on one of the five senses to discern the aesthetic qualities of their works, sensory experience is essential for some arts such as music and painting. Therefore theories about the operation of the senses have a standard place in aesthetics. The sense of taste is obviously crucial to the experience of eating, but traditional ways of understanding the exercise of taste have barred tasting from aesthetic experience and food from the regions of art proper. It is obvious that in most situations and cultures women are the ones who prepare food. What is less obvious—and more interesting—are the gendered ideas associated with body, eating, gustatory pleasure, and the sense of taste that function in opposition to the values that cluster around concepts of the aesthetic and the values of fine art. This is why the disputed status of "culinary art" reaches beyond custom and idiom and into philosophical strongholds and artistic traditions.

The five senses

The sense organs are the most immediate means by which we gather information about the world around us. We touch objects and discover their tactile qualities, smell them to detect their odors, see and feel them to discern their shapes, and listen to the sounds they make. They also have tastes, and the objects whose taste qualities interest us most are food and drink. The identification of five senses—vision, hearing, touch, smell, and taste—is ancient, transcultural, and relatively stable, although touch is sometimes divided into types of touch receptors (for pain and pressure, heat and cold), and some researchers prefer to join taste and smell in one coordinated system. Of most interest for the disposition of aesthetics is the hierarchy into which these five senses fall.[1]

Throughout the history of western philosophy, two of our senses have been accorded special status and ranked as superior to the other three. Vision and hearing are considered "higher" senses because of their relatively greater capacity to gather information about the world. Vision especially is capable of discerning a wide range of aspects of an object: its size, shape, color, movement, and relationship to other things both near and distant. So vivid and extensive is visual experience that it supplies the most common sensory metaphors for knowledge. Such metaphorical usage is by no means limited to philosophical texts, for in ordinary conversation we often say "I *see*" meaning "I understand." Other senses afford similar usage: "I *hear* you," "He doesn't *grasp* this concept," and so on; but visual images furnish by far the most common metaphors for knowledge and understanding.[2] Hearing has almost as capacious a receptive range as vision, and in addition it is crucial for convenient communication and hence for sharing experience, information, and learning. Thus both vision and hearing are considered the primary senses that contribute to cognition. Because the formation of knowledge is linked to the intellect and the operation of reason, vision and hearing are sometimes called the "intellectual" senses.

By comparison, touch, taste, and smell are considered "lower" senses, though the status of touch is complex. While any given touch sensation lacks the range and breadth of vision or even hearing (one can touch only a few parts of an object at a time, for example), it has an immediacy and reliability that one frequently resorts to in order to check the data received by vision. For example, if the surface of an object appears mottled and uneven, one might have to run one's fingers over it to discover if it is in fact rough or if color variation merely gives that impression on a surface that is actually smooth. A mirage or hallucination can be discovered to be an illusion by reaching towards it and encountering emptiness. The use of touch to confirm vision has led to the English maxim: "Seeing's believing, but touching's the truth." Moreover, the objects of touch can be ordered syntactically and assigned meaning and therefore can become the basis of written language such as Braille. In these capacities, touch is more like vision and hearing than it is like smell and taste, although other features qualify it as a lower sense.

Smell and taste, in contrast, appear to have little cognitive role to play, apart from imparting information about the odors and tastes of objects and relatedly about pleasantness, edibility, and rot. While these senses play an important role in protecting an organism by warning it of unhealthy substances and toxins, beyond this basic prophylactic function they don't seem to be required in the development of higher types of knowledge. Their apparent cognitive limits have kept taste and smell in the category of the lower, or "animal," or "bodily" senses. (Although I believe it is more accurate to consider taste and smell separate senses, the fact is they operate together in experiences of eating and drinking. When I speak of taste experience, I am including the full range of sensory experience that eating calls into play, including at least taste, smell, and touch.)

Collateral qualities of the different senses lend further support to the hierarchal ranking. Vision and hearing must operate at a distance from their objects. One can see and hear objects that are quite far away, and the farther away one stands, the more one can see of the world. The very physical distance between the object seen or heard and the perceiving subject is considered an advantage for the cognitive roles of these senses that places them above sense, taste, and touch. The latter three require proximity or physical contact to function. The body of the perceiver is involved, whereas with vision and hearing (even though a bodily sense organ is required) there is no physical contact with the object of perception. (Or, strictly speaking, there is no immediate physical contact. Sound waves are physical though invisible, and they travel through a medium such as air before reaching the aural receptors that permit us to hear.) The relative distance required for these two senses, and the absence of physical contact with their operation, impart to vision and hearing the impression of being less embodied, more ethereal, more abstract, and less messy than the bodily senses are. As intellectual senses, vision and hearing are allied with the mind, leaving touch, taste, and smell in the realm of the body and its physical sensations. Therefore the potent traditions that elevate mind over body also are at play in the status of the senses. Since these traditions are highly gender inflected, we need to ask whether concepts of masculinity and femininity are also at work in the hierarchy of the senses.

The values associated with the distinction between mind and body are deeply embedded in the sense hierarchy, for as a rule the mental is considered superior to the physical. It is in the range of mentality that specifically human qualities emerge that are not shared by animals, including the development of complex knowledge and artistic creativity. A bird may build a nice nest and display its feathers to advantage when mating, or a stag may sprout magnificent antlers. But these are products of its natural instincts and physiology rather than actual creativity. (Some theorists employ interpretations of evolutionary biology to argue that human creativity may have evolved from these sorts of animal dispositions.)[3] Similarly, eating is often regarded as an outgrowth of a natural tendency, for all animals must eat, and to a certain degree eating behavior is prompted by drives such as hunger and thirst. Eating and the food preparation that precedes it are to that extent regarded not so much as cultural accomplishments as activities propelled by natural drives, desires, instincts. And it is undeniable that food intake is essential to life and health. Even *haute cuisine* may be regarded as a refined and decorative version of satisfaction of an animal need, though as we shall see shortly this is disputed territory. Whatever one's views of the more elaborate versions of its preparation, food is suspect from the start as far as aesthetic status is concerned because of its inescapable association with practical bodily need.

Physicality has often symbolized the limits imposed on human life by the fact that we are embodied and mortal. (It is the female who is especially identified with nature and physical matter.) In the last several decades there has been a surge of celebration of "the body" and of physical nature, especially sexual nature, among both philosophers and artists; and many of the vigorous proponents of the body and its pleasures have been feminists revising the traditional western mind–body value structures, as we shall see further in Chapter 6. However, in previous times this was not a commonly held point of view, as we saw with philosophers such as Plato, Kant, and Schopenhauer, and which we also find in religious traditions such as Christianity. Rather, the aesthetic pleasures of art were valued partly for the relief they afforded from the demands of everyday, physical existence. As George Santayana wrote at the end of the nineteenth century:

> The pleasures we call physical and regard as low . . . are those which call our attention to some part of our own body, and which make no object so conspicuous to us as the organ in which they arise. There is here, then, a very marked distinction between physical and aesthetic pleasure; the organs of the latter must be transparent, they must not intercept our attention, but carry it directly to some external object. The greater dignity and range of aesthetic pleasure is thus made very intelligible. The soul is glad, as it were, to forget its connexion with the body and to fancy that it can travel over the world

with the liberty with which it changes the objects of its thought . . .
The illusion of disembodiment is very exhilarating, while immer-
sion in the flesh and confinement to some organ gives a tone of
grossness and selfishness to our consciousness.[4]

Santayana's comment reminds us that physicality has implications for two
particular features of the senses and their objects: the nature of the *pleasure*
taken in sense experience, and the *direction of attention* that the experience
induces.

Pleasure sensuous and aesthetic

Most theories of beauty and aesthetic appreciation are also theories of
pleasure, as we saw in Chapter 2; yet not every type of pleasure counts as
aesthetic. One reason why taste is disqualified from philosophical approval
has to do with the kind of pleasure that it delivers: a very dubious sort, by
most accounts, one that leads to self-indulgence in bodily sensation, which
if pursued with sufficient zeal, as Christian philosophy warns, eventually
leads to the deadly sin of gluttony. Indulgence in our animal nature (an inaccurate label, since most animals don't overeat the way humans do) is
unworthy of our higher, rational nature, and so this particular pleasure must
be taken only in moderation. Better yet, one ought not care about it at all. As
Socrates remarked on his deathbed, a philosopher should care neither for
food, nor drink, nor sex, for all can divert attention from the higher callings
of the mind to the pleasures of the body.[5] His ranking is an extreme version
of a rather common theme in western philosophy and religion, and he
reminds us that the pleasures of the table are often twinned with the pleasures of the bedroom, connecting with another type of sensual indulgence
and another deadly sin: lust.

The meanings attached to sensory pleasure are among the many elements
of taste, food, and eating that have a gender significance—including an overt
connection between eating and sex, between indulgence in taste pleasures
and in the sexual pleasures of touch. Not only is sex connected with eating
in many cultural systems (some would claim all),[6] it is evident in quite a lot
of art. Consider the number of paintings that arrange tasty-looking food in
proximity to nude female bodies. Edouard Manet's famous *Luncheon on the
Grass*, for example, features a picnic with a spilling basket in the foreground,
its contents leading to the figure of a nude women sitting with two clothed

male companions. Paul Gauguin's portrait of *Two Tahitian Women* adds the exoticism of Polynesia to his composition of two women, one of whom cradles a plate of fruit beneath her breasts. Many Biblical paintings feature Eve and her dangerous apple.

The connection between food and sex—with its overt acknowledgment of physical gratification—is one of several factors that disqualify taste experiences from genuinely aesthetic experience in the western aesthetic tradition that we are examining. Taste delivers sensual, bodily pleasure of sometimes questionable moral status, prone as it is to overindulgence. What is more, neither eating nor sex figures among the more intellectual and elevated cognitive experiences that human beings value, and so tied are they to animal pleasures (or what we imagine animal pleasures to be) that they are on occasion actually denigrated and shunned. Although both eating and sexuality are often the subject matter of works of art, aesthetic appreciation of art is supposed to transcend the sensuality depicted and reach a more distanced degree of enjoyment superior to physical and sensory pleasure.

In spite of all the cautions about the bodily senses, the gustatory sense of taste furnishes the model and central metaphor for the aesthetic theories that emerged in modern philosophy,[7] even though food itself is not a candidate for the kinds of objects treated by philosophies of art. Let us return briefly to the emergence of the idea of the aesthetic that was presented in Chapter 2. Aesthetics developed within a program of modern philosophy that was inclined to analyze beauty as a species of pleasure, and it is hard to taste something and remain utterly neutral as to whether or not one likes it. Not only is there an immediate pleasure or displeasure with the experience of taste, but the discriminating palate can be developed to discern traces and nuances of flavor, rather like aesthetic sensibility can be developed in a sophisticated critic. (In "Of the Standard of Taste" Hume employed this parallel in an anecdote comparing the delicate taste for wine with discerning ability to judge the quality of art.) Taste serves as a model for fine discrimination of the qualities of an object of appreciation, and metaphors of savoring and relishing aesthetic properties continue the gastronomic imagery. However, according to dominant tradition, taste is limited to metaphorical status. For most theorists—such as the influential Immanuel Kant—literal experiences of taste do not yield the kind of pleasure that is truly aesthetic; it remains bodily and sensual.

Unlike practical uses, moral approval, religious or civic ends, and physical pleasures, aesthetic pleasure is valued for its own sake alone. It is a response

Figure 8 Paul Gauguin, *Two Tahitian Women*. The Metropolitan Museum of Art, New York, gift of William Church Osborne, 1949 (49.58.1).

to the apprehension of intrinsic qualities, most centrally beauty. One does not ask what beauty is good for; it is its own excuse for being. In contrast, the pleasures of food cannot escape practicality, for we must eat in order to live; nor can they escape a degree of sensuousness that turns attention towards the satiation of hunger. Food and eating undoubtedly deliver pleasures, and those pleasures may be highly refined and discerning, for the palate is trainable. But accepted tradition asserts that food preferences are much more apt to be idiosyncratic and private rather than the target for joint critical acclaim. According to all of these orthodox terms of analysis, gustatory taste is not an aesthetic sense.

The hierarchy of the senses and the exclusion of taste from the domain of aesthetic pleasure is a centerpiece of several influential eighteenth-century philosophies of taste. A British author, Henry Home, Lord Kames, argued that pleasure is a "mental" phenomenon, which is to say it occurs in the experience of a perceiver rather than in the world at large. When pleasure is taken in an object of vision or hearing, he observed, it accurately appears to occur in the mind; but when the object is a taste or smell or touch, attention is drawn to the part of the body that is affected. The higher senses, in his view, are disposed to protect us against overindulgence in the bodily senses. The eyes and ears are the senses employed in the appreciation of the fine arts, and indeed they may act as a bridge away from corporeal pleasure to morality and religion. As he put it, "The fine arts are contrived to give pleasure to the eye and the ear, disregarding the inferior senses."[8] And in the *Critique of Judgment*, Kant explicated aesthetic pleasure by invoking its contrast with gustatory pleasure; the former demands a kind of universal agreement, he asserted, whereas with the latter we are content to pursue personal preferences.[9]

Subjectivity and objectivity

This rumination on sensuous pleasure has postponed discussion of the second reason Santayana mentions why physical pleasures are not aesthetic, namely, that the bodily senses direct attention inward towards the body of the perceiver rather than outward towards the external world. This is a complex claim that adds to the reasons that taste experiences have been excluded from aesthetic categories. The gustatory sense of taste is alleged to be too subjective to have either epistemic or aesthetic standing, and therefore it is not worthy of extended interest. The charge of subjectivity involves several contentions, all of them well-entrenched in philosophical tradition, most of them connected with gendered ideas, and many of them disputable.

First: taste sensations are experienced as states of one's own body. Sight and hearing operate with a distance between organ and object of perception, and as a consequence they serve to draw attention away from the body of the perceiving subject to the external object of perception. But with taste the sensation is experienced as "in" the body, specifically the mouth. For example, *red* is experienced as the quality of a strawberry, not of the eye, but *tart* is experienced as a sensation on the tongue. All three bodily senses are apt to lead the perceiver to an awareness of his or her own body. One way to put this difference is to say that vision and hearing are more "objective" (meaning they direct attention to their objects), whereas touch, taste, and smell are more apt to be "subjective" (meaning that they direct attention to the state of the perceiving subject). This contrast is reflected in the fact that the experience of touch, smell, and taste are commonly labeled "sensations," whereas there is unlikely to be an actual sensation of hearing or of vision; these are more apt to be called "perceptions." (In extreme cases there may be sensations accompanying hearing and sight. Deep bass sound, for example, may be felt in the soles of the feet; intense light may actually cause pain to the eyes.)

Second: taste is considered subjective because it appears to provide little information about the world. Inward directedness further reduces the cognitive value of a sense, as it diverts attention away from the diversities of the external world to the narrow focus of one's own being. Judgments about the objects of sight and hearing are necessarily relative to one's perspective and physical position, but sight and hearing are means of discovery about the world external to the body of the perceiver. In contrast, the proximal or bodily senses supposedly turn our attention inward to ourselves and the states of our bodies. Touch switches roles from time to time. As a source of physical pleasure, it shares the low rank of taste and smell; but it also has a greater cognitive role than taste and smell in exploring qualities of the world, and in this way it shares standing with vision and hearing. With this in mind, Immanuel Kant made this remark about three of the five senses— sight, hearing, and touch, which are:

> more objective than subjective, that is, they contribute . . . more to the cognition of the exterior object, than they arouse the consciousness of the affected organ. Two, however, are more subjective than objective, that is, the idea obtained from them is more an idea of enjoyment, rather than the cognition of the external object. Consequently, we can easily agree with others in respect to the three objective senses. But with respect to the other two, the manner in which the subject responds can be quite different.[10]

Third: this is why we so commonly assert that "there is no disputing about taste." Reports of taste concern one's own responses, available to no other. This is yet another sense of "subjectivity:" a judgment about whether something tastes good or not appears to be a purely personal, even idiosyncratic, judgment rather than something to be fruitfully debated. Unlike aesthetic judgments, differences in preferences concerning real, gustatory taste do not have sufficient importance to be worthy of dispute and standards, which is another reason this topic figured little in the modern search for a "standard of taste." What is more, searching for such standards would be fruitless, since individual bodily preferences are personal and not universal, another consequence of the bodily directedness of this subjective sense.

This leads to the fourth and most profound charge against taste: it bears no important meaning; it isn't *about* anything. More precisely, it isn't about anything but itself and the pleasure it arouses. Therefore those who make it their business to prepare food are nurturing the body and affording sensuous pleasure, but they are not contributing to interpretations of the world in the way that art does. As Frank Sibley remarks, in a context where he is actually defending the aesthetic status of the bodily senses, "Perfumes and flavours, natural or artificial, are necessarily limited: unlike the major arts, they have no expressive connections with emotions, love or hate, grief, joy, terror, suffering, yearning, pity, or sorrow—or with plot or character development."[11]

To sum up the case against taste: taste and eating experiences are traditionally disqualified from philosophical interest, specifically aesthetic interest, in part because of the nature of the pleasure that they deliver. Gustatory experience arouses sensuous rather than aesthetic pleasure; therefore it is less worthy of pursuit than other sense experiences that lead one's attention away from bodily concerns. It is only subjective and therefore not a matter for public or shared interest. Moreover, taste is cognitively weak because it does not inform us about the world in the way that the senses of hearing, sight, and even touch are equipped to do. This leads to the representational and expressive weakness of foods, tastes, and odors in comparison with works of art.

Shortly I shall offer a rebuttal to these charges, but first let us locate the gender implications of the hierarchy of the senses. Eyes are eyes and ears are ears, and although sense organs may function more or less acutely, the variants do not sort out by gender.[12] However, when it comes to the values associated with the different senses, gender significance abounds. First of all there is the intellectual–bodily division of rank that distinguishes higher from lower senses, for the category of intellectual prowess is gendered masculine. In addition, because of their extended role in the reproduction of the species, females are more connected with things "bodily" than are males— if not in fact then in symbol systems. This gives the sense hierarchy and the division between "higher" and "lower" senses a gendered message from the start. Moreover, as we have already seen in artistic contexts, women are traditionally considered more subjective than are men inasmuch as they supposedly are more apt to view the world through the distorting lens of feeling rather than the clear light of reason. These evaluations are part of the package of values that identify rationality as a masculine trait and assign femininity a more sensuous and emotional nature. The former fosters an artistic vision that can express feelings and ideas of universal resonance; the latter is apt to be more of a display of personal feeling.

The values associated with body, physical pleasures, and sensuous indulgence are the lower counterpart of values associated with mind, mental achievement, and austere discipline. The senses that are most associated with the masculine values of rationality, cognition, objectivity, and mentality are vision and hearing. Those most associated with the feminine values of emotion and feeling, subjectivity and the body are touch, taste, and smell. Reinforcing these conceptual divisions is the fact that the realm of food is emphatically domestic and feminine, not only in a symbolic dimension but literally, for those people whose lives are defined domestically are likely to assume the task of food preparation. Food preparation and eating are affiliated with nurturance and, insofar as feeding is physiologically driven, with nature. These observations may be considered the empirical manifestation of deeper gendered meanings of matters of taste and food. The aesthetic status of taste and of food is multiply hindered by all of these "feminine" traits.

A defense of taste

Even a brief consideration of the sense of taste will demonstrate that gendered patterns of thinking have led to some obvious oversights and well-entrenched errors in the history of aesthetics. I mentioned at the outset that gendered conceptual categories tend to separate subjects of philosophical weight from others considered less worthy of sustained theoretical examination. When one sets aside a topic because it isn't worth thorough investigation, one is apt to make mistakes about it that would be corrected with even a little more attention. This seems to have occurred with virtually all the dismissive claims made about the subjectivity of taste.

The error with the most far-reaching consequences is the idea that experiences of food are too subjective to bear the kinds of meanings that art does, an idea summed up by Sibley above when he contrasts foods with representational arts. This denial of meaning and cognitive significance to foods, which is a widespread claim in the literature on aesthetics and eating, is demonstrably inaccurate. Eating is an activity we freight with significance considerably beyond the pleasure it affords or the nutrition it provides.

Foods qualify as meaningful in a host of ways, for they are representational and expressive as well as nutritious and tasty.[13] Foods represent whenever they are shaped to resemble or refer to something else, a common practice that occurs with profound significance in special ritual or ceremonial foods and also more playfully in the things we eat every day. Consider how much of our food is made to resemble something else: gummy bears, candy canes, yule logs, hot cross buns, gingerbread men, animal crackers, and pretzels, for example. Many ordinary foods were first crafted with representational meaning that has long since disappeared. Who now recalls that croissants were invented by the bakers of Vienna after the successful defense of that city against the Turks? (The shape of the pastry is said originally to represent the crescent on the banners of the invaders.) Reflecting on these playful food-representations, one can see how readily what we eat and drink is put to use in our commerce with the world around us. This could not occur if food were incapable of expressive meaning and of summoning an "objective" direction of attention.

Foods can be expressive in the qualities that cooks and chefs emphasize when they prepare meals for different occasions, and as a rule these meanings are outgrowths of cultural practice. Sometimes the cognitive aspects of food—that is, its meanings—are pretty obvious. This is often the case with ceremonial meals such as the Jewish Passover Seder, where certain foods explicitly refer to aspects of the exodus from Egypt. (The matzoh that is eaten instead of leavened bread, for instance, represents the fact that in haste bread was baked before it had time to rise; bitter herbs convey sorrow in their sharp tastes.) On other occasions the meaning of food requires a little reflection, such as the pertinence of root vegetables at American Thanksgiving (a late harvest food appropriate for November and expressive of the season) and of course the turkey, bird of the North American woods. Symbolic foods such as dead man's bread and sugar skulls that are prepared for the Day of the Dead in Mexico are offerings of hospitality for the souls of the departed. The bone-images crafted for this meal represent death, and the entire feast is an expression of welcome and commemoration. The communion with the dead repeats the communion with the living that we experience every day in the sharing of food and drink.

Some religious rituals that employ food, such as the Christian Eucharist, engage the sense of taste in ways that have little to do with ordinary eating. However, the fact that it is taste that is employed in such a ritual is critical, for one takes sacred substances into one's body. This bodily aspect imparts to taste a peculiar and profound intimacy that can lend to eating a depth of participatory meaning wherein one attains insight through the very act of tasting and eating. (Rituals of fasting are similarly meaningful, requiring reflection on the body's pleasures by experiencing their absence.) More mundane situations offer something similar: hospitality, which often includes food offerings, entails a relationship of trust among people. One offers food in friendship and accepts it in faith that it is good to eat. It is a common gesture that has a kind of routine intimacy, and we may not always notice its meaning because it has become part of habit. Food and drink are quotidian elements of necessity and routine, and we often lose sight of their deep significance. Nevertheless understanding and meaning are present in the rhythms of living, and it takes only a little reflection to bring that fact into focused awareness.

In meals prepared especially for fine dining, foods exemplify all the qualities that the gourmet taster calls attention to in his or her assessments, and this, too, resists the charge of mere subjectivity. Praising a wine for its flowery bouquet, for example, is calling attention to the floral property manifest in the wine. It is not calling attention to the state of one's tongue. In fact, in none of these roles are foods and their tastes "merely" subjective. If they were, it would not make a lot of sense even to discuss the appropriate preparation of a dish and how it should taste. In fact, the common claim that "there is no disputing about taste" is probably challenged every day in kitchens and restaurants.

None of this is intended to deny that good food and drink can also deliver intense sensuous pleasure, but pleasure itself has been misunderstood as only private and subjective. The very flavors in our mouths are "about" something, and standard theory has been quite wrong in concluding that savoring them ensnares us in our own bodily sensations, oblivious to the social, cultural, and personal meanings that taste provides. Undeniably, taste is subjective because it occurs in one's own mouth and requires one's own experience. But that experience is just as communicable as more standard aesthetic judgments, and it may be debated and assessed. What is more, the strong social contexts in which we often eat make the joint experience of eating even more public. This domain of experience has as much claim on our philosophical attention as any other, and the venerable presumption that such matters are unphilosophical is a gender-inflected bias.

Food and/in/as art

At this point my analysis of food and its aesthetic import begins to split, for two distinct questions now arise. First: does the above defense of the aesthetic status of food lead to the conclusion that good food and its preparation ought to be classed as an art form? Second: although representations of food have often been subjects for art (as with still-life painting, for instance), a number of contemporary artists actually employ real foodstuffs as media in their works. Is this evidence of the recognition of the aesthetic standing of food that philosophical tradition has overlooked? These are far from simple questions, and each requires extended consideration.

Is cooking a form of art?

Defending the aesthetic status of taste might seem to invite a further argument that places food in the category of artworks, for one reason that food has been read out of philosophy of art is precisely that it is perceived by means of a nonaesthetic sense. However, I shall not make this case.

There are, of course, advocates for an "art" of cooking, especially if the type of cooking in question is especially refined *haute cuisine*. Jean-François Revel, for example, details the rise of influential cuisine in France—and it is surely not coincidental that this is the same period that saw the emergence of theories of the aesthetic in philosophy and art theory.[14] Revel argues that gastronomy ought to count as an art, and to that end he distinguishes between *haute cuisine* and ordinary eating in ways parallel to the distinction between the fine art of painting and domestic decoration. I have no argument with the claim that some food preparation requires a high degree of skill and artistry. That cooking is an art in the old sense of *techne* that we discussed in the first chapter has never been in question. But is it aptly considered a fine art and "elevated" (as it were) into the company of music and poetry? I would argue no, and moreover that this line of thought limits consideration of the importance of foods to a range that is unduly narrow.

First of all, the category of fine art that we have been investigating is simply inappropriate for actual food and meals, even in their gourmet varieties. The fine-art tradition is but one moment in the history of art, but it is one that emphasizes the autonomy of art and the contemplative distance between audience and artwork. Because of this emphasis, food simply does not qualify as a fine-art form in any recognizable sense. The preparation of food and other household labors have several features that are in a sense highly "aesthetic" in the customary meaning of that term. They have a decorative aspect, and one aim of both household management and the presentations of fancy restaurants is to make the table pleasing to the eye as well as the palate. But there are features of food preparation that violate traditional norms of artistic production, no matter how aesthetically satisfying they are along the way, for the presence of aesthetic qualities alone does not make something a work of art. Eating is an inescapably cyclic and repetitive process. One prepares food, eats, cleans up, digests, eliminates, gets hungry again, and starts the process all over—repeatedly, several times a day if one is fortunate and not living with scarcity. There is no point at which one can pause and say "this is finished and now can be left alone." Food, unlike paint or marble, decays and rots. And unlike music, it does not waft away into thin, clear air but requires clean-up and replacement. Neither its substance nor its form is stable, and its mutable physicality is inescapable. The practical dimensions of eating and the fact that it forms a necessary foundation for virtually everything else we do firmly root the basic aspects of food in the necessary and the routine. None of these qualities is favored by traditional concepts of fine-art.

There are a number of theorists who champion food and drink and who have launched campaigns to elevate culinary efforts to art status. Like Revel, most proponents for food as art consider fine dining and elaborate cuisine to be the best candidates for a culinary art form. The ornamental qualities of fancy preparation have indicated to some that food qualifies as an applied, decorative art.[15] The presumption is that particularly excellent examples of food stand as the artistic varieties of what is presented commonly as mere fuel. Because of their emphasis on the best examples of food, advocates of this approach usually focus on sophisticated discrimination and refined taste pleasures; the aesthetic qualities emphasized are flavors and savors rather than representational and expressive qualities. They defend the artistic status of food on the grounds that there is a way to taste and to eat that qualifies as genuinely "aesthetic" and not grossly sensual.[16] Their arguments do not achieve the conclusion that food ought to be considered a fine art, however, and they usually settle for something of less prestige. While the case for an aesthetic dimension of eating is well defended, this does not eventuate in a conclusion that food is a very important art form; even its advocates settle for the status of minor art.

One could decide to classify food among the applied or decorative minor arts, for such categories are less contentious in regard to the inclusion of food and cooking. On the other hand, they are also less tied to values of profundity and cognitive significance than is fine art, so one gains little by way of deeper understanding of the aesthetic status of food by this linkage. Nor does this approach provide a strong foothold from which to dispute all the mistakes summed up under the dismissal of taste as too subjective for philosophical attention. The symbolic, representational, expressive, cognitive roles for food do indeed have a parallel with the values manifest in fine art. While those parallels do not qualify food as itself art, they do redeem it from the scorned description of "merely subjective." In any event, classifying food as art is not my purpose, for food and drink need not depend on being counted among the arts in order that their aesthetic importance be recognized. That is, food has aesthetic importance in its own right and need not borrow status from art.

Food in art

What about food in art? Obviously food and drink have often been the subject-matter of art, especially in still-life painting that makes them the central subjects for study. (Incidentally, there is a gender import here as well, for still-life and flower paintings—regarded by academicians as the least important form of this art—were for years considered the only genres of painting in which women could excel.)[17] Often still-life painters explored the decay implicit in the physical substance of foods by featuring them in *vanitas* motifs—that is, pictures that remind the viewer of the insignificance of human accomplishment in the sweep of time. One could say that the very sense hierarchy is an implicit theme of such paintings, for rotting foods represent mortality and the fragility of physical life.

Literature and movies frequently feature food as well, often simply as part of the background and setting of plots, for it is a feature of eating that it needs to occur fairly frequently. This is one reason it is so easy to overlook its meanings, for often we eat only to satisfy a bodily requirement quickly. (On the other hand, if one is suffering scarcity from poverty or famine, the importance of routine fuel is hard to overlook.) But food is featured as a centerpiece of some works, such as both the stories and the movies of *Babette's Feast*, *Like Water for Chocolate*, *Chocolat*, or *Tampopo*. As with older still-life paintings, the sense hierarchy enters into the presentation of foods in literature and film—in these cases extolling the bodily pleasures in contrast to moralism and austere asceticism, and reversing the values usually assigned the senses. Food and drink are often explored in art as a means to reflect on the body and its fleeting pleasures, but their presence as subject-matter for depiction and narrative does not affect the theoretical consideration of food and eating outside of art.

Food as art medium

In recent years, food itself has been appropriated as a medium of art in the work of certain contemporary artists—not painted food but the real thing. Because food and eating are associated with the female, many artists exploit the gendered implications of this medium by deploying food in ways that emphasize rather than criticize its traditional philosophical standing. They highlight or exaggerate connotations of taste and eating and all of the associations of the lower, bodily senses. Performance artist Karen Finley notoriously smears her body with condiments and gooey substances, portraying not only food but excrement and exploiting the base, revolting mess that food connotes when it associates the female body with the disintegration of form. Janine Antoni's work *Gnaw* (1992) features huge blocks of chocolate and lard sculpted by the artist's teeth and tongue; this art not only uses food, but the actual mouth in its production.[18] Jana Sterbak's *Meat Chair* (1996) is a heavy pile of flank steak molded in the shape of an overstuffed chair. The very look of it stimulates a synesthetic damp chill on the back of one's legs. Her *Vanitas: Flesh Dress for an Albino Anorectic* (1987) is an entire dress stitched from slabs of beef and arranged around a mannikin. During the exhibit of this work the exposed meat, heavily salted, dries and cures in imitation of the aging process of human flesh. (This work will be discussed further in the next chapter.)

The goal of these and other works using food is evidently neither to rescue taste from philosophical neglect nor to raise cooking to the standing of art. Rather, they exploit the traditional meanings associated with food, its perishability and messiness, as well as the qualities that are associated with the female body. And they do this in part as a means to challenge aspects of the powerful fine-art tradition itself—a crucially important aspect of contemporary visual art that will be discussed in more detail in the next chapter. This is not the presentation of food that is invitingly tasty or even edible; it is food that emphasizes all the properties that have customarily disqualified it from regions of the aesthetic. Rather than questioning the traditional categorization of the lower senses and their objects, therefore, these artists invoke all the connotations of the "lower" senses to challenge fine art's ideals of autonomy, genius, perfection, and lasting value.

There is some irony in this development, because the innovation and impact of these pieces exploit an understanding of the bodily senses that represents a philosophical oversight that is rooted in deep gender bias, as I have argued. But they also remind us of the potent significance accorded the bodily senses and their objects as antonyms of the lasting achievements of intellect and of fine art. Feminist artistic appropriations of this traditional understanding of the bodily senses can perhaps make us more aware of that tradition in all its error and power. We shall consider them and their situation in the artworld more thoroughly in the next chapter.

Summary

This chapter has reviewed the features of sensory experience and of food, cooking, and eating that, according to the norms of traditional aesthetics and philosophy of art, disqualify taste pleasures from aesthetic experiences and foods from works of art. With the example of taste we have seen how excavating the gendered frameworks employed by theories can reveal systematic neglect of certain regions of experience. With this topic, so rarely discussed in terms of serious philosophy, we can see the operation of gender at a level of conceptualization where the very presumptions regulating philosophical importance are formulated.

I have argued for the inclusion of taste within the domain of the aesthetic but have not argued that food and drink should be considered art forms, especially if art is conceived along the lines of the fine arts.

Femininity is deeply connected with the body in all its meanings: sensual, enticing, disgusting, mortal. Recognizing this, some recent feminist and postfeminist artists have invoked the meanings of the bodily senses in their work, especially in pieces that incorporate actual foodstuffs as artistic media. Therefore we must not lose sight of the traditional significance accorded taste and eating, no matter how short-sighted it has been revealed to be. Ironically, a gender analysis of food and philosophy provides grounds for revising the hierarchy of the senses; yet feminists exploit the traditional assessment of the physicality of taste and eating in their own artistic explorations of gender. The low meanings of taste and of other aspects of bodily experience reach vivid display in the next two chapters, which deal with contemporary art and bring our review of philosophy of art into the twenty-first century.

5

WHAT IS ART?

(Art is what?)

In 1997 the *New York Times* published a survey of opinions about the nature of art compiled from interviews with seventeen established experts: art historians, museum curators, critics, a philosopher, artists, a newsperson, and a Congressman involved with the National Endowment for the Arts. The questions they were asked included our title subject: what is art? One might expect well formulated definitions to emerge from such a group, but the opinions ranged from noncommittal to skeptical. Most expressed the view that it is pretty difficult to say what art is these days, partly because it is more or less impossible to rule out anything that it is not. "There is no single definition of art that's universally tenable," stated William Rubin, former director of painting and sculpture at the Museum of Modern Art. "There's no consensus about anything today," concurred Philippe de Montebello, Director of the Metropolitan Museum. "Even the notion of standards are in question." Art historian Thomas McEvilley was somewhat bolder: "It is art if it is called art, written about in an art magazine, exhibited in a museum or bought by a private collection." But artist Barbara Kruger was skeptical even about this open-ended statement: "I have trouble with categories," she stated. "I do know just the idea that because something's in a gallery, instantly it's art, whereas something somewhere else is not art, is silly and narrow. I'm not interested in narrowing definitions."

Theorists and practitioners have never been in complete agreement about the way to answer broad and value-laden questions, so a certain amount of disagreement is to be expected. Art has always been hard to define, since there are so many forms, genres, periods, styles, intents, and purposes that mingle together in its making and its reception. Nonetheless, the hesitation and discomfort this question prompted for many of these professionals, who would seem above all others to be in good positions to pronounce on the issue, signal a moment of theoretical crisis. To many, any kind of definition at all seemed ill-advised. "Now the idea of defining art is so remote I don't think anyone would dare to do it," said art historian and Guggenheim curator Robert Rosenblum. "If the Duchamp urinal is art, then anything is."

Why would these experts refrain from committing themselves more substantively about the nature of art? What sorts of things did they have in mind that prompted them either to draw back from a definition or to offer an apparently vacuous formulation: art is whatever is called "art"? To understand their caution let us consider several examples of art that challenge traditional artistic concepts. These cases will introduce both feminist art and the reasons for philosophers' persistent urge—despite the odds—to formulate a definition.

I begin with an example introduced at the end of the last chapter. In 1987 Czech-born Canadian artist Jana Sterbak exhibited a piece she entitled *Vanitas: Flesh Dress for an Albino Anorectic*. A garment stitched together from sixty pounds of raw flank steak was displayed on a model arranged in a seated pose. In the course of the exhibition, the meat slowly darkened and spoiled. While other art using more orthodox media may represent decay and mortality, this work literally rots before one's eyes.

Despite its discomforting features, Sterbak's works are far from the most confounding that audiences face today. There are many more notorious, including the daring work of a number of other feminists. Among the most disconcerting is a piece that Carolee Schneemann performed and documented in the 1970s titled *Interior Scroll*. During this presentation Schneemann removed her wrap and stood naked before an audience; she smeared her body with mud, reading from a text. And then she slowly extracted a long, rolled strip of paper from her vagina, reading aloud the message written thereon.[2]

These two works—to which we shall return later—are entries in a feminist repertoire of art, and one agenda (among many) of some feminist artists has been to question the terms of classification and evaluation employed in art and to defy those standards in their own work—thereby resisting the gendered ideals that pervade art traditions. But the presentation of works that challenge tradition, categorization, and taste is hardly new. Probably the object most discussed in debates over the definition of art was produced in 1917, when Marcel Duchamp entered a urinal that he titled *Fountain* into the New York Armory show. While the jury for the show rejected his entry, it now stands as an icon of an important moment in twentieth-century art. But why?

Figure 9 Jana Sterbak, *Vanitas: Flesh Dress for an Albino Anorectic*, 1987. Collection of the
artist.

To one who is not well-acquainted with the artworld over the last century,
works such as these are likely to arouse consternation, bewilderment,
offense, or discomfort. They appear to be not so much difficult art as *not art at
all*.[3] What qualifies beef as an art medium? What makes *Flesh Dress* a work of
art? What qualifies Schneeman's performance as a exhibit of art rather than
ordinary exhibitionism? What transforms a plumbing fixture made for

entirely utilitarian purposes into a work of art? As Rosenblum noted, "If the Duchamp urinal is art, then anything is." But why should anyone accept this judgment? While they may be initially posed with outrage or naïvete, these are excellent questions. Critics, art theorists, and philosophers have grappled with them for decades, and not always with perfect confidence or success. It is art such as this that has brought the definitional question, what is art?, back into the center of aesthetic controversy. Feminist art, with its deliberate reversal of virtually all the aesthetic values that we considered in earlier chapters, has joined—and sometimes has led—movements within the artworld that perplex, astound, and exasperate, challenging the concept of art at its very core.

The role of feminism in these challenges dramatizes the fact that the historical situation of women artists that we reviewed in Chapters 1 and 3 has radically altered. The sheer numbers of women who participate in the arts today is considerably greater than in the past for most art forms. This is the outcome not only of the reduction of overt sex discrimination, but also of considerable struggle on the part of feminist activists. Women did not just slide into the artworld because long-standing prejudice waned; they battled their way in. The subversive group of artists called the Guerilla Girls, based in New York, spent years picketing, harassing, and embarrassing the art establishment for the lack of representation of women artists in galleries and museums.[4] Feminist artists in the US and Britain took on the art establishment with alternative exhibits and protests that garnered enough notice that they achieved a foothold in recognized art forums.[5] The energy of the Women's Movement of the 1970s, itself arising in the tumultuous atmosphere of political activism in the US and Europe, brought public attention to the social situation of women through events that were art and politics in equal measure.[6]

The influence of feminist movements has resulted not only in increased numbers of female artists, but also in many artists (women and men alike) who use art to investigate and explore gender itself. Other aspects of identity, including race, ethnicity, and sexual identification, are equally foregrounded by artists today. Art is a means to uncover aspects of social position that have been just as eclipsed and distorted as ideas about femaleness and maleness in cultural history. Music, literature, theater, dance—all have distinguished practitioners who express and explore race, sexual nonconformity, immigrant and diaspora status, social oppression, cultural identities, and cross-gender experiences. Sometimes in developing their own voices, these artists have been the avatars of new art forms, such as performance. Sometimes they defy traditional aesthetic norms, as does philosopher and artist Adrian Piper, who deliberately forecloses the pleasures afforded by aesthetic distance in her presentations exploring race and gender issues.[7]

In addition to an influx of artists with complex political and theoretical perspectives, other changes have also radically affected concepts of the arts in comparison to the way they had developed from the eighteenth through the early twentieth centuries. The distinction between art and craft that played so prominent a role in the emergence of the idea of fine art is now often deliberately breached. As we shall see in more detail shortly, a number of artists have incorporated craft materials such as fabric and fiber into their gallery works. Indeed, one now occasionally finds traditional craft objects such as quilts hung on gallery walls. (While recognition of an expanded repertoire of artistic contribution is to be applauded, this elevation of traditional crafts is a mixed blessing. Part of the artistry of quilts is their fine stitchery, and their promotion to art status prevents the viewer from getting close enough to see tiny stitches; and of course one must not touch.)

What is more, the barriers between fine art and entertainment, between "high" and "popular" culture, are not as sturdy as they used to be.[8] Jazz, blues, and rock music now receive almost as much theoretical attention as art music (and a good deal more of the market).[9] Narrative arts are by no means limited to literature or theater but include popular and lucrative cinematic media, television, and video. There are entire art forms based on technology that was not available when the concept of fine art was refined: most notably photography (which faced an early struggle to be considered an art form), film, and digital arts. The makers, performers, and audiences for these genres do not as a rule subscribe to the same aesthetic values that reigned when the concept of fine art developed in modern history. Such departures from older art traditions are noticeable in every art form, though philosophical theory has probably been most affected by the revolutions that have taken place within visual art, which has witnessed such radical changes that the very concept of art has been brought into question.

This is by no means to declare the older tradition dead. As we shall see, it yet wields considerable authority over the art scene today. Nonetheless, there has been a loosening of categories within the arts, such that the confidence that theorists used to have about their ability to characterize the essential qualities of art has dwindled considerably. This loss of confidence and its effects on philosophy of art is one of the subjects of this chapter.

The impact of feminist art, both its continuity with other iconoclastic art movements and its distinctiveness, needs to be placed in relation to debates about art that permeate philosophy, criticism, and art itself. This discussion could take a number of different directions. Because feminism is first of all a political stance, many theorists have utilized Marxist approaches or the ideas of the Frankfurt school of critical theory to analyze the impact of culture in contemporary society.[10] The influential work of British art historian Griselda Pollock is a case in point. Drawing on Marxist cultural theory, Pollock analyzes the patterns of exclusion that have erased women from the history of art and critiques the standards that underwrite the canons of "great art."[11] The works of philosophers and social theorists of these movements offer potent perspectives on the culture of the twentieth century, damaged by two world wars, that have been fruitful in uncovering the political message latent in the high art tradition and providing critiques of cultural norms. Even more directly, European psychoanalytic and deconstructivist theories have been put to use by feminists probing the very construction of gender. The latter approaches will be discussed in the next chapter. Here, however, I shall situate feminist art in relation to the largely analytic Anglo-American tradition, which has analyzed the concept of art in ways that indirectly illuminate feminist strategies in the artworld. As a preface to this discussion, let us review some background about the attempt to define art and to clarify the conceptual boundaries of the arts.

Definitions and their contexts

There have been concepts of art for as long as there has been art. For centuries the reigning assumption was that art is best considered a type of *mimesis* or imitation, and by some measures the more realistic the representation, the better the artist. (In Chapter 1 we saw how the Roman historian Pliny singled out realistic art for special admiration.) The mimetic concept of art, loosely understood, reigned from antiquity into early modern times in Europe.[12] To call these older discussions of art "imitation theories" is a retrospective judgment, however, for most writers presumed that it is the nature of poetry or painting or sculpture to be mimetic. Their controversies were focused on what it means to imitate, what kinds of relations obtain between subject and artwork, and the methods available to artists to render their subjects. By and large they did not ask the question, what is art? in the form in which we now pose that query. The studied attempt to formulate an actual definition of art is a modern project. It emerges from two directions: chronologically first was the project of clarifying the boundaries of fine art in order to distinguish art from craft or entertainment. We have already seen some efforts in this direction in our discussion of art theory in the eighteenth and nineteenth centuries. More recently, the impetus to define has stemmed from the need to account for objects created within the fine-art tradition that appear deliberately to violate its norms and borders, including examples of feminist art such as Sterbak's and Schneemann's.

The emergence of a fine-art tradition involved reconceiving the purposes of painting, sculpture, poetry, music, and so on, and clustering these genres within a genus "art." With the development of the notion of fine art, the aesthetic value of artworks often became definitionally central. There are too many theories of art to review them all here, but let us briefly consider two major movements in modern aesthetics that include definitions of art: expression theory and formalism, which in different ways carry significance for the gendered concepts of art, artist, and aesthetic value. Both of these theories are also departures from the older presumption that art is essentially imitative.

Expression theory was introduced in our earlier discussion of artistic creativity and genius. This approach to art emerged in the Romantic period and persisted through the twentieth century, and in most of its versions it places special weight on the artistic imagination that brings art into being.[13] Expression theories hold that a keenly expressive work is something of power and lasting value that imparts to the viewer, reader, or listener a vision or idea or intuition that is unique. This use of the concept of expression furthered the distinction between the fine art of high culture, and both popular entertainment and utilitarian crafts. Despite their many differences, most expression theories are interested in the nature of the kinds of products that are categorized as artworks within the fine-art tradition. Most of them are general theories about the defining character of all artworks, whether music or poetry, painting or architecture, as with Suzanne Langer's definition that "Art is the creation of forms symbolic of human feeling."[14]

Another major departure from the idea that the essence of art is mimesis is formalism. The centrality of form—structure, composition, and so forth—is an important aspect of aesthetics since the early eighteenth century and plays a major role in the development of the very concept of the aesthetic. But "form" does not constitute the core of an actual philosophy of art until later with the rise of modernist art.[15] In various disciplines, artists called "modernist" dramatically opposed traditions of artistic imitation by deliberately departing from familiar representational techniques, distorting figure and space in painting, narrative chronology in literature, harmony and tonality in music. An emphasis on aesthetic form rather than the meaning of represented content provided a means of promoting these stylistic innovations.

We can distinguish two sides to the formalist movement: the theoretical definition of art in terms of its form, and a powerful branch of criticism that evaluates artworks, especially music, painting, sculpture, dance, and architecture, in formalist terms. The formalist definition of art was relatively short-lived. Philosophers usually single out the English art critic Clive Bell as the quintessential formalist, because his theory of art was so extreme and clear. Bell argued that it is the essence of art to be "significant form," by which he meant a compositional arrangement that arouses aesthetic emotion.[16] Bell advanced his theory as a general description of all visual art, though an important secondary agenda was the defense of post-Impressonist painting. The works of painters such as Picasso and Cézanne, whose work collapsed perspective, flattened space, and distorted figures, baffled much of the general public in the early twentieth century because such paintings did not represent objects the way they actually look. Bell issued a scathing rejection of the values of imitation and realistic representation, defending all art purely on the grounds that the possession of significant form qualifies an object as art. His theory is primarily a theory of painting, though he allowed that music might be similarly dependent upon form. (The way was already well paved for this idea; a theorist of the previous generation, Eduard Hanslick, had argued influentially on behalf of formalist values in music.)[17] Incidentally, though formalism is an assiduously aestheticist theory, it is not interested in rejecting craft and separating it out from fine art. Bell explicitly includes craft among his examples of significant form. However, the craft object is evaluated solely for its form: its shape, balance, harmony, and so on; its use value is utterly ignored if it is to be considered art. So in a sense the idea of craft is set aside, since the form of beautiful artifacts alone can make them art.

The formalist approach to the definition of art goes hand in hand with formalist art criticism, which evaluates compositional qualities above all others in assessment of works of art. (Such attention to form paved the way for appreciation and appropriation of objects created in other cultures, notably Africa; interest in African masks is evident in some of the paintings of Picasso and Modigliani, for instance.) Formalists locate aesthetically pertinent qualities among the intrinsic properties of artworks; they reject as irrelevant extrinsic properties that relate to matters beyond the work, such as representational meaning or social import.[18] This was part of an agenda to defend the anti-mimetic innovations of modernism; but it also reduced the relevance of art as a comment about life or society or the world at large. Thus anything like a political or religious message expressed by means of art would be irrelevant to its import as a work of art, whatever its political or religious significance. Therefore, attention to the sexual politics of representation is smothered by formalist approaches, which is why they are rejected by many feminist critics.

Both formalist and expressionist concepts of art are interested in accounting for the creation of a product that has high aesthetic value, whether that value be described in terms of beauty of form or expressive insight. Both "expression" and "significant form" accord honor to artworks and their makers. Definitions based upon these approaches are attempts to delineate the features of genuine art from other things that may be similar, such as entertainment, but which lack some pertinent defining features, features that also separate artistic excellence from mediocrity.

The philosophical drive to formulate a definition of art, that is, to stipulate necessary and sufficient conditions such that all and only objects meeting those conditions qualify as art, has often been at the center of aesthetic theory in the analytic tradition. This kind of endeavor, however, reached a hiatus of sorts in the mid-twentieth century. Some theorists, influenced by ideas derived from Wittgenstein that emphasize context and use in understanding concepts rather than the formulation of definitions, actually argued that art neither admits nor requires a strict definition. We know what art is when we encounter it, some claimed, and we don't recognize it by applying a theory or a set of criteria to distinguish art from non-art. Our ability to use the term is what is important, and the ability to speak coherently about art and to behave appropriately in relation to it is the measure of our understanding. What is more, art objects are too various to admit a meaningful set of necessary and sufficient conditions, which is another reason why the search for a definition is wrongheaded, by this line of thought.[19] However, this confidence about "our" working understanding of art is stymied by some kinds of art itself. The complacency implicit in the assumption that we don't need to formulate a concept of art because we already know it when we see it, seems an inadequate response to the puzzles that the artworld amply delivers nowadays.

Art and anti-art

Challenges to artistic traditions, methods, and styles are part of the history of art; indeed, one could say that they are the reason that art has a history at all. But some challenges are so radical that they appear to undermine not only stylistic traditions but the entire idea of art itself. One of the earliest and most dramatic of these movements called itself "Dada."[20] The Dadaist movement began during World War I in Switzerland among a group of expatriate artists who were opposed to the war and critical of the social, economic, and political forces that had brought Europe into brutal conflict. Their deliberately outrageous performances and exhibits were designed, in part, to taunt the industrialist machinery of wartime, although their most obvious targets were the values of high culture. Those who identified themselves as Dadaists (the origin of the name is obscure; some claim that it derives from "dadada": the meaningless prattle of a baby) were disaffected from proper society generally and challenged social and aesthetic values at every front. Most importantly, they did not necessarily conceive of their exhibitions and performances as art at all. The term "anti-art" perhaps describes them more accurately, because of the extreme degree to which their works defied familiar aesthetic and artistic norms.

Dadaist reversal of traditional values of art can be seen in Marcel Duchamp's presentation of what he called "readymades." Duchamp selected manufactured items, titled them, and presented them as "art." Some of the titles were whimsical, such as In Advance of the Broken Arm, the title he gave a snow shovel. The urinal of Fountain, his most notorious piece, was purchased from a plumbing supply house. The manufacturer's name, "R. Mutt," was sloppily painted as an artist's signature on the base of the urinal (initially Duchamp kept his role anonymous). This piece has become one of the major referents of twentieth-century art history, not only despite but because of the fact that it flouts the traditional expectation that art should be an expression of the artist's original imagination, that it should be unique, that it should express profound insight, that it should have beautiful form and aesthetic value. Fountain was calculated to outrage; it was not presented as part of an artistic agenda to attune the public to the beauties of factory-produced porcelain plumbing. Ironically, art historians and artists returned to Dada and hailed it as an important moment in the history of art. This outcome was hardly part of the original intent. Decades later, Duchamp was still protesting: "I threw the urinoir in their faces," he complained, "and now they come and admire it for its beauty."[21]

One might think that an object made as anti-art simply is not art at all. But the power of history trumps individual intent, and there are numerous performances and objects originally made to challenge, insult, taunt, and annoy the art establishment that have been incorporated into the annals of art and criticism and that therefore demand some place in the concept of art. Moreover, these movements supply an important context for understanding feminist art, for many feminists share the agenda of anti-art inasmuch as they diagnose elements of cultural practice that require critique or rejection. In Peggy Phelan's succinct summary:

> Emerging in the 1960s and 1970s, feminist art was itself framed by simultaneously occurring art movements and by the discourses that surrounded it. Pop and Conceptual art, Minimalism, Happenings, body art, Land art, photography, experimental film and public art were all vying for attention when feminist art began to be recognized as a specific aesthetic practice, a recognition that was rooted in a political awakening.[22]

It is far from easy to formulate a definition of art that includes Dada or its heirs such as conceptualism and performance art. It is just to address this conceptual chaos that a definition known as the "institutional theory" was developed.

Institutional theory

The institutional theory is most associated with American philosopher George Dickie, who devised his definition of art to accommodate the kinds of objects such as Fountain that appear to violate traditional norms. He argues that objects become art in virtue of the relationships they bear to a complex set of institutions and participants. His first formulation was quite simple:

> A work of art in the classificatory sense is (1) an artifact (2) a set of the aspects of which has had conferred upon it the status of candidate for appreciation by some person or persons acting on behalf of a certain social institution (the artworld).[23]

In response to critics and to clarify his meaning further, Dickie eventually supplied five component definitions in his formulation of the concept of art within an artworld: (1) "An artist is a person who participates with under-standing in the making of a work of art." (2) "A work of art is an artifact of a kind created to be presented to an artworld public." (3) "A public is a set of persons the members of which are prepared in some degree to under-stand an object which is presented to them." (4) "The artworld is the totality of all artworld systems" (that is, art forms such as painting, sculpture, per-formance, music, novels, and so on). And (5) "An artworld system is a framework for the presentation of a work of art by an artist to an artworld public."[24] These five stipulations together define what makes an object or event a work of art. It is a philosophical rendition of the kind of approach that McEvilley expressed to the *New York Times* when he said that "It is art if it is called art, written about in an art magazine, exhibited in a museum or bought by a private curator."

The components of the institutional theory exemplify some of the diffi-culty that the uninitiated are likely to confront with artworks such as Duchamp's, Schneeman's, and Sterbak's. To understand art at any time in his-tory one needs to be familiar with a tradition. The contemporary scene, however, puts special demands on audiences because it includes numerous anti-traditional movements that are quite difficult to comprehend at first encounter. In fact some theorists have argued that since the mid-twentieth century the role of the expert art critic as mediator between artist and public has become essential.[25] If one is not already acquainted with the contempo-rary artworld, either as artist or as adept member of the art public, one is apt to feel excluded from the conversation.

This approach to art calls attention to the power of institutions of all sorts—formal and informal—to exclude or include objects as art and their makers as artists. It was the power of the artworld that drew Dada kicking and screaming into its precincts, and it is the authority of formal institutions such as museums and galleries that the Guerrilla Girls address in their protests. In the first chapter we noted how earlier concepts of the artist, of creativity, and of the nature of art products systematically tended to exclude women and their works. Though the institutional theory can be faulted for a somewhat uncritical endorsement of the authority of established artworld institutions, it is not overtly exclusionary—partly because there is little in it that settles on the value that art supposedly has. This is deliberate; Dickie set out to produce a "classificatory" rather than an "evaluative" theory. What interests him is not what makes a work aesthetically valuable but what qual-ifies it to be called "art" at all.[26] This definition tells us what conditions make something art, not what makes it good art. It does not, therefore, tell us why we should care about it.

Art as a mirror: Arthur Danto

Among those interviewed by the *New York Times* in 1997 was philosopher and art critic Arthur Danto. While Danto agrees that the definitional question is especially difficult these days, he does not believe that this difficulty lets theorists off the hook. On the contrary, precisely because so many objects of art confound our traditional separation of objects into art and non-art categories, the definitional task is far more pressing than it appeared to be when we thought we knew art when we saw it.

> There used to be a time when you could pick out something perceptually the way you can recognize, say, tulips or giraffes. But the way things have evolved, art can look like anything, so you can't tell by looking. Criteria like the critic's good eye no longer apply.
>
> Art these days has very little to do with esthetic responses. It has more to do with intellectual responses. You have to project a hypothesis: Suppose it is a work of art? Then certain questions come into play—what's it about, what does it mean, why was it made, when was it made and with respect to what social and artistic conversations does it make a contribution? If you get good answers to those questions, it's art.[27]

The emergence of anti-traditional artworks from Dada through conceptualism and Pop Art, Danto observes, forced theorists' attention away from the features of art that had previously been the focus of attention precisely because those works possessed no such features—no beauty of form, no expression of feeling, no evident representation, sometimes even no original artifact. And yet, despite these efforts to repudiate every value of the art establishment, these works are now included in the chronicle of twentieth-artworld.[28] One reason for this is that such works are comments *within the artworld*—about aesthetic judgment and mass culture, about value and property, about the role of the artist and the public. They are profoundly *about* art itself.[29] As such, they provide a means by which we can understand our own historical times, our values, our social identities. Danto himself alludes to the old notion of mimesis when he calls art a mirror turned upon the world:

"externalizing a way of viewing the world, expressing the interior of a cultural period, offering itself as a mirror to catch the conscience of our kings."[30]

It is Danto's contention that art—all art at any time or place—must be about something, must bear meaning, have content; and that its meaning must be embodied in the artwork itself.[31] This is not and cannot be done the same way at all periods of history, a fact that indicates the role of *concepts of art* in the production of art. Sophisticated New Yorkers of the 1960s were just barely able to see Andy Warhol's *Brillo Box* as art, for example; such a conceptual feat would have been not only impossible but nonsensical at an earlier period of history. Requisite conceptions of art were not in place to produce or to recognize Pop Art until the mid-twentieth century. As Danto puts it, "to see something as art at all demands nothing less than this, an atmosphere of artistic theory, a knowledge of the history of art."[32]

By this point in history the embodiment of meaning is virtually unrestricted in terms of the form or means that can be employed. Danto acknowledges that unprecedented diversity characterizes the contemporary artworld, and hence he agrees with the consensus reviewed at the start of this chapter that one simply cannot draw lines between the kinds of objects that can become art and those that cannot. Many installations are situated not in galleries but in public spaces such that their identity as works of art is deliberately confused, and in fact people often do not recognize things like Jenny Holzer's billboards as artworks. But this heterogeneity does not imply that art is indefinable. Rather, it forces us to realize that what artworks share is not any perceptual quality (such as beauty or significant form or the expressed visions of artistic genius) but is rather a relational quality within art traditions and unfolding culture. All art possesses meaning and is about—however obliquely—some subject, whether event, person, object, or idea; and it manifests and exemplifies that meaning to the spectator who asks the right questions. Acknowledging this helps to situate feminist art and other contemporary works that are so perplexing to understand on first encounter.

Feminist work and changing concepts of art

Just as "feminism" does not describe a monolithic politics nor a single point of view about the role of women in society, so "feminist art" does not label one type of art, nor even a class of artworks that share similar themes or perspectives.[33] Art critic Lucy Lippard observes:

It is useless to try to pin down a specific formal contribution made by feminism because feminist and/or women's art is neither a style nor a movement, much as this idea may distress those who would like to see it safely ensconced in the categories and chronology of the past. It consists of many styles and individual expressions and for the most part succeeds in bypassing the star system. At its most provocative and constructive, feminism questions all the precepts of art as we know it.[34]

What feminist artists do share is a sense of the historic social subordination of women and an awareness of how art practices have perpetuated that subordination. That perpetuation has been accomplished by such things as ignoring women's work, objectifying women's bodies in painting and film, romanticizing the sexual exploitation of women in narrative, employing exclusionary criteria for women's creativity, or carrying on the symbolic systems that regard the feminine as a dark rival to the masculine.

With such issues in mind, not only do feminist and postfeminist artists participate in the complex self-reference that characterizes virtually all postmodern work, but they challenge and overturn patriarchal traditions, often with highly theoretical agendas aiding their creative production.[35] Nancy Spero, for example, paints registers of delicately limned figures taken from ancient mythic traditions (Greek and Celtic) and installs them racing across gallery walls. Sometimes the images are juxtaposed to classic texts, presented as partially erased fragments; sometimes the texts allude to contemporary writings about women.[36] This sort of play with tradition calls attention to the norms of the genre that are being queried or subverted, and hence a "knowledge of the history of art" is a special necessity. Sally Potter's film *Thriller* (1979) is a reprise and revision of the story of the popular Puccini opera *La Bohème*. Laura Mulvey and Peter Wollen's movie *Riddles of the Sphinx* (1976) recounts the Oedipus myth from the point of view of the Sphinx whose riddle launched Sophocles' drama, thus invoking not only Greek myth but also the psychoanalytic theory that Mulvey used to such influential effect in articulating her theory of the gaze.

In addition to questions and challenges raised within the genres of familiar art forms, there are two trends much employed by feminists that refuse the expectations of traditional arts: the use of nonstandard materials and the presentation of the body as a component of art.

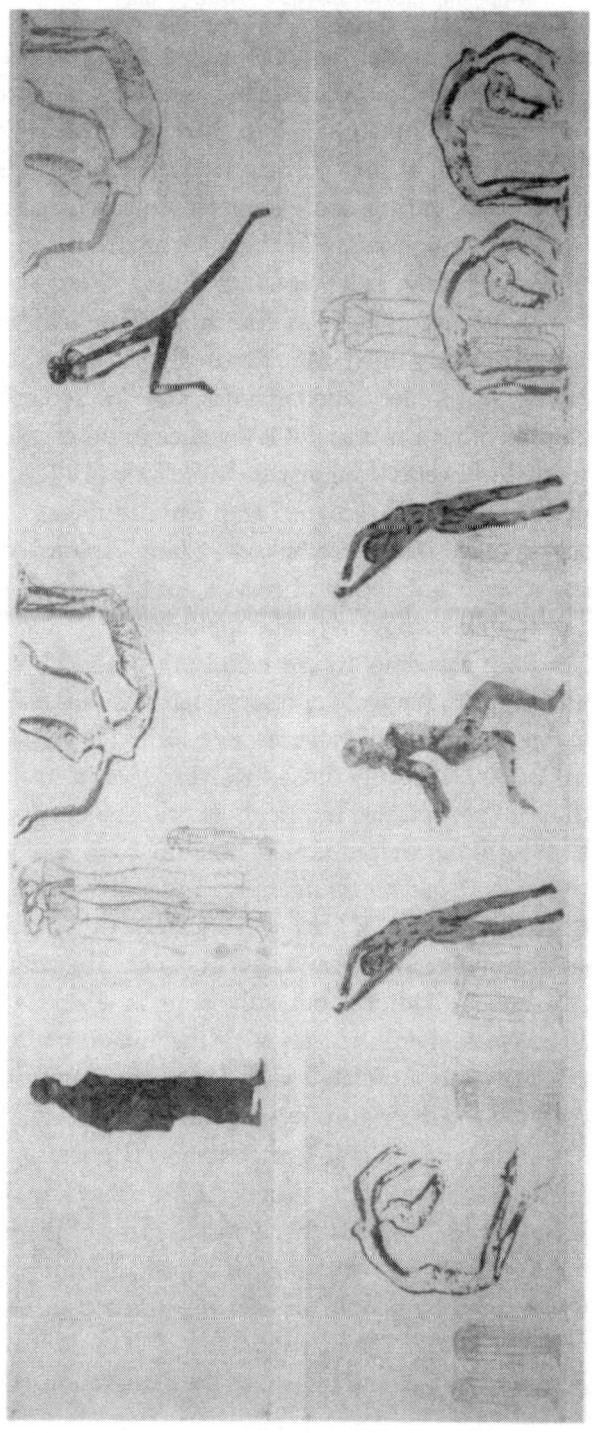

Figure 10 Nancy Spero, Egyptian figure/Acrobat/Dancing (1988). Photograph by David Reynolds.

The medium and the message: fiber and food

Since the fine-art tradition was fairly strict about excluding utilitarian craft objects, including things made for domestic use, many feminist artists have deliberately incorporated craft materials into their work. Moreover, since some craft traditions in which women participated were joint efforts and did not single out an individual creator, some feminist projects have been similarly collaborative, even though many of them are attributed to the artist who "directed" the whole show, as it were. Judy Chicago's large project *The Dinner Party* (1974–9), for example, is an enormous triangular table with place settings commemorating thirty-nine female figures from history and myth. It uses weaving, embroidery, and ceramics, and Chicago enlisted the skills of over a hundred other artists to put it together. Another collaborative installation on the part of twenty-four artists, *Womanhouse* (1972), set up an entire house with different rooms designed with feminist themes. Chicago's room in this project is called *Menstruation Bathroom*, a blood-splotched lavatory. We can regard it as a wry counterpoint of *Fountain*, for Duchamp's attention-getting urinal is, of course, a singularly male appliance.

Cloth and other fiber materials figure heavily in the work of Miriam Schapiro and Faith Ringgold. Ringgold employs quilts, a traditional women's craft form, in the fine art context of galleries, as vehicles for messages about politics and social issues, especially those involving race in America. This work uses the idiom of sewn fabric implicitly to criticize the exclusion of women's craft items from the art tradition by pointing back to objects commonly made for domestic use on the frontier, under slavery, in ordinary domestic necessity. Feminist uses of fiber, ceramics, and other craft materials may be seen as a challenge to the fine art–craft divide. The very materials employed *subvert* the fine-art tradition; but at the same time cloth and woven items refer to and revive women's artifacts *within* the fine-art tradition.

The use of craft materials associated with home and comfort to make painful and difficult social statements produces some interesting dissonance in the product. One thinks of quilts as benign items for warmth and decoration. But their designs are often more than decorative; they have long been used as family records or to depict historical events, many of them tragic or painful. The largest quilt on record is the AIDS quilt, a joint project that connected squares quilted by people all over the globe commemorating loved ones who died of AIDS.[37] The incorporation of craft in fine art defies the distinction between the two and questions the denigration of domestic creativity. And as Ringgold's work makes evident, it also can be employed to confront another standard modernist aesthetic divide: the separation of aesthetic value from political significance.

The artistic employment of food is even more radically subversive of familiar concepts of art, for while craft materials represent artifacts that have been squeezed out of the fine-art tradition, foods represent substances that have been considered to have little or no artistic import at all. In the last chapter we analyzed how values of the body involving the sense of taste and eating are especially excluded from philosophical domains. There I argued that the ascription of nonaesthetic status to the bodily senses is a product of theoretical neglect of those senses. But the fact remains that the low philosophical standing of taste, smell, and eating is powerfully embedded in cultural symbols, and it is these associations that contemporary "food artists" usually exploit. The use of foodstuffs as art media simultaneously explores aesthetic traditions and sabotages them. It probes at the concept of art and the values associated with high culture traditions, at the same time that it presents provocative reflections on gender, sexuality, and death.

Sterbak's *Vanitas: Flesh Dress for an Albino Anorectic*, to return to our initial example, is an interesting bridge between traditions of painting and the contemporary interrogation of those traditions. Its references are directed to the history of art itself, and it can be read as a manifesto against that history and its aesthetic values. Moreover, it reaches into political realms and embodies commentary on the worth attributed to the female body.

We can begin by placing *Flesh Dress* in a continuum of artistic production. Sterbak gives us some help with the title: *Vanitas*. This term alludes to a genre of European still-life painting popular in the sixteenth through eighteenth centuries. *Vanitas* motifs feature objects such as decaying foodstuffs, skulls, broken musical instruments, spilled coins, torn pages—any item that once was accorded value and is destroyed with the passage of time and therefore symbolizes the ultimate waste of worldly endeavors. (The label is taken from the first line of the book of Ecclesiastes: "*Vanitas vanitatis, et omnia vanitas* [Vanity of vanities, all is vanity]".) *Vanitas* pictures are highly moralistic reminders of the fruitlessness of human effort and the error of placing value on things of this world that inevitably will be destroyed. The title places *Flesh Dress* in the same tradition as still-life painting, declaring its kinship with a long-recognized genre of art.

At the same time, its insistent literalness, for the dress is actually made of flesh, rejects the traditions of that medium, for Sterbak has chosen to work not with paint on canvas but with butchered meat. Her work will not survive to hang alongside its forebears in art museums; it decays rapidly and declares its decay in the very course of an exhibit. (It is preserved only through reports and photographic documentation.) In so doing, it mimics the aging of human flesh—in this case female flesh: a "flesh dress for an albino anorectic." Allusions multiply as we realize that the flesh is hanging outside the emaciated body of a very pale woman, her thinness indicating an extreme fashion that rejects too much female fleshiness.[38] The meat is heavily salted, but all meat has an odor. Even looking at a picture of this piece arouses uncomfortable synaesthetic feelings: *What would it feel like against one's skin? Do age and rot smell the same? In the final analysis, is human flesh really just so much butchered meat?* Sterbak's work is not itself anti-art, but it partakes of the spirit of anti-art in its choice of medium.

The employment of meat and other foodstuffs is different from the incorporation of craft materials into venues of high culture, though it similarly questions fine-art traditions. But food and eating, for all the reasons discussed in the last chapter, are associated with femininity in a most extreme and disturbing way. The female body in many symbol systems is linked with both life and death. All bodies die, but the maternal body is also a source of life, and the decay of women's flesh is a kind of betrayal—beauty and sexual attraction are lost, the ability to produce life has withered, and the comfort and sustenance of a mother are no longer available. The flesh of *Flesh Dress* isn't even naked (we are used to that in art); it is *skinned*—disgusting, vulnerable, and impermanent. One difference between food in a traditional *vanitas* motif and in Sterbak's work is that the first is a theme explored within *art* and the second is a statement about the nature of *art itself*. What began as the object of an associative reference employed for moral and aesthetic purposes to convey messages about the transience of life, has been transmogrified into an actual art medium.

Artists' bodies

Employing large quantities of beef in an exhibit is not a notably abstract enterprise; because the meat decays, its specificity is manifest in the art: this particular meat, this particular body. In Chapter 2 we noted how feminist theory participates in the critique of Enlightenment ideas, including skepticism about the universality of aesthetic values. This critical approach rejects the idea that the artist should create with an abstract, universal vision that

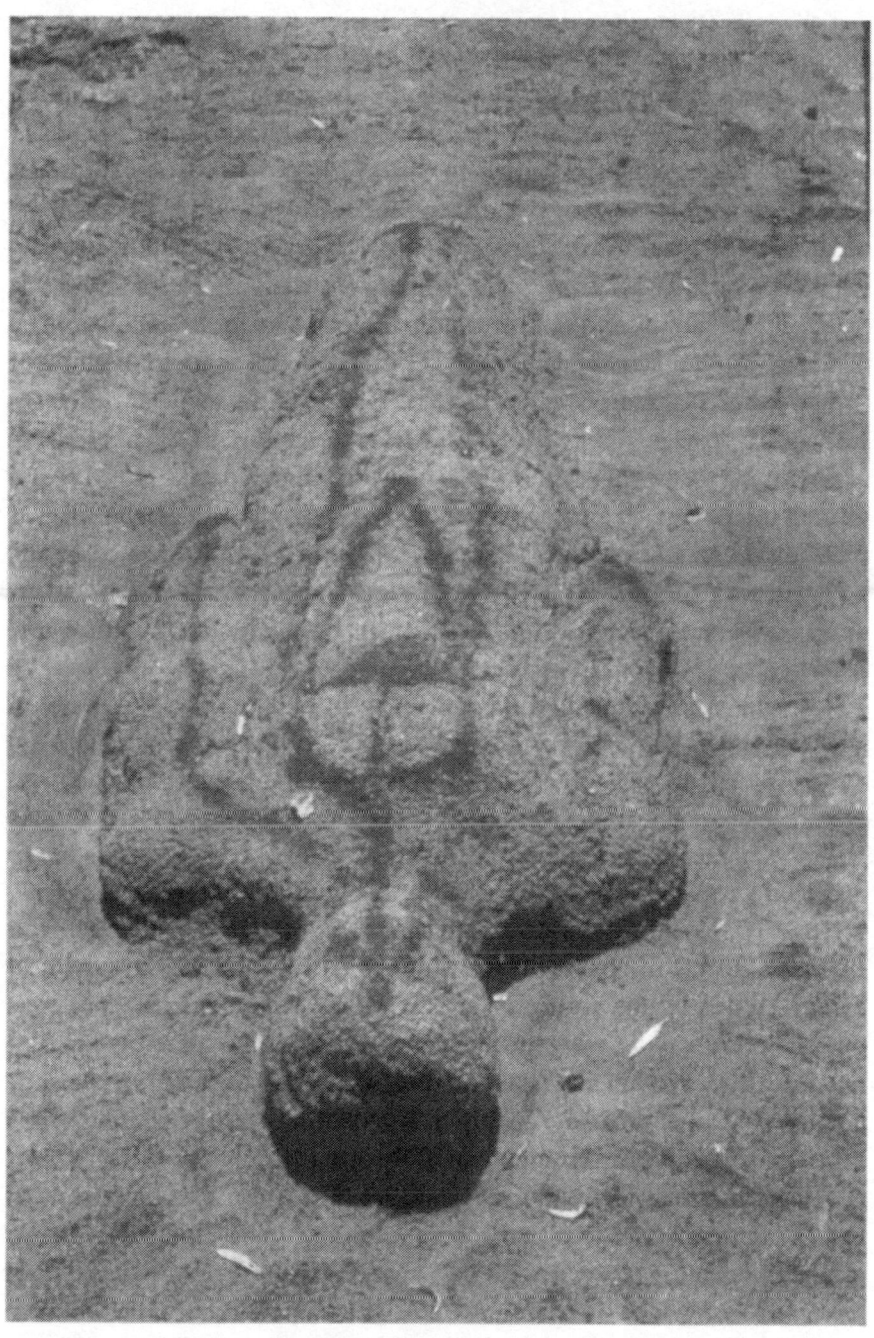

Figure 11 Ana Mendieta, *Silueta Works in Iowa*, 1976–1978/1991. Courtesy of the Estate of Ana Mendieta and Galerie Lelong, New York.

eclipses his or her personal perspective, and replaces it with the insistence that all creativity has "position" inflected by history, gender, sexuality, social position or class, race, nationality, and so forth.

One means by which artists draw attention to specificity and positionality is by using their own bodies in their works. Ana Mendieta imprinted her body into the land art she created in the 1970s and 1980s as a means of expressing her views about the affinity between women's bodies and the earth. Virtually all of Cindy Sherman's works of the 1970s, 1980s, and into the 1990s include her own image, sometimes standing in for figures in compositions reminiscent of famous old master paintings, as with her series of History Portraits. Her Untitled #224 (1990) is unsettling partly because of an implied gender cross-over, for her face appears in the motif of the classical Bacchus or wine-god figure. Renée Cox's work Yo Mamma is a photograph of herself holding a child, an image that resonates with paintings and sculptures of the Virgin Mary and the Christ child, most especially Michelangelo's Pietà.[39] In the act of substituting her own image for a familiar icon of art and biblical narrative, Cox calls attention to the fact that she creates from a particular subject position identified in history by gender, race, culture, and sexuality.[40]

It is evident even from just these three examples that this specificity of position means that the use of "the body" on the part of artists does not always signify the same thing. This fact is particularly dramatic when one considers the political impact of body images made by women artists from different nonwestern cultural traditions. Alongside the male–female dichotomy these works allude to additional oppositions between occident–orient, past–present, tradition–revolution.[41] Just which cultural context is employed further diversifies the meanings of female flesh. The covered-over bodies hidden by the chador in Sherin Neshat's photographs of Iranian women holding guns, whose visible flesh is inscribed with Persian poetry, reference both Muslim tradition and revolution. The artificial, mechanized figures of Lee Bul evoke the highly technocratic society of contemporary urban Asia. Additional examples would further multiply the different types of eroticism, gender meanings, and social challenge that the presentation of bodies can signify. Needless to say, these meanings are not limited to the use of female bodies. Male artists have also used their own flesh—depicted or presented—to heighten awareness of sex, gender, eroticism, and identity.

The literal use of flesh and the body of the artist has also become a major feature of performance art, a relatively new form in which feminist artists

Figure 12 Cindy Sherman, *Untitled* #224, 1990. Courtesy of the artist and Metro Pictures.

have been especially daring.[42] Performance art affords an immediate means to engage with audiences and to explore and enact ideas about identity and the cultural construction of femininity.[43] Since so much of the Euro-American visual-art tradition depicts female bodies (usually young and voluptuous), much performance art upsets that tradition by means of exaggeration, parody, violence, and reversal. Artists have used their own bodies as means to explore the pornography industry (risking confusion with pornography itself), violence against women, the sexual marketplace, race identification, aging, and mortality.[44] Performance art employs the living flesh of the artist, and some have shed their own blood in their works, sometimes with irreversible effects. The French artist Orlan, for example, has undergone numerous plastic surgeries, broadcast on video links, that have permanently made her own body into an exemplar of a series of references to artistic renditions of idealized feminine appearance.[45] Orlan's works refer to specific paintings and sculptures. But more generally, when women employ their bodies in performance, they can hardly avoid evoking echoes of the entire art tradition at the same time. Speaking of performance artist-musician Laurie Anderson, Susan McClary says:

> The fact that hers is a *female* body changes the dynamics of several of the oppositions she invokes in performance. For women's bodies in Western culture have almost always been viewed as objects of display. Women have rarely been permitted agency in art, but instead have been restricted to enacting—upon and through their bodies—the theatrical, musical, cinematic, and dance scenarios constructed by male artists. Centuries of this traditional sexual division of cultural labor bear down on Anderson (or any woman performer) when she performs.[46]

Performance art has met with a high degree of controversy partly because of the directness of its presentations and the exposure of the bodies of the artists in ways that are unprecedented in the fine arts (though not in pornography). The work of Karen Finley, who calls attention to the sexual exploitation of women by smearing her body with foodstuffs resembling blood and excrement, gained special notoriety because of her participation in a lawsuit filed against the National Endowment for the Arts, some of whose members found her work too offensive to merit public expenditures.[47] The performance of Carolee Schneemann mentioned earlier, *Interior*

Scroll, shockingly made use of taboo interior space of the artist's body, from which she extracted a wound strip of paper—like both tampon and sacred scroll. The idea that there are secrets hidden within women's sex is an ancient conceit of myth, and the enactment of myth in and by a living woman both explodes and employs venerable symbols, collapsing the distinction between mythic body and real flesh, and also between representation and reality.

For some theorists, performance signifies the social and psychological production of gender itself. They adopt a strong version of social construc-tionism, which maintains that gender identity is not given by nature as a developmental feature of sexual dimorphism, but is imposed by social norms with which children are inculcated through education, manners, upbringing, and cultural discourse. The connections between gender iden-tity and performance have entered feminist thinking from several philo-sophical entry points. Marilyn Frye, writing in the analytic tradition, has formulated an analysis of female and lesbian identity that employs the idea of performatives developed in speech-act theory.[48] Judith Butler, more influ-enced by European philosophy, has developed an explicit theory of gender and sexuality as performance.[49] In fact, related ideas can be traced back sev-eral generations, for (as Butler notes) in 1929 Joan Rivière, a Freudian psy-choanalyst, wrote a suggestive essay on "Womanliness as Masquerade."[50] Thus from multiple theoretical starting-points one can explore the idea that female identities are less given by nature than formed through patterns of culture.

The feminist uses of the real body in art are among the challenges directed to traditional distinction between art and reality. At first glance, it does indeed seem difficult to distinguish art from reality if the art object is not a representation but a real thing.[51] Strictly speaking, however, the ontological distinction between artwork and real object, however one articulates it, still obtains with even the most radical of body arts. It is the artwork that is described by means of aesthetic predicates: daring, graceful, packed with meaning, etc. Schneemann's performing body may be co-extensive with her actual body, which is to say that physically they are one and the same (which is part of the impact of her performances). But it is the body-in-performance that is the referent for aesthetic judgments, not Schneemann herself. In this respect performance art, however radical in other respects, is comparable to dance, where the dancer's body creates the dance but is not identical to it. The ontological distinction between art and reality, strictly speaking, cannot be erased. One must grant, however, that it has been rendered nearly imperceptible; moreover, the idea that gender itself can be viewed as performance further blurs the borders between art, artifice, and "reality."[52] Uses of the body in feminist performance art have the dramatic effect of obliterating the familiar distance between art and life, and in terms of the challenges posed to the concept of art, this apparent ontological shrinkage has had stunning impact.

Summary

The last century has witnessed radical alterations to the earlier picture of art and aesthetic opportunities discussed in the first three chapters. To what extent do the philosophical, aesthetic, and artistic traditions that peaked in the eighteenth and nineteenth centuries still affect artists in the twenty-first century? This is a complicated question, and answering it is made more difficult by the fact that we are actually living in the time under assessment. We don't have the benefit of hindsight to judge the effects of the present art scene on developments yet to happen. Analyzing the artworld of today is necessarily tentative, for no one can foresee what the present will resemble from the perspective of the future.

We do not find with contemporary philosophical concepts of art and of the artist the same kinds of exclusionary categories that prevailed as the fine-art tradition developed. (This is not to say that standards of evaluation and selection in the artworld today have erased all of the skewed value structures that excluded women's accomplishments of the past. That is a matter for a study of the critical reception of art, which I have not done here.) Women—of diverse ethnic and racial and national backgrounds—have been major presences in postmodern and feminist art and are among the pathbreaking innovators on the contemporary art scene. Their presence adds impact to the fact that the concept of art itself continues to be under scrutiny, and women artists embody in their very persons a challenge to the fine-art tradition. This we can see vividly in performance art as well as in the expansion of art to encompass nontraditional media.

Amid all these changes, have the concepts of artist and art also utterly changed, such that their implicit masculine gender has all but faded away? With due observance of the caveats expressed above, I suspect that this is not the case. The most noticeable reason for this judgment is that tradition remains the overarching point of reference for feminist and postmodern artists, who refer continually to the past, whether ironically, parodically, or confrontationally. Tradition unavoidably frames the work of even the most iconoclastic artists, for only God creates *ex nihilo*. The breakaway movements in art remain to that extent bound to rejected legacies, which therefore retain much of their power in these acts of confrontation. What will emerge from the collision of innovation and tradition that propels cultural history we have yet to see.

6

DIFFICULT PLEASURES

Sublimity and disgust

Several examples of feminist art mentioned in the last chapter dramatically draw attention to physical, bodily nature, whether by means of the actual body of a performer or the surrogate body of butchered meat. The mortality and facticity of physical being are emphasized in these works, sometimes with unsettling, even revolting effect. One can find many additional instances of art that deliberately disturbs and disgusts, such as Kiki Smith's *Tale*, a sculpture of a crawling woman trailing excrement, or Cindy Sherman's faces which appear to rot into their backgrounds. And there are numerous other examples in contemporary art—both feminist and nonfeminist—where mortality, gross physical effects, and decay are presented, not only by representation in traditional media, but sometimes also through the use of actual blood or urine or body parts, as with Damien Hirst's vitrines of animal carcasses or Andres Serrano's Piss Christ.[1] The body in all its terrible vulnerability has become a major presence in literature, television, and film as well. The advancement of special effects in film and video has made possible particularly extreme representations of violence, dismemberment, and monstrosities, and has brought death, injury, and decay right before the eyes of the audience. If beauty and the sublime were touchstones of aesthetic value of the eighteenth and nineteenth centuries, one might wonder if the parallel value at the advent of the twenty-first might be the disgusting.

At first glance, the presence of themes involving blood, death, excrement, and rot in art of our times might appear to be utterly discontinuous with the values of previous eras, might even seem to be the inordinate extension of anti-art that has broken with the roots of the western cultural tradition. But in fact there are numerous continuities in aesthetic theory and artistic aims that bind these artworks to the traditions of the past, even as they criticize it, reject it, and break new ground in expressing what some refer to as an "anti-aesthetic."[2] Especially with the feminist presence, which has been an important propellant for difficult, even repellent, explorations in art, we can see employment of theoretical frameworks that are outgrowths as well as critiques of the philosophical traditions we have been reviewing. There is an oscillation between rejection and adaptation of traditional values and styles, which is why the past is never completely laid to rest but remains available for resurrection, reinterpretation, and inspiration. Here we shall pursue several more topics that manifest this dynamism, reviewing continuities with and departures from philosophical traditions in feminist art and theory, and culminating in consideration of art that evokes disgust.

The first section of this chapter presents a brief update of philosophical treatments of mind and body as a general backdrop for understanding the emphasis on corporeality that we see in art today. Then we shall return to an aesthetic concept that was introduced in Chapter 2: the sublime. Theories of the sublime probe questions about aesthetic response and the limits of expressibility that are continued by some of the psychoanalytic and deconstructivist approaches that have become major features of feminist theory, interpretation, and art. This will lead us to consider the appropriation of certain philosophical theories among feminist artists who explore the body and sexuality, sometimes by exposing and exploring aspects of bodies that are standard examplars of the disgusting. By no means do I mean to imply that feminists make art simply by taking theory and applying it in some art-making project; that occasionally happens, but seldom. Rather, we can see in philosophy and art tandem investigations of shared questions that have become urgent to both at this particular time in history. The attention paid to matters of the body in feminist and postfeminist art, and in contemporary art in general, should be understood against the background of philosophical theories about the ways the mind and the body are conceived in relation to each other. Indeed, the question of the body and its place in subjectivity is so central in both philosophy and art today that it renders especially vivid a claim of Arthur Danto's: "Philosophy and art are not discontinuous fragments of a divided subject, but facets of a single unitary philosophy, which thinks of art philosophically and of philosophy from the perspective of art."[3]

Mind and body revisited

The previous chapter situated feminist art in the context of theories of art and their challenges. But there are other philosophical issues that equally illuminate such phenomena as the use of foodstuffs in art or the new significance of the body in installation and performance, among them the distinction between mind and body that plays so important a role in conceptual frameworks of the western tradition. At this juncture in history the old divisions that underwrite the major gendered concepts in philosophical discourse are themselves undergoing challenge and revision. The venerable (if contentious) distinction between mind and body has gradually been eroded by the advancement of neuroscience, the decline of theological metaphysical commitments, and perennial philosophical skepticism. Indeed the distinction between mind (mental) and brain (physical), which always has been a matter of some controversy, has become increasingly complex. While debates concerning the distinction between the mental and the physical continue, old-fashioned substance dualism (the kind espoused by Descartes, for example) is no longer a contender in philosophical circles.[4] The role of physical phenomena—such as the brain, its neural pathways, and its chemistry—in producing consciousness plays an increasingly central role in contemporary debates about the interaction of mind and body and of thought and action. And the role of the entire body, including its sexual morphology, has an increasingly important place in the analysis of subjectivity, identity, and what it means to be "a person."

Feminist theorists have a particular stake in mind–body debates. The binary opposites that were outlined in Chapter 1 have served to frame issues in western philosophy for centuries in ways that overdetermine the neglect or denigration of the side of the duality that is associated with "feminine" elements; one of the most enduring and powerful of these pairs is mind versus body. This system of concepts usually assumes that the mind is the most important human attribute, that it houses reason and ideally governs emotions and the senses, and that the body itself is merely the material container for the most essential traits of an individual. This division has served to sideline sex, gender, and any other aspect of identity that involves bodily morphology or behavior from analyses of the "self."[5] The division between mind and matter or body has always been philosophically problematic, generating a host of debates and arguments about just how to separate the two, whether they represent two distinct substances, and how they are supposed to interact. For our purposes, the important point to note is that the values associated with the persistence of that pair of opposites are gendered values that feminists have subjected to probing skepticism. Querying the mind–body distinction leads in many directions: metaphysics, epistemology, political analysis, aesthetics, and art practice, and there are plenty of controversies among those who challenge dualistic assumptions. But few feminist theorists have left the traditionally conceived mind–body dualism unquestioned. Some have argued that what has standardly been considered "natural," namely physical bodies, are in fact highly cultural constructions of social discourse.[6] Others employ insights available from other philosophies of the past or present to speculate about physical embodiment in ways that resist the traditional dualist conceptualization of mind and body.[7] As Moira Gatens observes: "The claim here is *not* that dichotomous thought is bad or oppressive *per se*, but rather that it can covertly promote social and political values by presenting a conceptual division as if it were a factual or natural division."[8] It is ironic that although the value distinctions associated with mind and body are still pretty well entrenched—for habits of abstract evaluation seem hard to break—the metaphysics that used to subtend them is no longer in place. The gendered values that traditional concepts assumed in philosophies of the past apparently fade less speedily than the explicit philosophical tenets adopted at any given period.

The previous chapter noted how current interest in the body is manifest in art by means of the presentation of flesh and artists' bodies in installations and performance works. And as noted above, the use of real bodies in art is paralleled in the representation of things bodily in graphic art, film, video, and narrative, especially experiences that emphasize the *grossness* of the bodily, the aspects of physical existence that seem most to contrast with the rarified ether of "mind." The evocation of bodily elements that provoke disgust is intimately tied to the philosophical re-evaluation of the body, for disgust is above all others the most physical, visceral emotion. The evocation of disgust on the part of art is a shocking disruption of traditions of aesthetic value, but at the same time it may be seen as continuous with a venerable and exalted aesthetic category: the sublime.

Sublimity again

As we saw in Chapter 2, the concept of the sublime developed in the eighteenth century in terms that compared it to the beautiful, a contrast that often classed the latter as "feminine" and the former "masculine." A woman's mind was considered by theorists such as Kant to be limited to an affinity for the charming or the beautiful, while Burke actually modeled the qualities of beautiful objects on the female body. We might consider this a descriptive means by which concepts take on gender, because the two aesthetic terms are associated with stereotyped ideas about feminine and masculine characteristics. But I think at this point in our study this aspect of binary disparity is sufficiently familiar, and there are other ways to look at the sublime that will illuminate and deepen the ways that femaleness can be explored in art. Because of the emotional difficulty entailed by sublimity, understanding the sublime will eventually also help us understand the role of aversions in art, including disgust.

The modern discourse of aesthetics is rooted in theories of pleasure, even to the extent that many philosophers identify beauty as a type of pleasure. Some aesthetic values appear paradoxical, however, for they involve a fair degree of displeasure as well. The sublime itself appears to be grounded in the profound emotional pain of terror. "Whatever is qualified to cause terror, is a foundation capable of the sublime," as Burke put it.[9] It seems perverse to seek out terror, but that is precisely what we do when we pursue the sublime. Burke surmises that a measure of protective distance is required for the terrifying to convert to the delight of the sublime, for no one enjoys being in the real grip of fear. That it converts at all indicates the profound *meaning* contained in the sublime, which is an experience that thrusts the perceiver to the imagined edge of danger and even death. Burke regards death—which he dubs "this king of terrors"—as the ultimate object of the sublime.[10] Relatedly, confrontation with mortality can put one in mind of its opposite, and Burke was one of many who saw in the experience of sublimity a glimpse of God—an experience of transcendence that terrifies, thrills, and awes.

The magnetism of the sublime indicates something excellent in human character and its quest for knowledge of the most difficult sort. Burke is somewhat unusual for his time in admitting that there may be something just a little depraved in this paradoxical curiosity. He observes that we find the same fascination about death in real life as in artistic experience, speculating that a theater readied for a performance of a tragedy would empty with the news that a public execution was being held nearby. One vividly pictures the well-dressed audience flocking to the foot of the gallows to get even closer to the mystery of death. Just why human beings are drawn to extreme experiences such as this is puzzling, though Burke speculates rather vaguely that we are constituted such that placidity easily slides to boredom, so every now and then a brush with terror heightens one's sense of life.

Kant found the psychological description that Burke presents to be philosophically unsatisfying. Safety from death produces not delight but relief, he observes, so the explanatory power of distance from danger does not explain what he called the strong "negative pleasure" of the sublime. His own explanation elaborates the conditions of the mind that make the experience of sublimity possible.

There are two sorts of situations that give rise to the sublime. What he calls the "dynamical" sublime is experienced in situations where one confronts a dangerous object of great might or size. Not only does the object threaten to overwhelm one (thereby prompting terror), but also its might and vastness exceed the abilities of perception to apprehend it all at once. Our imagination fails to grasp completely such magnitude, and we realize the profound limitations of the human faculties. The "mathematically sublime" is similar, though here it is the intellectual faculties that are confounded. Contemplating infinity, for example, we realize that numbers progress endlessly, but we cannot place that endlessness under a concept with definite numerical value. Once again, we realize that the universe extends far beyond the ability of the human mind to grasp. With that realization we have a sense of the world beyond our own phenomenal experience; the sublime hints at the noumenon that lies unknown beyond the reaches of human imagination and understanding.

Both of these experiences induce the perceiver to reflect on the limits of the human mind and to realize that we are unable to comprehend the might and size of nature in its totality. Part of recognizing our weakness before natural forces is feeling that death is a possibility when we are brought near objects of might and magnitude. Initially this arouses fear, though this emotion is surmounted with more profound realizations about what it means to be human. For in the experience of the sublime we also realize that the mind is not completely bounded by nature. It is free from the causal forces that govern everything else in the world. And this is the basis of the fact that we are moral beings, capable of willing that our actions be different from the way that natural causes, including the forces of desire, would intend. As Kant puts it:

> [T]hat magnitude of a natural object to which the imagination fruitlessly applies its entire ability to comprehend must lead the concept of nature to a supersensible substrate (which underlies both nature and our ability to think), a substrate that is large beyond any standard of sense and hence makes us judge as sublime not so much

the object as the mental attunement in which we find ourselves
when we estimate the object . . .

[T]rue sublimity must be sought only in the mind of the judging
person, not in the natural object the judging of which prompts this
mental attunement.[11]

By this analysis, the attention of the person experiencing the sublime is re-
directed from the external object that initially provokes fear and awe to the
autonomous self, the "mind of the judging person." In so doing, terror is
diminished and the sovereignty of the human mind is sustained. The sublime is an experience of paradoxical mastery: the vastness of its objects
threaten to master the self, and yet the self recovers its integrity in the realization of its own freedom.

The importance of mastery and domination in this account of sublimity
suggests additional elements to the gendered concept of the sublime. Christine Battersby remarks: "In Kant's mind-constructed reality, the 'I' keeps itself
at a regulated—and respectful—distance from the 'object' and 'nature' which
acts as a kind of unknowable 'excess'. Nature, matter and the 'transcendental
object' are feminized."[12] Barbara Freeman posits a complementary "feminine" sublime in which the subject accepts its relation with other forces and
a certain loss of individuation:

The feminine sublime is neither a rhetorical mode nor an aesthetic
category but a domain of experience that resists categorization,
in which the subject enters into relation with an otherness—social,
aesthetic, political, ethical, erotic—that is excessive and unrepresentable. The feminine sublime is not a discursive strategy,
technique, or literary style that the female writer invents, but rather
a crisis in relation to language and representation that a certain subject undergoes.[13]

Several features of these treatments of the sublime are pertinent to keep in
mind as we make our way towards the topic of disgust: first, not all aesthetic
"pleasure" is notably pleasurable at all. Much art, and indeed the most profound art, evokes emotions that are not entirely comfortable, and that indeed
may be difficult, painful, and aversive.[14] Whatever their other differences,
both Burke and Kant agree that the sublime provides a taxing but ultimately
fulfilling experience, one that the more easily satisfied pleasure of beauty

does not match. What is more, this aesthetic experience goads the mind to try to grasp something that is in fact impossible fully to comprehend: the mysteries of life, death, and the limits of human understanding. And finally, Kant's theory turns analytical attention away from the external object that is the trigger for sublime experience and directs it instead to reflection on the mind of the subject experiencing this powerful aesthetic emotion. The aspect of the sublime that surpasses understanding and exceeds sensible experience has been captured in a description of the sublime by Jean-François Lyotard, who calls art that attempts the sublime "presenting the unpresentable."[15] This sounds paradoxical, but art that attempts to present what is "unpresentable"—or what does not (yet) have a presence in cultural expression—also aptly describes certain of the more difficult and enigmatic feminist art of recent years.

Although at the time of the development of modern theories of the sublime, the female mind was widely held to be incapable of sublime experience, there are other aspects of sublimity that place femininity of an entirely different sort *within* that concept.[16] The classic experience of sublimity is an encounter with the overwhelming might of nature. Nature itself, in contrast to culture, is one of the old binary terms that has long held a feminine association.[17] We can see vestiges of this association in metaphors of "mother nature" or "mother earth," as well as with the practice, abandoned only recently, of giving women's names to tropical storms. The gender metaphors here are untidy and inconsistent, for certainly the concept of God manifest in Burke's sublimity is a patriarchal divinity. Yet at the same time, certain discussions of sublimity imply that the glimpse of the noumenon that it affords is a brush with a region of life and death long associated mythologically with terrible feminine forces.

We can see this interpretation developed in a text that is not directly about sublimity, but whose terms echo the distinction between the sublime and the beautiful, Nietzsche's *Birth of Tragedy* (1872) in which he distinguishes two creative impulses, the Apollonian and the Dionysian. The arts of painting and sculpture (especially those of classical Greece, the focus of Nietzsche's analysis) are formally contained and well-ordered; Nietzsche names them after the sun god Apollo. They represent the imposition of order and form on inchoate nature and nonrational impulses. Nietzsche wishes to bring forward the more ancient, wilder impulses that he identifies with the name of the cult of Dionysus, whose female followers, the Bacchantes, are forces of both destruction and life. Unlike the Apollonion impulse, the Dionysian violates order and rationality, even transgresses individual identity. It is the wild spirit of dance and music, in which dancers surge in orgiastic rites, that epitomizes the Dionysian spirit of art.

Nietzsche recognizes that the different arts partake of both aesthetic impulses, emphasizing one or another. The highest artistic achievement, represented in ancient tragedy, offers a perfect balance between the two. But there are two points to glean from his theory that pertain to interpretations of what we might call a feminine aspect of sublimity.[18] One is his claim that the dominant thrust of western culture—patriarchal culture in feminist idiom—has been to repress the Dionysian impulse. The values of order and dominance over nature have quashed disorder and unruliness, but have also impoverished a sense of life and primal energy. And secondly, there is the insinuation of a brand of feminine nature in the Dionysian spirit, for although the god Dionysus is male, his followers are female; indeed, they are female devourers who, in their rites, re-enact the myth in which the god was murdered and consumed by the enthusiasts of his cult.[19] Nietzsche himself invokes the voice of feminized nature when he speaks for the spirit of Dionysus:

> In Dionysian art and its tragic symbolism the same nature cries to us with its true, undissembled voice: "Be as I am! Amidst the ceaseless flux of phenomena I am the eternally creative primordial mother, eternally impelling to existence, eternally self-sufficient amid this flux of phenomena."[20]

This is hardly the type of "femininity" that Burke associated with the beautiful, for his bounded curves and dainty forms are Apollonian aesthetic qualities that appeal to highly socialized and contained feminine traits: women in dutiful social roles, obedient and decorative. Insofar as the Dionysian impulse is feminine it refers to uncontrolled nature, matter as opposed to form, chaos unleashed. It is not pretty but fearsome, indeed more terrible than sublime. The Dionysian is unbound, uncivilized, and a threat to the social order because it propels species to kill, consume, and propagate, without heed for any individual being.

Its violation of the principle of individuation (as Nietzsche puts it) means that there is a sense in which the Dionysian aesthetic realm exceeds human ability to describe it with exactitude, for linguistic labels are tools for singling out things for categorization. A purely Dionysian experience (should one even be possible, and if it were should one survive it) would be a terrible frenzy beneath rational compartmentalization, an experience of pure drive that is both death and life in one, a loss of self in the swirl of inchoate nature; it would escape the ordered grammar and syntax of language.

Both Kant's treatment of the sublime, which cannot be captured with determinate concepts, and Nietzsche's idea of a Dionysian aesthetic energy that exceeds formulation in language, adumbrate certain of the ideas developed in postmodern philosophies. The distinction between that which can and cannot be captured in language is critically important for Lyotard's treatment of ineffable aesthetic experiences (the "unpresentable"). And the capability of language to capture experience is guardian of the border of what psychoanalyst Jacques Lacan calls the "symbolic order."

Many feminist theorists have found psychoanalysis to offer a useful theoretical approach because of its attention to sexuality and gender in the formation of subjective identities. The exploration not only of consciousness but of the realms of the unconscious has been especially provocative for feminists who seek in that which has been repressed or sublimated answers to the enigmas of the self. Lacan's version of psychoanalysis has been enormously influential for certain critical disciplines, especially literary and film theory. Feminist appropriations and adaptations of psychoanalysis have a major presence in performance, literature, film, and visual arts, as well as in critical interpretations of all of the arts.

Lacan's concept of the symbolic order can be interpreted to capture the "patriarchy" that dominates society and that has been the subject of so much feminist diagnosis.[21] The symbolic order refers to the world of human experience that has been brought into the kind of comprehension that is only possible with language, in which category distinctions and individual subjective identities—language users—have come into being. But the symbolic order does not contain all there is. Utterly outside it lies the real, as inaccessible as Kant's noumenon. One is not born into the symbolic order but enters it in stages of development that also bring the self into being. In infancy there is no clear boundary between one's own identity and everything else around; the most important object with which the infant identifies is the body of the mother. Lacan rereads Freud's Oedipal complex, which is a stage that the developing child must go through in order to subdue the pleasure principle and participate in society under the reality principle, as the gate to entering the symbolic order superintended by language. As the infant develops, he attains a sense of the difference between "me" and "not-me," which entails an awareness of absence or lack, as he can no longer identify himself with the mother's body. Entering the symbolic order of language (the name-of-the-father, the patriarchal order) entails forever leaving the maternal plenitude of the infant imaginary behind.

Because symbolic discourse is patriarchal discourse according to this approach, there is a sense in which woman and the feminine are articulated only as lack or absence; female subjectivity is not positively present within the symbolic order at all. On this most abstract of levels the feminine escapes representation altogether.[22] This aspect of Lacan's theory—itself highly patriarchal—has galvanized feminist psychoanalytic theorists to modify this aspect of his work and fill this "lack." Relatedly, insofar as feminist artists and theorists have wanted to break free of the constricting concepts that repeatedly reinscribe experience in terms of stereotyped and familiar images of femininity and masculinity, many have attempted to resist patriarchal discourse and speak from other subject positions, reaching for new possibilities for understanding female subjectivity. Lacan's, and before him Freud's, theories have been springboards for much feminist thinking that seeks somehow to revise and redress the absence of the feminine. These include the psychoanalytic versions of critical theories of the dominant male gaze mentioned in Chapter 2.[23] And they also include the work of theoretically minded artists, such as Mary Kelly, whose *Postpartum Document* explores the mother–son relationship and queries the analytical categories posited to mark stages in infant development.

Within the symbolic order the patriarchal perspective reigns; hence the prescribed vantage point (for art and for everything else) is gendered male. But gender might not be so uniform and omnipresent; we might find openings for other points of view, other desires, other genders, other developments out of the imaginary that rest less easily within the patriarchal order. One theorist who pursues these possibilities and who has had particular influence over feminist thinking about art is Luce Irigaray.

Luce Irigaray: sexuate subjectivity

Although her direct interests are not in aesthetics, philosopher and psychoanalyst Luce Irigaray has been influential for the practice of artists and of critical scholars because of her provocative suggestions about how language—and by extension art and expression generally—might be a means to articulate a feminine subjectivity. Irigaray radically extends critiques of the patriarchal traditions of philosophy to language itself, advancing the idea of *parler femme*: speaking as a woman, from and with the body of a woman. (This claim is often paired with the idea of *l'écriture féminine* advocated by another French theorist, Hélène Cixous.)[24] What it means to speak or write "as" a woman involves Irigaray's own analysis of how language is placed at the formation of subjectivity and a sense of self. Subjectivity emerges in and through language use; without this signifying tool, there is no differentiation between self and other. That is, the self should not be pictured as a previously existing, independent entity who "chooses her words" to match her particularly female experience. Rather, the self and subjectivity are actually produced through social relations and language. The problem lies in the fact that the social and symbolic order does not provide language adequate for women's subjectivities, partly because the mother–daughter relationship has been eclipsed by father–son struggles in myth, philosophy, and psycho-analysis.

The body and its morphology are central to Irigaray's philosophical method, as she insists that "sexuate" being pervades one's identity, and that the pretense of shedding one's sex when writing or speaking in standard, familiar style and syntax causes the feminine to disappear into the masculine/neutral discourse that dominates the patriarchal order. As she puts it in the title of one of her widely-read essays, "any theory of the subject has always been appropriated by the masculine."[25] Writing "from the body" potentially overturns this appropriation, as it would elude the structures of patriarchal discourse and order that have defined the feminine as the not-masculine, lacking positive subjectivity of its own.

> [W]hat I want, in fact, is not to create a theory of woman, but to secure a place for the feminine within sexual difference. That difference—masculine/feminine—has always operated "within" systems that are representative, self-representative, of the (masculine) subject . . . For one sex and its lack, its atrophy, its negative, still does not add up to two. In other words, the feminine has never been defined except as the inverse, indeed the underside, of the masculine. So for woman it is not a matter of installing herself within this lack, this negative, even by denouncing it, nor of reversing the economy of sameness by turning the feminine into the standard for "sexual difference"; it is rather a matter of trying to practice that difference.[26]

Irigaray uses female morphology as a model for understanding the boundary between that which is representable within the symbolic order and the
unrepresentable. Her most famous trope here is "lips," which signals both
the mouth and the labia, and the moisture that both produce. She sees the
female body as formed in "twoness"—the twoness of lips—rather than in
phallic "oneness," and this basic distinction leads her to explore realms of
sexuality and pleasure—heterosexual and homosexual—and identity, which
are outside the mandate of patriarchal society and demand their own
expression.[27] The mucus and viscosity of the mouth and vagina are
metaphors for the fluidity of the feminine, which in contrast to the masculine resists boundary and form.[28] Mucus and fluid are signs of liminality, that
which slides between two orders—inside and outside, unrepresented and
symbolic. One of Irigaray's tasks is to evoke feminine subjectivity that can
be represented in its own terms, not just as an "absence" in the symbolic
order. Responding to a query about what it means to write "as a woman,"
Irigaray says:

> I am a woman. I write with who I am. Why wouldn't that be valid,
> unless out of contempt for the value of women or from a denial of
> a culture in which the sexual is a significant subjective and objective
> dimension? . . . Only those who are still in a state of verbal automa-
> tism or who mimic already existing meaning can maintain such a
> scission or split between she who is a woman and she who writes.
> The whole of my body is sexuate.[29]

This statement indicates one of the elements of Irigaray's theory that has led
her critics to describe her as an "essentialist," that is, a theorist who assumes
that all women are alike and share some essential trait that unites them.[30]
Since women are demonstrably not all alike in their histories, cultural identities, and social positions, and since their subjectivities are bound up with
these contingent factors, the label of essentialism is almost always a criticism
within feminist theory. However, Irigaray is not implying that women's writing does or could express all the same things, or that any expression of the
feminine body could take its place in the symbolic order under its own category heading. In a sense such expression is presenting the unpresentable, to
use Lyotard's term, though it is more in keeping with Irigaray's project to say
that it represents a new order of presentability.[31] Writing that eludes the symbolic order might be compared to what Kant, in the context of discussing the

sublime, called an aesthetic idea: "An aesthetic idea cannot become cognition because it is an intuition (of the imagination) for which an adequate concept can never be found" (reading "concept" in this passage as referring to determinate concepts within patriarchal discourse).[32] The world of the feminine that is "beyond" stable, univocal representation may yet be presented, I would venture, through accumulated singular aesthetic experiences of art.

A number of artists have pursued Irigaray's suggestions. Theirs is not a simple application of her advice or enactment of her theories in practice, for there are different ways to read her difficult, enigmatic, and sometimes murky texts. Her evocative style is more suggestive than directive. Margaret Whitford aptly characterizes the exchange between Irigaray and her readers when she suggests that

> Her work is offered as an object, a discourse, for women to exchange *among themselves*, a sort of commodity, so that women themselves do not have to function as the commodity, or as the *sacrifice* on which sociality is built. Instructions for use of Irigaray would include the message: Do not consume or devour. For symbolic exchange only.[33]

When the female body provides the locus of articulation, given all of its associations with materiality and mortality, the visceral and disturbing elements of the body are the ones that are apt to be targeted for artistic expression. And now we are positioned to see the slide between the classic sublime, the "unpresentable," and disgust. Writing and speaking from the body is suggested in Joanna Frueh's performance pieces, for example, in which she both uses her own body and describes others. The following passage evokes the uneasy border between that which should and should not be put into language, that which has and has not been named, or thought, or felt.

> The girl pulled her menstrual pad to one side and dipped two fingers into her blood. Forcing herself, because she was doing something she had neither read nor talked to anyone about, and seducing herself with the pleasure of knowledge through sensation, she licked the fluid from her fingers. It tasted like blood from a cut, but the flavor was denser, the texture thicker. Part of her felt that this act was nothing unusual, that it had been nothing to fear, so she did it again. As she repeated the dipping and licking, a feeling earlier submerged by her sense of the ordinary overwhelmed her.

Words tumbled over one another, waves that seemed to knock the wind out of her like imagined breakers that would swell, then draw her underwater, groin first.

The words in her mind, made by her lips with no sound, went on and on, impossible to remember later. Arms around her knees, rocking back and forth, then side to side, she listened to the language brought by her blood, the liquid world of words.[34]

We are verging into the territory where the sublime—perhaps understood now as that which has been sublimated—slides towards the disgusting. Something that is "unpresentable," not because of any noumenal mystery but because it ought not to be presented, being base and beneath public acknowledgment, has been spoken of and brought into the light. That which is familiarly characterized as disgusting is transformed here into something taboo but sensuously alluring. Menstrual blood, long considered so unspeakable that it never entered public discourse let alone art, is one of the subjects that feminist artists have opened in literary, visual, and performance art. It still likely raises discomfort; indeed it is raised in order that the discomfort be exposed and plumbed. Frueh transforms it into a sensuous opening of a previously hidden aspect of female sexuality, probing at the relation between the erotic and the disgusting. Just how the aversion of disgust converts into a positive aesthetic recognition is one of the puzzles facing contemporary aesthetic analysis.

Disgust as an aesthetic response

Sometimes one claims to be disgusted by art simply because one does not like it; this is not a species of approval but of rejection. Of far greater interest for understanding aesthetic emotive responses are cases where the actual emotion of disgust is aroused by art as part of understanding and appreciation. If one is drawn to the above fragment of Frueh's performance piece, any disgust aroused in reading it—and I assume there will be at least a little—is a component of recognizing the border she has crossed and her imaginative incorporation of something usually regarded as shamefully female into a piece of transgressive poetry. In this instance, disgust is an element of positive aesthetic apprehension. That such a basic aversion can be elevated to an aesthetic response is as paradoxical as the transfiguration of terror into the sublime. Indeed it may be even more paradoxical, for by traditional understanding disgust is the one emotion that cannot undergo a positive aesthetic conversion. Kant was emphatic on this point: "There is only one kind of ugliness that cannot be presented in conformity with nature without obliterating all aesthetic liking and hence artistic beauty: that ugliness which arouses *disgust*."[35] Yet as we noted at the beginning of this chapter, disgust has evidently entered into contemporary "aesthetic liking" from several directions.

Probably there is no emotion that rivets attention to the body as dramatically as does disgust, for it is a profoundly visceral emotion. It is closely connected to physical responses, such as gagging and nausea, and it seems to require a trigger from one of the senses. The two primary senses for disgust are taste and smell, but the aversion may arise by means of any of the senses or by imagining sensations. As William Ian Miller observes, "What the idiom of disgust demands is reference to the senses. It is about what it feels like to touch, see, taste, smell, even on occasion hear, certain things."[36] As an aesthetic response, disgust is especially suitable for arts that exaggerate, distort, and explore the body—not the beautiful body of classicism, but the lived body that gets dirty, is prey to illness and injury, and that ages, dies, and rots. Just as terror is a means to plumb the transcendent meaning of the sublime, the emotive response of disgust recognizes meaning carried by physical embodiment. To quote Miller once more:

> Here we have the most embodied and visceral of emotions, and yet even when it is operating in and around the body, its orifices and excreta, a world of meaning explodes, coloring, vivifying, and contaminating political, social, and moral meanings. Disgust for all its visceralness turns out to be one of our more aggressive culture-creating passions.[37]

If we consider the array of art that employs disgust, we can confirm Miller's assessment that we have here an emotion that rapidly takes on and perpetuates cultural meaning. This makes the feminist employment of disgust, particularly as it attaches to female bodies, an especially interesting but also delicate and risky enterprise. Feminist uses must thread their way carefully through the minefield of standard misogynist responses in order to deploy disgust, and other difficult emotions as well, in ways that disrupt rather than reinforce old myths and stereotypes.

Feminist presentation of embodiment and disgust has had at least two dimensions with political import, in addition to the artistic innovations it has occasioned. First of all, it invites the inversion of the sorts of "feminine ideals" that frame restrictive norms for personal appearance: beauty norms relying on elegance, diminutiveness, and propriety mandating that women appear neat, that they possess certain body types, and that they exaggerate the bodily traits considered most alluring in the societies they inhabit. This is an aspect of beauty and appearance that bridges the styles adopted in art and in life: not only are women depicted with certain types of idealized bodies, but women emulate ideal body attributes themselves. In extreme cases, this leads to tiny waists constricted by corsets, breasts enlarged by surgery, or feet bound to infantile diminutiveness.[38] Such a narrow band of aesthetic values excludes all but a small range of characteristics from the acceptable sphere of public exposure. But insofar as such values are cultural norms, there is hardly anyone who escapes their authority. In counterpoint, feminist artists have portrayed bodies that do not conform to these standards. This can be done humorously, boldly, sadly, aggressively, casually; much depends on the individual work of art. Jenny Saville, for example, employs her own body in casts and paintings, making the finished product a topological map of excess flesh. These complex works invert the traditional aesthetic values expected in the nude, with a disturbing emotional effect that makes us question those values and their comprehensiveness.

Artists may also move from the smooth and lovely exterior of the body to the warm, dark, sticky interior where unmentionable substances are kept hidden away. The deliberate cultivation of that which is not pretty but is grossly material presents tableaux of emancipation from the quotidian but powerful oppression of social norms of appearance. It also is the occasion for presenting some of the utterly taboo aspects of women's bodies, such as the vaginal images presented in Judy Chicago's monumental *Dinner Party* (1979).[39] Of course, the material body presents more than sexual morphology. Mona Hatoum's *Entrails Carpet* (1997) is an installation that mimics the look of eviscerated intestines that have proliferated and filled a room. The same artist used her own body in her video installation *Corps étranger* (1994).[40] Images taken with a medical endoscopic camera from both the surface of her body and inside it are projected onto the floor of an enclosure, beneath the feet of the viewer, who not only discovers herself standing on magnified close-ups of internal body tissues but also hears the artist's breath and beating heart.

The exploitation of the visceral moves from the grossly physical to the mysterious and uncanny. It opens a complex and delicate territory for feminist investigation: the ancient category of the "feminine" that includes the element of untamed nature and the gross matter of existence. Feminist uses of these types of objects of disgust and other aversions play upon myths of nature and culture, of horror and sublimity, and of death and life. The female body is simultaneously the icon of human beauty—when it is young and healthy—and the symbol of death and the inexorable grip of mortality. Though these qualities are opposites, both function in the aesthetic operation of disgust, simultaneously repelling and attracting, just as the sight of something horrific causes us both to turn away and then to take a second look. Julia Kristeva refers to this oscillation as "a vortex of summons and repulsion," a paradoxical force that opens her analysis of disgust and its relation to the "abject." Kristeva's notion of abjection affords a theoretical analysis of disgust and of the female body that has been employed by a number of feminist critical interpreters of art.

Disgust and abjection: Julia Kristeva

Kristeva modifies psychoanalysis to foreground the roles of female figures in subjective development, offsetting the emphasis on the development of the male child in relation to the father that characterizes both Freud and Lacan.[41] Kristeva examines the mother–child dyad and its lingering shadows in language and art, and it is here that her work has relevance for another approach to what might be considered "feminine" in aesthetic questions. Kristeva discovers in certain expressive forms lingering traces of relations with the primal body of the mother that obtain for males and females alike. There are two principal aesthetic phenomena that betray this relation, one of which is a key to her analysis of disgust.

One phenomenon has to do with language and sound.[42] Kristeva posits that poetic writing proceeds from pre-Oedipal experience of the mother–child dyad (before language develops and patriarchal discourse predominates) that breaks through or "irrupts" into language. While Lacan theorizes that in entering the symbolic order one takes on the mantle of language, and that the pre-symbolic world of the imaginary is unutterable, Kristeva pushes back the boundaries of language to include intimations of the time in which the young child feels little or no differentiation between himself or herself and the mother's body. She refers to this phenomenon as the "semiotic chora," indicating a space with meaning but no determinate articulation. As language develops and the child enters the symbolic, whispers of the semiotic linger in the sounds that attend articulation. Sounds that echo pre-articulate verbalizations irrupt in language, especially poetic language and the literature of artists who violate the proper bounds of patriarchal values. Poetic language contains, as it were, aesthetic traces of archaic memory of maternal plenitude, union with the mother before separate subjectivity formed. Such semiotic traces would obtain for everyone, male and female alike, for at that stage of development gender distinctions are not in place.

The lingering sense of the maternal body is far less comforting in confrontations with the "abject," a theoretical term that does not mean disgust, but that signals phenomena that are manifest in the experience of disgust. The complicated term "abject" is used as noun, verb, and adjective. It refers to the process of expelling the Other, beginning with the mother's body, which the young child does not differentiate from itself; this expulsion is necessary in order that subjective identity develop, for otherwise there is no sense of lack or absence, no gap by which to measure the difference between oneself and everything else. Once it emerges in the symbolic order, the self remains a dynamic but tenuous system that needs continuously to sustain its independence. But certain experiences present threats to the self that are manifest in the emotion of disgust. Disgust is prompted by objects whose own boundaries are indeterminate and fluid. Typical exemplars of the abject are things undergoing the changes of spoilage, rot, and decay. One of Kristeva's favorite examples is the skin that forms on warm milk. It is a "between" thing that slides between air and liquid, and that is and is not solid, is and is not fresh, is and is not milk. And, of course, the milk itself is a maternal substance. But other more standard examples of the disgusting also manifest that uneasy border where something's self-identity is changing and disappearing: decaying corpses are no longer alive, and they vividly present their disintegrating passage from being to non-being. Anything that rots, and that stinks of decay, is more than disgusting to the senses; it is abject—losing its proper form, and thereby presenting a threat to subjectivity with the terrible reminder that the subject shall lose its identity as well. This is why the abject is central to horror, indeed the book in which Kristeva pursues this analysis is titled *The Powers of Horror*. Elizabeth Grosz interprets the abject and the disgust it evokes as a recognition of embodiment itself:

> Abjection is a reaction to the recognition of the impossible but necessary transcendence of the subject's corporeality, and the impure, defiling elements of its uncontrollable materiality. It is a response to

the various bodily cycles of incorporation, absorption, depletion, expulsion, the cycles of material rejuvenation and consumption necessary to sustain itself yet incapable of social recognition and representation.[43]

Despite the base, revolting aversive character of disgust, we can see some parallels with the sublime in this description of the abject: both are unbounded, formless, threatening.[44] The sublime, however, is possessed of might and magnitude, and it therefore tends to the magnificent. It arouses fear, but also thrill, and awe. The attraction to the sublime is therefore relatively easy to understand, for it is bound up with admiration, and in classical forms even a sense of the divine. And for Kant, as we saw, the sublime puts us in mind of our moral autonomy. This sounds far from the revulsion that disgust indicates. Whence, then, comes the attraction of the abject?

According to the analysis Kristeva provides, because abjection is requisite for subjective identity to develop, it is a necessary process for a self to come into being. But there is also a loss in becoming an independent self, for one is forever separated from the maternal plenitude that originally sustained one. That sense of loss is retained in the allure of the abject, for there is a desire to be reunited with that oneness; at the same time, reuniting with oneness entails extinguishing one's individual identity. That is, it entails the death of the subject, which is a horrifying and terrible prospect as well. And yet, there is a terrible magnetism to the idea that one might relax back into plenitude, even while losing one's identity in so doing. (Freud described what he called the "death-wish" in rather similar terms.)[45] No one wants to lose one's identity, to die; and yet there is an unconscious attraction that lingers in the abject. It is fascinating, mesmerizing, revolting, horrifying. Kristeva puts this powerfully in the opening paragraph of her study:

There looms, within abjection, one of those violent, dark revolts of being, directed against a threat that seems to emanate from an exorbitant outside or inside, ejected beyond the scope of the possible, the tolerable, the thinkable. It lies there, quite close, but it cannot be assimilated. It beseeches, worries, and fascinates desire, which, nevertheless, does not let itself be seduced. Apprehensive, desire turns aside; sickened, it rejects . . . But simultaneously, just the same, that impetus, that spasm, that leap is drawn toward an elsewhere as tempting as it is condemned. Unflaggingly, like an inescapable

149

boomerang, a vortex of summons and repulsion places the one haunted by it literally beside himself.[46]

There are many aspects of disgust that do not fit the notion of the abject. But the deployment of disgust on the part of artists who present the female body so as to foreground its material excess and mortality, whether intentionally or not, dovetail with Kristeva's theoretical concerns, which is why the notion of abjection has been adapted for the interpretation of certain kinds of art. The evocation of the powerful aversion of disgust is a daring artistic enterprise, for it risks both alienation of audiences and misinterpretation of intent and meaning.

Disgust: context and ambiguity

The employment of disgust in art featuring women's bodies is complex, multi-layered, and risky. Feminist exploitation of disgust faces an especially complicated context of reception because of the enormous role that disgust assumes in movies and television (not to mention another genre that lurks in the background of horror: pornography). Part of the risk involves the fact that some of the very images of the body that feminists reclaim are also widely used in art forms with no feminist intent. Like it or not, the difficult appreciation of the disgusting in feminist and postfeminist art reaches into a context of reception that includes popular horror and science fiction. (In her film *Office Killer* [1997], Cindy Sherman extended her trademark disgusting images into a horror-movie format.) This eclecticism signals the pervasiveness of such images in our visual culture and memory banks and confirms the fact that art derives its reception from the powerful images that pervade other venues as well. There is a tension between—and also a commonality of—the feminist uses of disgust and those that pervade mass culture. While these sometimes have a quasi-feminist aspect themselves, they often reinforce gender stereotypes by means of perhaps the most powerful device for doing so: entertainment.

A number of feminist critics have applied Kristeva's theory of abjection to interpreting horror genres.[47] The number and variety of female monsters in popular movies are noteworthy, and they are often portrayed with terrible jaws like a vagina dentata and morphology that suggests sexual origins—a vivid employment of the fearsome power of sexuality transformed into the monstrous.[48] These disgusting creatures threaten annihilation; the plot of horror turns on vanquishing these forces of annihilation and restoring order to the world of the plot. Few horror movies can be described as feminist,[49] and it almost seems as though the horror genre were ready-made for externalizing fears of the abject in the form of devouring females.

At the same time, abjection illuminates other works that are ascribed a feminist content, such as the disturbing photographic works of Cindy Sherman, whose exaggerated faces often traverse the borders between human and nonhuman, sane and insane, life and death.[50] How can the abject be employed both as a feminist tool of analysis and in art, and as a means to retain the image of woman as monstrous and threatening? As with any art objects, which are singular by nature, this question needs to be addressed case by case. Nonetheless, a few general distinctions separate the mere repetition of the terrible or mythic images from feminist counterpoints: With the slicker versions of horror, the disgust is aroused as a sort of perverse entertainment. It is attached to the body of the Other, the creature whom one must escape; it is different from oneself. With the monster of horror fiction, the disgusting and terrible object is external to oneself, indeed is usually utterly alien.

When the familiarly human body is presented in a way that arouses disgust, however, the emotion takes on a more pensive, reflective tone. We have seen one instance of its use with Joanna Frueh's piece, where a standard object of disgust (menstrual blood) is eroticized and made fascinating (which is not to say that it loses its disgust quotient; rather, the disgust enhances the unusual eroticism.) Still more difficult is the use of disgust to provoke intimate and immediate realizations of the vulnerability of the flesh and the nearness of death. Now we are in a region not so far removed from the reality that awaits us all: illness, age, and mortality. The artist Hannah Wilke, after she was diagnosed with cancer, candidly documented the stages of her illness in unflinching photographs of her body bloated and bruised from treatments, sometimes posed in positions that, since she was so obviously dying, dreadfully mimicked the elegant pornography of the nude in classics of painting. Her pictures confront and display the terrible import of decaying and violated bodies: they are full of dread and inevitability and mortality. This kind of art does not permit the escape of entertaining horror; it forces the viewer to stay within the disgust-appreciation, for such images force a painful identification with the depicted body. Here disgust does not indicate a threat from the outside that is therefore something to be vanquished and banished; now disgust is a threat from within. Powers of life and death are no longer mythologized and attributed to a monstrous force; they are immediate and intimate and all too familiar.

Summary

This chapter has emphasized a particular aspect of some feminist art and its relation to changing philosophical ideas about the mind and the body. As we have seen, philosophy, feminist theory, and art have proceeded along similar paths that sometimes cross and sometimes diverge. All three display an interest in analyzing the body and its roles in experience, emotion, and subjectivity.[51]

My emphasis on art that disgusts is intended to clarify the continuities of tradition that often are obscured by dissimilarities in theoretical terminology employed by different philosophical approaches. Without denying the important disagreements among rival schools of thought, we can also see how contemporary philosophy of all stripes continues quests and debates that have a long history in the western philosophical tradition. Using feminist issues as a focus, we can link the transcendence of the sublime with the aesthetic use of aversive affects such as disgust.

Feminist artists have explored many avenues of expression, from outright political messages to allusive, indeterminate "writing from the body." Feminist art is situated in the midst of the complex terrain of contemporary art in general, both the "high" art traditions and popular entertainment. Because it employs venerable images while subjecting them to critique and exploration, the works tread a treacherous border between the new and the old, the unfamiliar and the stereotyped. This makes understanding theoretical approaches to art all the more urgent, for often ambiguity cannot be resolved without the context that theoretical aesthetics provides for the practice of art.

Discovering gender in aesthetics, therefore, traverses a long road, beginning with the investigation of the conceptual frameworks that excluded women from the central aesthetic concepts of art, creativity, and artist. We have ended this study with theories that surmise an even more profound exclusion: an absence of the feminine in patriarchal discourse altogether. The efforts of feminist theorists and artists can be read as contributions of distinctive and unique voices, ideas, and images to fill the absences of history and to combat the distortions of myth, perhaps to discover, in the words of poet Adrienne Rich, "the thing I came for: / the wreck and not the story of the wreck / the thing itself and not the myth."[52] If the approach of the philosophers reviewed in this chapter is sound, it is unlikely that there is any "thing itself" with regard to gender and sexuality and desire, but rather ceaseless striving to articulate a subjectivity that is always compromised and partially formed by history and society. This quest is undertaken by artists and investigated by philosophers in the combination of efforts that are gathered under the label "aesthetics."

NOTES

INTRODUCTION

1 Judith Butler, *Gender Trouble: Feminism and the Subversion of Identity* (New York: Routledge, 1990) and *Bodies That Matter: On the Discursive Limits of "Sex"* (New York: Routledge, 1993); Elizabeth Grosz, *Volatile Bodies: Toward a Corporeal Feminism* (Bloomington: Indiana University Press, 1994). For a biological slant on sexual identity and indeterminacy, see Anne Fausto-Sterling, *Sexing the Body: Gender Politics and the Construction of Sexuality* (New York: Basic Books, 2000).

2 Susan Bordo, "The Feminist as Other" in Janet Kourany (ed.), *Philosophy in a Feminist Voice: Critiques and Reconstructions* (Princeton, NJ: Princeton University Press, 1998): 296–312.

3 Rita Felski, *Beyond Feminist Aesthetics: Feminist Literature and Social Change* (Cambridge, MA: Harvard University Press, 1989). Discussions for and against feminine artistic traditions, with particular attention to Germany, may be found in Gisela Ecker (ed.), *Feminist Aesthetics*, trans. Harriet Anderson (Boston: Beacon Press, 1986). See also Cornelia Klinger, "Aesthetics" in Alison M. Jaggar and Iris Marion Young (eds), *A Companion to Feminist Philosophy* (Malden, MA: Blackwell, 1998): 343–52; Anita Silvers, "Feminism: An Overview" in Michael Kelly (ed.), *Encyclopedia of Aesthetics*, vol. 2 (New York: Oxford University Press, 1998): 161–7. A number of the newer philosophy reference books have sections on feminism and aesthetics. The *Encyclopedia of Aesthetics* contains a set of essays presenting different perspectives on feminism and philosophy of art.

4 Peggy Phelan, "Survey" in Helena Reckitt (ed.), *Art and Feminism* (London: Phaidon Press, 2001): 18.

5 In the United States, the National Museum for Women in the Arts in Washington, DC has gathered together an enormous collection of works by women; the Feminist Press at the City University of New York has re-edited and republished many works by near-forgotten women writers of the past.

6 A word is in order about the prefix "post" that I have used above. Sometimes the addition of this prefix to a term suggests rejection or revision of the past, but it also indicates a development out of a movement or tradition that appreciates rather than rejects it. When I refer to "postanalytic" philosophy, I mean to indicate contemporary philosophy in the analytic tradition that has retained its rigor

and relationship to science but has expanded its borders to methods and subjects beyond the relatively narrow, ahistorical conceptual analysis that characterized analytic philosophy in the mid-twentieth century. (I would characterize as post-analytic all feminist philosophy in the analytic tradition.) "Postfeminist" art rarely rejects feminism, though it is often less overtly political than earlier feminist art was, as it sometimes explores gender in a playful or fantastic manner. The "post" that has received the most heated diagnosis is "postmodern," a designation that refers to departure from or rejection of many tenets and stylistic values of the modern European Enlightenment, but which also may be considered to contain ideas to be found within modernism itself. See Jean-François Lyotard, *The Postmodern Condition*, trans. Geoff Bennington and Brian Masumi (Minneapolis: University of Minnesota Press, 1984). There is never a clear border between a period and the subsequent one designated "post."

1 ARTISTS AND ART

1 References to some of this work may be found in Chapter 3.

2 A succinct survey of how reason and gender operate in some influential philosophies is Genevieve Lloyd, *The Man of Reason: "Male" and "Female" in Western Philosophy* (Minneapolis: University of Minnesota Press, 1984).

3 A review of feminist critiques of different areas of philosophy may be found in Janet Kourany (ed.), *Philosophy in a Feminist Voice* (Princeton, NJ: Princeton University Press, 1998).

4 Prudence Allen, RSM, *The Concept of Woman: The Aristotelian Revolution, 750 BC–AD 1250* (Montreal: Eden Press, 1985); Cynthia Freeland (ed.) *Feminist Interpretations of Aristotle* (University Park, PA: Pennsylvania State University Press, 1998); Bat-Ami Bar On, *Engendering Origins: Critical Feminist Readings in Plato and Aristotle* (Albany: State University of New York Press, 1994).

5 Moira Gatens notes, "the dichotomies which dominate philosophical thinking are not sexually neutral but are deeply implicated in the politics of sexual difference." *Feminism and Philosophy: Perspectives on Difference and Equality* (Bloomington: Indiana University Press, 1991): 92.

6 Larry Shiner, *The Invention of Art: A Cultural History* (Chicago: University of Chicago Press, 2001): 5.

7 Katharine Everett Gilbert and Helmut Kuhn, *A History of Esthetics* [1939] (New York: Dover Publications, 1972): Chapter 1 and 19–23.

8 For a point of view that would include products from across the globe in a unified category of art, see Richard L. Anderson, *Calliope's Sisters* (Upper Saddle River, NJ: Prentice-Hall, 1990).

9 Eugenie Sellers, Introduction to *The Elder Pliny's Chapters on the History of Art* [1896], trans. K. Jex-Blake (Chicago: Argonaut, 1968): xiii–xiv.

10 Pliny, *History of Art*: 7. The combination of familiar and unfamiliar treatments of the arts in texts such as Pliny, and also in the philosophical works of Plato and Aristotle, feeds the continuing controversy over how similar are concepts of art

across the centuries. One author who emphasizes similarities between Greek and modern ideas about art is Christopher Janaway, *Images of Excellence: Plato's Critique of the Arts* (Oxford: Clarendon Press, 1995), Introduction.

11 Pliny, *History of Art*: 171, 227.

12 Aristotle, *Poetics*, trans. D. W. Lucas (Oxford: Clarendon Press, 1968). Although Aristotle is criticized for the systematic way that he subordinates female to male in his philosophy and biology, his philosophy is also regarded by many feminists as a potential ally, in part because he recognizes emotional range in moral character. For some feminist readings of Aristotle on tragedy, see Angela Curran, "Feminism and the Narrative Structures of the *Poetics*" in Freeland, *Feminist Interpretations of Aristotle* 289–326; and Cynthia Freeland, "Plot Imitates Action: Aesthetic Evaluation and Moral Realism in Aristotle's *Poetics*" in Amélie Rorty (ed.), *Essays on Aristotle's Poetics* (Princeton, NJ: Princeton University Press, 1992): 111–32.

13 Pliny, *History of Art*: 125.

14 Simone de Beauvoir presents an argument to this effect in her existential analysis of woman as "Other" in *The Second Sex* [1949], trans. H. M. Parshley (New York: Vintage Books, 1989), esp. Chapter 9.

15 For feminist debates over the import of Diotima's speech see Susan Hawthorne, "Diotima Speaks through the Body" in Bar On, *Engendering Origins*: 83–96; Page duBois, "The Platonic Appropriation of Reproduction;" Wendy Brown, "'Supposing Truth were a Woman . . .': Plato's Subversion of Masculine Discourse;" Luce Irigaray, "Sorcerer Love: A Reading of Plato's *Symposium*, Diotima's Speech;" and Andrea Nye, "Irigaray and Diotima at Plato's *Symposium*;" all in Nancy Tuana (ed.), *Feminist Interpretations of Plato* (University Park, PA: Pennsylvania State University Press, 1994): 139–215.

16 For a sympathetic exposition of Plato's famous denunciation of poets and painters, see Janaway, *Images of Excellence*.

17 For arguments that the concept of art does obtain cross-culturally, see Anderson, *Calliope's Sisters*; Stephen Davies, "Non-Western Art and Art's Definition" and Denis Dutton, "'But They don't Have our Concept of Art'," both in Noël Carroll (ed.), *Theories of Art Today* (Madison: University of Wisconsin Press, 2000): 199–216 and 217–38.

18 Paul Osker Kristeller, "The Modern System of the Arts: A Study in the History of Aesthetics," Parts I and II, *Journal of the History of Ideas* 12 and 13 (1951, 1952) 496–527, 17–46. Widely reprinted, including in Peter Kivy (ed.), *Essays on the History of Aesthetics* (Rochester, NY: University of Rochester Press, 1992) 3–64. Larry Shiner, in *The Invention of Art*, also argues that the concept of fine art is a modern notion.

19 Władysław Tatarkiewicz, *A History of Six Ideas: An Essay in Aesthetics* [1975], trans. Christopher Kasperek (Warsaw: Polish Scientific Publishers, 1980): 13, 16–17.

20 One of the first treatments of perspective is Leon Battista Alberti's treatise, *On Painting* [1435], trans. John R. Spencer (New Haven, CT: Yale University Press, 1966).

21 The evolution of products such as needlework from art to craft status is reviewed

in Rozsika Parker and Griselda Pollock, *Old Mistresses: Women, Art and Ideology* (New York: Pantheon Books, 1981), Chapter 2.

22 Victor Cousin, *Lectures on the True, the Beautiful, and the Good* [1818], trans. O. W. Wright (New York: D. Appleton and Co., 1870): 141.

23 Ibid.: 162–3.

24 Immanuel Kant, *Critique of Judgment* [1790], trans. Werner Pluhar (Indianapolis: Hackett, 1987): 174.

25 Christine Battersby, *Gender and Genius: Towards a Feminist Aesthetics* (Bloomington: Indiana University Press, 1989).

26 Ibid.: 33. Battersby does not accept the usual judgment that history has produced no to few female geniuses; she argues for traditions of female artistic creativity and a revision of the notion of genius.

27 The destructive aspects of a life of genius are portrayed in the movie *Pollock* about the life and career of the abstract expressionist painter Jackson Pollock, directed by and starring Ed Harris, Sony Pictures Classics, 2000.

28 Battersby, *Gender and Genius*: 22.

29 Friedrich Schiller, *On the Aesthetic Education of Man in a Series of Letters* [1793], trans. Elizabeth M. Wilkinson and L. A. Willoughby (Oxford: Clarendon Press, 1967) esp. Letter XXVII.

30 For a sampling of different approaches to artistic expression, see Leo Tolstoy, *What Is Art?* [1898], trans. Aylmer Maude (New York: Liberal Arts Press, 1960); Benedetto Croce, *The Aesthetic as the Science of Expression and General Linguistic* [1902], trans. Douglas Ainslie (New York: Noonday Press, 1963); Wassily Kandinsky, *Concerning the Spiritual in Art, and Painting in Particular* [1912] trans. Michael Sadleir, amended Francis Golffing (New York: Wittenborn, Schultz, 1947); Suzanne Langer, *Feeling and Form: A Theory of Art* (London: Routledge and Kegan Paul, 1953); Alan Tormey, *The Concept of Expression* (Princeton, NJ: Princeton University Press, 1971); Guy Sircello, *Mind and Art: An Essay on the Varieties of Expression* (Princeton, NJ: Princeton University Press, 1972); Malcolm Budd, *Music and the Emotions* (London: Routledge and Kegan Paul, 1985); Stephen Davies, *Musical Meaning and Expression* (Ithaca, NY: Cornell University Press, 1994

31 R. G. Collingwood, *The Principles of Art* (Oxford: Clarendon Press, 1938), Book I.

32 As Larry Shiner observes, this delineation of cultural products reflects and perpetuates a host of social divisions: "When the genres and activities chosen for elevation and those chosen for demotion reinforce race, class, and gender lines, what once looked like a purely conceptual change begins to look like an underwriting of power relations as well." *The Invention of Art*: 7.

33 Tolstoy, *What Is Art?*

34 Catherine M. Soussloff, *The Absolute Artist: The Historiography of a Concept* (Minneapolis: University of Minnesota Press, 1997): 4. See also Ernst Kris and Otto Kurz, *Legend, Myth, and Magic in the Image of the Artist* [1934], trans. Alastair Lang, revised Lottie M. Newman (New Haven, CT: Yale University Press, 1979).

2 AESTHETIC PLEASURES

1 Alexander Baumgarten introduced the term in his *Reflections on Poetry* [1735], trans. Karl Aschenbrenner and William B. Holther (Berkeley and Los Angeles: University of California Press, 1954). "Aesthetic" comes from a Greek root referring to sense perception. The term entered English in the early nineteenth century.

2 Plato's most extended discussion of beauty occurs in the *Symposium*, especially the speech of Diotima discussed in Chapter 1.

3 John Locke, for example, *Essay Concerning Human Understanding* [1690] (Freeport, NY: Books for Libraries Press, 1969) Book 2, Chapter 12, Section 5: 281.

4 Peter Kivy, "Recent Scholarship and the British Tradition: A Logic of Taste—the First Fifty Years" in George Dickie and R. J. Sclafani (eds), *Aesthetics: A Critical Anthology* (New York: St Martin's Press, 1977): 626–42.

5 Some conducted a joint search for aesthetic and moral foundations, such as Francis Hutcheson, *An Inquiry into the Original of Our Ideas of Beauty and Virtue* (1725).

6 Francis Hutcheson, *An Inquiry concerning Beauty, Order, Harmony, Design* [1725], ed. Peter Kivy (The Hague: Martinus Nijhoff, 1973): 40; William Hogarth, *The Analysis of Beauty* [1753], ed. Ronald Paulson (New Haven, CT: Yale University Press, 1997).

7 Hume is somewhat unusual in that he does not rely chiefly on reason, a position that some feminists have found congenial. See Anne Jaap Jacobson (ed.), *Feminists Interpretations of David Hume* (University Park, PA: Pennsylvania State University Press, 2000). For gender in "Of the Standard of Taste," see Carolyn Korsmeyer, "Gendered Concepts and Hume's "Standard of Taste" in Peggy Zeglin Brand and Carolyn Korsmeyer (eds), *Feminism and Tradition in Aesthetics* (University Park, PA: Pennsylvania State University Press, 1995): 49–65; Marcia Lind, "Indians, Savages, Peasants, and Women: Hume's Aesthetics" in Bat-Ami Bar On (ed.), *Modern Engendering: Critical Feminist Readings in Modern Western Philosophy* (Albany: State University of New York Press, 1994): 51–67.

8 Edmund Burke, *A Philosophical Enquiry into the Origin of our Ideas of the Sublime and Beautiful* [1757], ed. James T. Boulton (Notre Dame, IL: University of Notre Dame Press, 1968): 15.

9 Ibid.: 42.

10 Ibid.: 49. See also 92–107.

11 Ibid.: 115.

12 See Simone de Beauvoir, *The Second Sex* [1949], trans. H. M. Parshley (New York: Vintage Books, 1989): 729–30. For a critique of the rejection of beauty in both feminism and modernism, see Wendy Steiner, *Venus in Exile: The Rejection of Beauty in Twentieth-century Art* (New York: The Free Press, 2001). For beauty of persons and the values of feminism, see Peg Zeglin Brand (ed.), *Beauty Matters* (Bloomington: Indiana University Press, 2000); Diana Tietjens Meyers, *Gender in the Mirror: Cultural Imagery and Women's Agency* (New York: Oxford University Press, 2002).

13 Kant, "Conjectural Beginning of Human History" [1786], trans. Emil L.

Fackenheim, in *Kant on History*, ed. Lewis White Beck (Indianapolis: Hackett, 1963): 57.

14 Kant, *Critique of Judgment* [1790], trans. Werner Pluhar (Indianapolis: Hackett, 1987) §59. See Ted Cohen, "Why Beauty is a Symbol of Morality" in Ted Cohen and Paul Guyer (eds), *Essays in Kant's Aesthetics* (Chicago: University of Chicago Press, 1982): 221–36; for feminist analyses of this claim, see Jane Kneller, "The Aesthetic Dimension of Kantian Autonomy;" Marcia Moen, "Feminist Themes in Unlikely Places: Re-reading Kant's *Critique of Judgment*;" Kim Hall, "*Sensus Communis* and Violence: A Feminist Reading of Kant's *Critique of Judgment*;" all in Robin May Schott (ed.), *Feminist Interpretations of Immanual Kant* (University Park, PA: Pennsylvania State University Press, 1997): 173–89, 213–55, 257–72.

15 Kant, *Grounding for the Metaphysics of Morals* [1785] trans. James W. Ellington (Indianapolis: Hackett, 1993).

16 This point is developed in Chapter 4. See also Chapter 2 of Carolyn Korsmeyer, *Making Sense of Taste: Food and Philosophy* (Ithaca, NY: Cornell University Press, 1999). Also Carolyn Korsmeyer, "Perceptions, Pleasures, Arts: Considering Aesthetics" in Janet Kourany (ed.), *Philosophy in a Feminist Voice* (Princeton, NJ: Princeton University Press, 1998): 145–72. Some of the ideas of the present chapter were first developed in this essay.

17 Kant, *Critique of Judgment*: 53. For a history of this term, see Jerome Stolnitz, "On the Origin of 'Aesthetic Disinterestedness'," *Journal of Aesthetics and Art Criticism*, Winter, 1961: 131–43.

18 In Kant's idiosyncratic terminology, the judgment of taste is based on the form of purposiveness of an object without any concept of purpose. *Critique of Judgment*, §11.

19 David Bindman, *Ape to Apollo: Aesthetics and the Idea of Race in the 18th Century* (Ithaca, NY: Cornell University Press, 2002); Lind, "Indians, Savages, Peasants, and Women,"; Adrian M. S. Piper, "Xenophobia and Kantian Rationalism" in Schott, *Feminist Interpretations*, 21–73; Hall, "*Sensus Communis* and Violence."

20 Hutcheson, *An Inquiry*: 77.

21 Kant, *Observations on the Feeling of the Beautiful and Sublime* [1763], trans. John T. Goldthwaite (Berkeley and Los Angeles: University of California Press, 1960): 78–9. See Mary Bittner Wiseman, "Beautiful Exiles" and Jane Kneller, "Discipline and Silence: Women and Imagination in Kant's Theory of Taste," both in Hilde Hein and Carolyn Korsmeyer (eds), *Aesthetics in Feminist Perspective* (Bloomington: Indiana University Press, 1993): 169–78 and 179–92; Paul Mattick, Jr., "Beautiful and Sublime: 'Gender Totemism' in the Constitution of Art" in Brand and Korsmeyer, *Feminism and Tradition in Aesthetics*: 27–48; Cornelia Klinger, "The Concepts of the Sublime and the Beautiful in Kant and Lyotard" in Schott, *Feminist Interpretations*: 191–211. Some scholars reject the exclusion of women from sublimity and argue for a "feminine sublime." See Chapters 3 and 6.

22 "Effeminacy . . . is a misogynist construct whereby the sexuality of men is policed through the accusation of sliding back from the purposeful reasonableness that is supposed to constitute manliness, into the laxity and weakness

conventionally attributed to women." Alan Sinfield, *Cultural Politics—Queer Reading* (Philadelphia: University of Pennsylvania Press, 1994): 32. For a more historical study of this term, see Sinfield's *The Wilde Century: Effeminacy, Oscar Wilde, and the Queer Moment* (New York: Columbia University Press, 1994): Chapter 2.

23 Paul Mattick, Jr. (ed.), *Eighteenth-century Aesthetics and the Reconstruction of Art* (Cambridge: Cambridge University Press, 1993); Terry Eagleton, *The Ideology of the Aesthetic* (Cambridge, MA: Blackwell, 1990); Luc Ferry, *Homo Aestheticus: The Invention of Taste in the Democratic Age*, trans. Robert de Loaiza (Chicago: University of Chicago Press, 1993); Pierre Bourdieu, *Distinction: A Social Critique of the Judgment of Taste*, trans. Richard Nice (London: Routledge, 1994 [1979]).

24 Arthur Schopenhauer, *The World as Will and Representation* [third edition 1859], vol. I, trans. E. F. J. Payne (New York: Dover, 1969): 209.

25 Schopenhauer, "The Weakness of Woman" in Rosemary Agonito (ed.), *History of Ideas on Women* (New York: G. P. Putnam's Sons, 1977): 199.

26 Jerome Stolnitz, from *Aesthetics and the Philosophy of Art Criticism* (1960). This quote taken from portions reprinted in Philip Alperson (ed.), *The Philosophy of the Visual Arts* (New York: Oxford University Press, 1992): 10.

27 Rebecca Schneider, *The Explicit Body in Performance* (London: Routledge, 1997): 14.

28 Stolnitz, *Aesthetics*: 12.

29 Susan McClary, *Feminine Endings: Music, Gender, and Sexuality* (Minneapolis: University of Minnesota Press, 1991): 4.

30 "The subject matter of art and the concept of a philosophical aesthetics are closely bound to the same metaphysical, universalist, and esssentialist assumptions of the Western philosophical tradition that appear highly suspect from a feminist perspective in relation to other fields of male-dominated theory formation." Cornelia Klinger, "Aesthetics" in Alison M. Jaggar and Iris Marion Young (eds), *A Companion to Feminist Philosophy* (Malden, MA: Blackwell, 1998): 344.

31 Lynda Nead, *The Female Nude: Art, Obscenity and Sexuality* (London: Routledge, 1992), Part I. Nead critiques Kenneth Clark's influential analysis of the nude in *The Nude: A Study of Ideal Art* (London: John Murray, 1956). For an analysis of the display of the influential nudes of twentieth-century art, see Carol Duncan, "The MoMA's Hot Mamas" in Carolyn Korsmeyer (ed.), *Aesthetics: The Big Questions* (Malden, MA: Blackwell, 1998): 115–27.

32 Linda Nochlin examines Gérôme's slave markets and other paintings in which sexual power is a theme, in "Women, Art, and Power" in *Women, Art, and Power and Other Essays* (New York: Harper and Row, 1988): 1–36. See also the discussion of multiple "looks" in painting and literature in Rosemary Geisdorfer Feal and Carlos Feal, *Painting on the Page: Interartistic Approaches to Modern Hispanic Texts* (Albany: State University of New York Press, 1995): 202–5.

33 Theories of the gaze developed most extensively in feminist film theory. The galvanizing essay for this perspective is Laura Mulvey, "Visual Pleasure and Narrative Cinema," *Screen* 16: 3 (Autumn, 1975): 6–18. For this as well as refinements of her original views, see Mulvey's *Visual and Other Pleasures* (London: Macmillan, 1989). For selected feminist film theory, see Mary Ann Doane, *The*

Desire to Desire (Bloomington: Indiana University Press, 1987) and Femmes
Fatales: Feminism, Film Theory, Psychoanalysis (New York: Routledge, 1991); E. Ann
Kaplan (ed.), Psychoanalysis and Cinema (New York: Routledge, 1990); Constance
Penley (ed.), Feminism and Film Theory (New York: Routledge, 1988). For painting,
see Griselda Pollock, Vision and Difference: Femininity, Feminism and the Histories of Art
(London: Routledge, 1988).

34 Mulvey, "Visual Pleasure and Narrative Cinema."

35 Naomi Scheman, "Thinking about Quality in Women's Visual Art" in Engenderings: Constructions of Knowledge, Authority, and Privilege (New York: Routledge, 1993):
159.

36 See also John Berger, Ways of Seeing (New York: Penguin, 1972); James Elkins, The
Object Stares Back: On the Nature of Seeing (San Diego, CA: Harcourt Brace, 1996);
Nead, The Female Nude; Norman Bryson, Michael Ann Holly, and Keith Moxey
(eds), Visual Theory: Painting and Interpretation (Cambridge: Polity Press, 1991).

37 Kaja Silverman complicates theories of the gaze in Male Subjectivity at the Margins
(New York: Routledge, 1992). See also bell hooks, "The Oppositional Gaze" in
Black Looks (Boston: South End Press, 1992): 115–31. Cynthia Freeland, "Film
Theory" in A Companion to Feminist Philosophy (Malden, MA: Blackwell, 1998): Chap-
ter 35. Mary Devereaux, "Oppressive Texts, Resisting Readers, and the Gendered
Spectator" in Brand and Korsmeyer, Feminism and Tradition in Aesthetics: 121–41.

38 Situatedness or positionality is a component of much postmodern philosophy.
An influential feminist statement is Donna Haraway, "Situated Knowledges: The
Science Question in Feminism and the Privilege of Partial Perspective," Feminist
Studies 14:3 (Fall, 1988) 575–96.

39 Some feminists argue that the distance of vision perpetuates an ideal of mastery.
For various perspectives on vision, see Barb Bolt, "Shedding Light for the
Matter," Hypatia 15:2 (Spring, 2000): 202–16; Luce Irigaray, An Ethics of Sexual Dif-
ference, trans. Carolyn Burke and Gillian C. Gill (London: Athlone Press, 1993);
Martin Jay, Downcast Eyes: The Denigration of Vision in Twentieth-century French Thought
(Berkeley and Los Angeles: University of California Press, 1993); Evelyn Fox
Keller and Christine R. Grontkowski, "The Mind's Eye" in Sandra Harding and
Merrill B. Hintikka (eds), Discovering Reality: Feminist Perspectives on Epistemology, Meta-
physics, Methodology, and Philosophy of Science (Boston: D. Reidel, 1983): 207–24;
Cathryn Vasseleu, Textures of Light: Vision and Touch in Irigaray, Levinas, and Merleau-Ponty
(London: Routledge, 1998).

3 AMATEURS AND PROFESSIONALS

1 Virginia Woolf, A Room of One's Own [1929] (New York: Harcourt, Brace, Jovanovich, 1981).

2 For gender and music in traditional cultures across the globe see Marcia Herndon and Susanne Ziegler (eds), Music, Gender, and Culture (Wilhelmshaven: Florian
Noetzel Verlag, 1990).

3 Jane Bowers and Judith Tick (eds), Women Making Music: The Western Art Tradition,

1150–1950 (Urbana: University of Illinois Press, 1986) contains essays studying women's musical contributions during 800 years of European history. One of the most prolific female composers of the Middle Ages was Hildegard of Bingen (1098–1179) a Benedictine nun and abbess, who also left many drawings of her mystical visions. See *Illuminations of Hildegard of Bingen* (Santa Fe: Bear and Company, 1985).

4 Marcia J. Citron, *Gender and the Musical Canon* (Cambridge: Cambridge University Press, 1993): Chapter 1.

5 Sally Banes, *Dancing Women: Female Bodies on Stage* (London: Routledge, 1998): 64. Women on stage were professionals, and Banes' study of dance emphasizes that women dancers have always exercised agency in their careers and stage presence, despite the social roles they occupied and the sexual ideologies of the dance plots they performed.

6 Carol Neuls-Bates (ed.), *Women in Music: An Anthology of Source Readings from the Middle Ages to the Present* (New York: Harper and Row, 1982): 143.

7 Gustave Kerker from the *Musical Standard* (1904), in ibid.: 202–3.

8 Ethel Smyth, from "Female Pipings in Eden" in ibid.: 285. Smyth assesses women and music as Virginia Woolf surveys women and literature in *A Room of One's Own*. Woolf and Smyth were contemporaries and friends.

9 *The New Grove Dictionary of Music and Musicians*, second edition, ed. Stanley Sadie (London: Macmillan, 2001), vol. 26: 577.

10 Bowers and Tick, "Introduction," *Women Making Music*: 3.

11 Citron, *Gender and the Musical Canon*: 80.

12 Neuls-Bates, *Women in Music*: 223.

13 Jean Jacques Rousseau, *Lettre à M. d'Alembert*, mentioned in Citron, *Gender and the Musical Canon*: 262.

14 Arthur Schopenhauer, "Of Women" in Rosemary Agonito (ed.), *History of Ideas on Women* (New York: G. P. Putnam's Sons, 1977): 200–1.

15 George Upton (1880) in Neuls-Bates, *Women in Music*: 207.

16 Susan McClary, *Feminine Endings: Music, Gender, and Sexuality* (Minneapolis: University of Minnesota Press, 1991): 17.

17 Citron, *Gender and the Musical Canon*: Chapter 4.

18 McClary, *Feminine Endings*: 7–8.

19 Sue Campbell, *Interpreting the Personal: Expression and the Formation of Feelings* (Ithaca, NY: Cornell University Press, 1997): 135.

20 Michelle LeDoeuff observes how women in philosophy have also been perpetual amateurs: *The Philosophical Imaginary*, trans. Colin Gordon (London: Athlone Press, 1989): 105 ff.

21 Dorothy Mermin, *Godiva's Ride: Women of Letters in England, 1830–1880* (Bloomington, Indiana University Press, 1993): 13–16.

22 Martha Woodmansee, *The Author, Art, and the Market: Rereading the History of Aesthetics* (New York: Columbia University Press, 1994). Woodmansee's study is especially illuminating regarding the market for literature in Germany and England.

23 Sue Campbell defends sentimentality in *Interpreting the Personal*: 172–80.

24 Mermin, *Godiva's Ride*: 43.

25 Maria V. Coldwell, "*Jougleresses* and *Trobairitz*: Secular Musicians in Medieval France" in Bowers and Tick, *Women Making Music*: 47.

26 Mermin, *Godiva's Ride*: 53.

27 Woolf, *A Room of One's Own*: 77.

28 Woodmansee, *The Author, Art, and the Market*: Chapter 2. For another analysis of the genesis of authorship, see Michel Foucault, "What is an Author?" in Paul Rabinow (ed.), *The Foucault Reader* (New York: Pantheon Books, 1984).

29 Jane Tompkins analyzes the shifting assessment of popularity vs quality in the American literary market in *Sensational Designs: The Cultural Work of American Fiction 1790–1860* (New York: Oxford University Press, 1985).

30 Woodmansee, *The Author, Art, and the Market*: Chapter 1.

31 Linda Nochlin, "Why Have there Been No Great Women Artists?" in *Women, Art and Power and Other Essays* (New York: Harper and Row, 1988): 145–78. This essay, first published in 1971, is credited with launching feminist art history.

32 Lynda Nead, *The Female Nude: Art, Obscenity and Sexuality* (London: Routledge, 1992): 47.

33 Eunice Lipton, *Alias Olympia: A Woman's Search for Manet's Notorious Model and Her Own Desire* (New York: Charles Scribner's Sons, 1992).

34 Whitney Chadwick notes that after Kauffmann and Moser, no women were admitted to the Royal Academy until 1922: *Women, Art, and Society* (London: Thames and Hudson, 1990): 7. On amateur and professional status, see also Chadwick, Chapter 5; and Germaine Greer, *The Obstacle Race: The Fortunes of Women Painters and their Work* (New York: Farrar, Strauss, Giroux, 1979): Chapter 14.

35 Chadwick, *Women, Art, and Society*: 64–8. See also Susan L. Feagin, "Feminist Art History and de facto Significance" in Peggy Zeglin Brand and Carolyn Korsmeyer (eds), *Feminism and Tradition in Aesthetics* (University Park, PA, Pennsylvania State University Press, 1995): 305–25.

36 Linda Nochlin points out how frequently women painters of the past were the daughters of painters who personally taught them: "Why Have There Been No Great Women Artists."

37 John Rubens Smith, *Juvenile Drawing Book No. 1* (New York, 1822): preface.

38 Carolyn Korsmeyer, "Instruments of the Eye: Shortcuts to Perspective," *Journal of Aesthetics and Art Criticism* 47:2 (Spring, 1989) 139–46.

39 Simeon DeWitt, *The Elements of Perspective* (Albany: Southwick, 1813): xxii.

40 E.g. Maria Turner, *The Young Ladies' Assistant in Drawing and Painting* (Cincinnati: Corey and Fairbank, 1833).

41 Anne Higgonet, *Berthe Morisot* (New York: Harper and Row, 1990).

42 Ibid.: 29.

43 See for example Barbara Claire Freeman, *The Feminine Sublime: Gender and Excess in Women's Fiction* (Berkeley and Los Angeles: University of California Press, 1995); Christine Battersby offers a critique and revision of Kant along with her argument for a sublime developed for a female subject in "Stages on Kant's Way: Aesthetics, Morality, and the Gendered Sublime" in Brand and Korsmeyer,

Feminism and Tradition in Aesthetics: 88–114; Patricia Yaeger, "Toward a Female Sublime" in Linda Kauffman (ed.), Gender and Theory (Oxford: Basil Blackwell, 1989); Susan Howe, My Emily Dickinson (Berkeley, CA: North Atlantic Books, 1985).

44 See Chapter 6 for more about the concept of the sublime.

45 Mary Garrard, Artemisia Gentileschi: The Image of the Female Hero in Italian Baroque Art (Princeton, NJ: Princeton University Press, 1989).

46 On the role of women artists in modernism, see Griselda Pollock, "Inscriptions in the Feminine" in M. Catherine de Zegher (ed.), Inside the Visible: An Elliptical Traverse of 20th-century Art in, of, and from the Feminine (Cambridge, MA: MIT Press, 1996): 67–87.

Not all artists have appreciated the attention directed to them: painter Georgia O'Keeffe was discomforted by the interpretation of her sensuous flower paintings in terms of female sexual imagery, whether by her contemporaries or by her feminist interpreters. San MacColl, "A Woman on Paper" in Hilde Hein and Carolyn Korsmeyer (eds), Aesthetics in Feminist Perspective (Bloomington: Indiana University Press, 1993): 150–66.

47 As was noted at the beginning of this study, these speculations are the subject of controversy among feminist scholars. See Mary Devereaux, "Feminist Aesthetics" in Jerrold Levinson (ed.), The Oxford Handbook of Aesthetics (New York: Oxford University Press, 2003): 647–66 and Introduction, note 3.

4 DEEP GENDER

1 Many of the ideas of this chapter are explored in more detail in Carolyn Korsmeyer, Making Sense of Taste: Food and Philosophy (Ithaca, NY: Cornell University Press, 1999). See also David Howes (ed.), The Varieties of Sensory Experience (Toronto, University of Toronto Press, 1991); Constance Classen, Worlds of Sense: Exploring the Senses in History and across Cultures (London: Routledge, 1993).

2 For feminist analysis of the primacy of vision, see Chapter 2, note 39.

3 Geoffrey Miller, The Mating Mind: How Sexual Choice Shaped the Evolution of Human Nature (New York: Doubleday, 2000); Nancy Etcoff, Survival of the Prettiest: The Science of Beauty (New York: Doubleday, 1999).

4 George Santayana, The Sense of Beauty: Being the Outline of Aesthetic Theory [1896] (New York: Dover, 1955): 24.

5 The scene of Socrates' death is recounted in Plato's Phaedo. Earlier in the narrative Socrates had dismissed his wife Xantippe, for her tears and lamentation interfered with his contemplation of immortality, a subject of conversation with his male friends until he drank the cup of hemlock.

6 Claude Lévi-Strauss, The Raw and the Cooked, trans. John and Doreen Weightman (New York: Harper and Row, 1969); Jack Goody, Cooking, Cuisine, and Class (Cambridge: Cambridge University Press, 1982).

7 One contemporary analyst refers to the eighteenth century as a "century of taste." George Dickie, The Century of Taste: The Philosophical Odyssey of Taste in the Eighteenth Century (New York: Oxford University Press, 1996).

8 Henry Home, Lord Kames, *Elements of Criticism* [1762], vol. I (Hildesheim, NY: Georg Olms Verlag, 1970): 6–7.

9 Immanuel Kant, *Critique of Judgment* [1790], trans. Werner S. Pluhar (Indianapolis: Hackett, 1987): 47–55.

10 Immanuel Kant, *Anthropology from a Pragmatic Point of View* [1798], trans. Victor Lyle Dowdell (Carbondale: Southern Illinois University Press, 1978): 41.

11 Frank Sibley, "Tastes, Smells, and Aesthetics" in John Benson, Betty Redfern, and Jeremy Roxbee-Cox (eds), *Approach to Aesthetics: Collected Papers on Philosophical Aesthetics* (Oxford: Clarendon Press, 2001): 249.

12 Actually, color-blindness is a sex-linked characteristic that requires both parents to carry a gene in order for a female offspring to be color-blind; genes from only one parent may cause the condition in a male child.

13 For a fuller argument for this point see Chapter 4 of Korsmeyer, *Making Sense of Taste*.

14 Jean-François Revel, *Culture and Cuisine: A Journey through the History of Food*, trans. Helen R. Lane (New York: Doubleday, 1982).

15 Mary Douglas, "Food as an Art Form" in *In the Active Voice* (London: Routledge and Kegan Paul, 1982): 107.

16 Elizabeth Telfer, *Food for Thought: Philosophy and Food* (London: Routledge, 1996): 57.

17 Rozsika Parker and Griselda Pollock, *Old Mistresses, Women, Art, and Ideology* (New York: Pantheon Books, 1981), especially Chapter 2.

18 Mignon Nixon, "The Gnaw and the Lick: Orality in Recent Feminist Art" in Helena Reckitt (ed.), *Art and Feminism* (London: Phaidon Press, 2001): 275–6. Laura Trippi, "Untitled Artists' Projects by Janine Antoni, Ben Kinmont, Rirkrit Tiravanija" in Ron Scapp and Brian Seitz (eds), *Eating Culture* (Albany: State University of New York Press, 1998): 132–60.

5 WHAT IS ART?

1 *New York Times*, "Is it Art? Is it Good? And Who Says So?" "Arts and Leisure," October 12, 1997: 36.

2 Helena Reckitt (ed.) *Art and Feminism* (London: Phaidon Press, 2001): 82. This book presents four decades of feminist art from the 1960s to the end of the twentieth century.

3 Cynthia Freeland, *But is it Art? An Introduction to Art Theory* (New York: Oxford University Press, 2001).

4 Ibid., Chapter 5.

5 Rozsika Parker and Griselda Pollock (eds), *Framing Feminisms: Art and the Women's Movement 1970–1985* (London: Pandora, 1987). The editors' introductory essay details the struggles, some of them legal, of the feminist art movement in Britain. See also Lucy R. Lippard, *From the Center: Essays on Women's Art* (New York: E. P. Dutton, 1976): 28–37.

6 For example, the Los Angeles anti-rape performance project of Suzanne Lacy and Leslie Labowitz, *In Mourning and in Rage* (1977). On art and social activism, see

Nina Felshin, But Is It Art? The Spirit of Art as Activism (Seattle: Bay Press, 1995); Arlene Raven (ed.), Art in the Public Interest (Ann Arbor, MI: UMI Research Press, 1989); Lucy R. Lippard, Get the Message? A Decade of Art for Social Change (New York: E. P. Dutton, 1984).

7 Adrian M. S. Piper, "Monologues from 'Four Intruders Plus Alarm Systems' and 'Safe'"; Peggy Zeglin Brand, "Revising the Aesthetic–Nonaesthetic Distinction: The Aesthetic Value of Activist Art," both in Peggy Zeglin Brand and Carolyn Korsmeyer (eds), Feminism and Tradition in Aesthetics (University Park, PA: Pennsylvania State University Press, 1995): 235–44, 245–72.

8 Noël Carroll, A Philosophy of Mass Art (Oxford: Clarendon Press, 1998); Colin McCabe (ed.), High Theory/Low Culture: Analysing Popular Television and Film (Manchester, UK: Manchester University Press, 1986); Tania Modleski, Loving with a Vengeance: Mass-produced Fantasies for Women (New York: Metheun, 1982).

9 Theodore Gracyk, Rhythm and Noise: An Aesthetics of Rock (Durham, NC: Duke University Press, 1996); I Wanna Be Me: Rock Music and the Politics of Identity (Philadelphia, PA: Temple University Press, 2001).

10 For example, Maggie O'Neill (ed.), Adorno, Culture, and Feminism (London: Sage Press, 1999).

11 Griselda Pollock, Vision and Difference: Femininity, Feminism and the Histories of Art (London: Routledge, 1988).

12 The history of imitation is denser and more complicated than can be presented here. For a fuller discussion of development and change in the idea of mimesis, see Władysław Tatarkiewicz, The History of Aesthetics (3 vols) (The Hague: Mouton, 1970).

13 Sue Campbell defends expression theory in Interpreting the Personal: Expression and the Formation of Feelings (Ithaca, NY: Cornell University Press, 1997): 67–74.

14 Suzanne Langer, Feeling and Form: A Theory of Art (London: Routledge and Kegan Paul, 1953): 53.

15 Larry Shiner summarizes modernism in this way: "Although notoriously hard to define and date, the establishment of modernism is often identified with the period 1890–1930, which witnessed a profound stylistic disruption of repre sentational modes in painting (Picasso), traditional narrative techniques in the novel (Woolf), the standard tonal system in music (Schoenberg), classical balletic movements in the dance (Duncan), and traditional architectural forms (Le Corbusier)." The Invention of Art: A Cultural History (Chicago: University of Chicago Press, 2001): 246.

16 Clive Bell, Art (London: Chatto and Windus, 1914).

17 Eduard Hanslick, On the Musically Beautiful [8th edition, 1891], trans. Geoffrey Payzant (Indianapolis: Indiana University Press, 1986).

18 The so-called form–content distinction is difficult to articulate precisely. Bell eliminated representation from form; his colleague Roger Fry argued that how a subject is represented is a formal property (Transformations: Critical and Speculative Essays on Art [London: Chatto and Windus, 1926]). On feminist revisions of intrinsic vs extrinsic value, see Anita Silvers, "Has Her(oine's) Time Now Come?" in Brand and Korsmeyer, Feminism and Tradition: 279–304.

19 Two influential essays arguing these points are Morris Weitz, "The Role of Theory in Aesthetics" *Journal of Aesthetics and Art Criticism* 15 (1956) and William Kennick, "Does Traditional Aesthetics Rest on a Mistake?" *Mind* 67 (1958), both reprinted in John W. Bender and H. Gene Blocker (eds), *Contemporary Philosophy of Art: Readings in Analytic Aesthetics* (Englewood Cliffs, NJ: Prentice-Hall, 1993): 191–8 and 134–44.

20 For discussions from and about Dada, see Robert Motherwell, *The Dada Painters and Poets* (New York: Wittenborn, Schultz, 1951).

21 Related by Hans Richter, "In Memory of a Friend," *Art in America* (July/August, 1969), quoted in Ursula Meyer (ed.), *Conceptual Art* (New York: E. P. Dutton, 1972): ix.

22 Peggy Phelan, "Survey" in Reckitt, *Art and Feminism*: 19.

23 George Dickie, *Art and the Aesthetic: An Institutional Analysis* (Ithaca, NY: Cornell University Press, 1974): 34.

24 George Dickie, "The Institutional Theory of Art" in Noël Carroll (ed.), *Theories of Art Today* (Madison: University of Wisconsin Press, 2000): 98–101. For a feminist critique of current theories of art, see Peg Zeglin Brand, "Glaring Omissions in Traditional Theories of Art," also in Carroll, *Theories of Art Today*: 175–98. See also Stephen Davies, *Definitions of Art* (Ithaca, NY: Cornell University Press, 1991).

25 Phelan, "Survey": 25.

26 Richard Wollheim criticizes Dickie's separation of classification and evaluation in "The Institutional Theory of Art," *Art and Its Objects*, second edition (Cambridge: Cambridge University Press, 1980).

27 *New York Times*, "Is it Art?"

28 Danto coined the composite term "artworld" in his 1964 essay "The Artworld," *Journal of Philosophy* 61 (1964): 571–84. It has since been widely adopted.

29 The degree to which contemporary visual art comments on its own past has led Danto to assert that in a sense we have reached the "end of art." This controversial statement has received possibly more discussion than any other aspect of his theory, though I shall not deal with it in this study. See Arthur C. Danto, *The Philosophical Disenfranchisement of Art* (New York: Columbia University Press, 1986) and *After the End of Art: Contemporary Art and the Pale of History* (Princeton, NJ: Princeton University Press, 1997). For a sampling of critical discussion, see David Carrier (ed.), *Danto and his Critics: Art History, Historiography and After the End of Art* (Middletown, CT: Wesleyan University Press, 1998).

30 Arthur C. Danto, *The Transfiguration of the Commonplace: A Philosophy of Art* (Cambridge, MA: Harvard University Press, 1981): 208.

31 Arthur C. Danto, *Philosophizing Art: Selected Essays* (Berkeley and Los Angeles: University of California Press, 1999): 8.

32 Danto, *Transfiguration*: 135.

33 Mary Devereaux, "Feminist Aesthetics" in Jerrold Levinson (ed.), *Oxford Handbook of Aesthetics* (New York: Oxford University Press, 2003): 647–66.

34 Lucy R. Lippard, *The Pink Glass Swan: Selected Essays on Feminist Art* (New York: The New York Press, 1995): 172.

35 On "post" see Introduction, note 6.

36 Spero has called her work *la peinture féminine*, adapting the idea of *l'écriture féminine* from Hélène Cixous. See Elizabeth Ann Dobie, "Interweaving Feminist Frameworks" in Brand and Korsmeyer, *Feminism and Tradition*: 215–34; Judy Purdom, "Nancy Spero and Women in Performance" in Penny Florence and Nicola Foster (eds), *Differential Aesthetics: Art Practice, Philosophy, and Feminist Understandings* (Aldershot, UK: Ashgate, 2000): 161–74. Artists from many traditions have reinterpreted cultural imagery from a female perspective, including Shahzia Sikander, who re-employs figures from traditional Indian miniature painting, and Ghada Amer, who embroiders and paints over ancient Islamic texts.

37 Such quilts may be compared with the *arpilleras* made by women in Chile in memory of their disappeared family members. *Arpilleras* are wall-hangings or pillow covers. At first glance they are colorful and pleasant folk decorations. But on closer inspection one sees that the appliquéd scenes picture torture and execution. Marjorie Agosin, *Scraps of Life: Chilean Arpilleras*, trans. Cola Franzen (Trenton, NJ: Red Sea Press, 1987).

38 Susan Bordo, *Unbearable Weight: Feminism, Western Culture, and the Body* (Berkeley and Los Angeles: University of California Press, 1993).

39 Edward Lucie-Smith, in Judy Chicago and Edward Lucie-Smith (eds), *Women and Art: Contested Territory* (New York: Watson-Guptill, 1999): 63.

40 Lisa Bloom (ed.), *With Other Eyes: Looking at Race and Gender in Visual Culture* (Minneapolis: University of Minnesota Press, 1999).

41 Eleanor Heartney, "Beauty, Bodies, and Burquas," presentation to the American Society for Aesthetics, October 31, 2002.

42 Moira Roth (ed.), *The Amazing Decade: Women and Performance Art in America, 1970–1980* (Los Angeles: Astro Artz, 1983); Greil Marcus, *Lipstick Traces: A Secret History of the Twentieth Century* (Cambridge, MA: Harvard University Press, 1989).

43 Petra Kuppers, "Living Dialectics, *Aufhebung* and Performance Art" in Florence and Foster, *Differential Aesthetics*: 141–57.

44 Rebecca Schneider, "Binary Terror and the Body Made Explicit." Chapter 1 of *The Explicit Body in Performance* (London: Routledge, 1997).

45 Orlan, "Intervention" and Tanya Augsberg, "Orlan's Performative Transformations of Surgery" in Peggy Phelan and Jill Lane (eds), *The Ends of Performance* (New York: New York University Press, 1998): 315–27, 285–314; Peggy Zeglin Brand, "Disinterestedness and Political Art" in Carolyn Korsmeyer (ed.), *Aesthetics: The Big Questions* (Malden, MA: Blackwell, 1998): 155–71; and Brand, "The Virtual Body: Orlan and Morimura" in Annette W. Balkema and Henk Slager (eds), *Exploding Aesthetics*, L&B: *Series of Philosophy of Art and Art Theory* 16 (2001): 92–104.

46 Susan McClary, *Feminine Endings: Music, Gender, and Sexuality* (Minneapolis: University of Minnesota Press, 1991): 137–8.

47 *National Endowment for the Arts, et al., Petitioners v. Karen Finley et al.* (1998).

48 Marilyn Frye, *The Politics of Reality: Essays in Feminist Theory* (Trumansburg, NY: The

Crossing Press, 1983), especially the chapters "Sexism" (17–46) and "To See and Be Seen" (152–74).

49 Judith Butler, *Gender Trouble: Feminism and the Subversion of Identity* ((New York: Routledge, 1990) and *Bodies that Matter: On the Discursive Limits of "Sex"* (New York: Routledge, 1993).

50 Joan Rivière, "Womanliness as Masquerade," *The International Journal of Psychoanalysis* 10 (1929), reprinted in Victor Burgin, James Donald, and Cora Kaplan (eds), *Formations of Fantasy* (London: Methuen, 1986): 35–44.

51 See Danto, *Transfiguration*, Chapter 1.

52 Peggy Phelan, "The Ontology of Performance: Representation without Reproduction" in *Unmarked: The Politics of Performance* (London: Routledge, 1993): 146–66.

6 DIFFICULT PLEASURES

1 Cynthia Freeland, *But is it Art: An Introduction to Art Theory* (Oxford: Oxford University Press, 2001): Chapter 1, "Blood and Beauty."

2 Hal Foster (ed.) *The Anti-Aesthetic: Essays on Postmodern Culture* (Port Townsend, WA: Bay Press, 1983).

3 Arthur Danto, *The Body/Body Problem: Selected Essays* (Berkeley and Los Angeles: University of California Press, 1999): ix–x.

4 On varieties of dualism see Suzanne Cunningham, *What is a Mind?* (Indianapolis: Hackett, 2000): Chapter 1.

5 Exploration of the self has been a major project of feminist philosophers. See Diana Tietjens Meyers (ed.). *Feminists Rethink the Self* (Boulder, CO: Westview Press, 1997).

6 See Introduction, note 1.

7 E.g. Moira Gatens and Genevieve Lloyd, *Collective Imaginings: Spinoza Past and Present* (London: Routledge, 1999); Gatens, *Imaginary Bodies: Ethics, Power, and Corporeality* (New York: Routledge, 1996). See also Elizabeth Grosz' use of Deleuze and others in *Volatile Bodies: Towards a Corporeal Feminism* (Bloomington: Indiana University Press, 1994); Tamsin Lorraine, *Irigaray and Deleuze: Experiments in Visceral Philosophy* (Ithaca, NY: Cornell University Press, 1999); Janet Price and Margrit Shildrick (eds), *Feminist Theory and the Body* (Edinburgh: Edinburgh University Press, 1999). Christine Battersby revises Kant's legacy in *The Phenomenal Woman: Feminist Metaphysics and the Patterns of Identity* (New York: Routledge, 1998). Many feminists have adopted a variety of social constructionism, arguing that bodies as much as minds are products of culture and discourse. For an argument against this position that puts evolution and the physical body at the center of a feminist analysis, see Maxine Sheets-Johnstone, *The Roots of Power: Animate Form and Gendered Bodies* (Chicago: Open Court, 1994).

8 Moira Gatens, *Feminism and Philosophy: Perspectives on Difference and Equality* (Bloomington: Indiana University Press, 1991): 92.

9 Edmund Burke, *A Philosophical Enquiry into the Origin of our Ideas of the Sublime and Beautiful* [1757], ed. James T. Boulton (Notre Dame, IL: University of Notre Dame Press, 1968): 131.

10 Ibid.: 40.

11 Immanuel Kant, *Critique of Judgment* [1790], trans. Werner S. Pluhar (Indianapolis: Hackett, 1987): 112–13.

12 Battersby, *The Phenomenal Woman*: 79.

13 Barbara Claire Freeman, "Feminine Sublime" in Michael Kelly (ed.), *Encyclopedia of Aesthetics*, vol. 4 (New York: Oxford University Press, 1998): 332.

14 This phenomenon was first explored by Aristotle in the *Poetics*, where he wonders why the painful tragic emotions of pity and terror contribute to pleasurable experience. He concludes that we discharge these emotions in a "cathartic" imaginative act that is necessary to understand terrible truths. Pleasure in learning accounts for enjoyment of tragedy. For an extension of his approach to disgust, see Noël Carroll, *The Philosophy of Horror: or Paradoxes of the Heart* (New York: Routledge, 1990).

15 Jean-François Lyotard, "Presenting the Unpresentable: The Sublime," *Artforum*, 20: 8 (April, 1982): 64–9. See also *The Postmodern Condition*, trans. Geoff Bennington and Brian Masumi (Minneapolis: University of Minnsesota Press, 1984). Lyotard comments on Kant in *Lessons on the Analytic of the Sublime*, trans. Elizabeth Rottenberg (Stanford, CA: Stanford University Press, 1994).

16 Although sublimity is supposedly an experience that women rarely achieve, it requires a certain submission to power and a receptivity that complicates any simple equation of masculinity with active force. This argument is made by Timothy Gould, "Intensity and its Audiences: Toward a Feminist Perspective on the Kantian Sublime" in Peggy Zeglin Brand and Carolyn Korsmeyer (eds), *Feminism and Tradition in Aesthetics* (University Park, PA: Pennsylvania State University Press, 1995): 72–3. See also Jeremy Gilbert-Rolfe's claim that the sublime is "androgynous" in *Beauty and the Contemporary Sublime* (New York: Allworth Press, 1999): xvii, 47 and passim.

17 Many scientific treatises of the modern period assigned nature a feminine gender, mastered by the (male) scientist. Evelyn Fox Keller, *Reflections on Gender and Science* (New Haven, CT: Yale University Press, 1984); Paul Mattick, Jr., "Beautiful and Sublime: 'Gender Totemism' in the Constitution of Art" in Brand and Korsmeyer, *Feminism and Tradition*: 27–48.

18 Luce Irigaray, whose views are discussed later in this chapter, ruminates on Nietzsche in *Marine Lover of Friedrich Nietzsche*, trans. Gillian C. Gill (New York: Columbia University Press, 1991). See also Ellen Mortensen, "Woman's (Un)Truth: The Dionysian Woman," Chapter 4 of *The Feminine and Nihilism: Luce Irigaray with Nietzsche and Heidegger* (Oslo: Scandanavian University Press, 1994).

19 This myth is the basis of Mary Renault's popular novel, *The King Must Die*. Euripides featured the story in *The Bacchae*. For a reading of gender in this and other ancient plays, see Froma I. Zeitlin, "Playing the Other: Theater, Theatricality, and the Feminine in Greek Drama" in John J. Winkler and Froma I. Zeitlin (eds), *Nothing to Do with Dionysos? Athenian Drama in its Social Context* (Princeton, NJ: Princeton University Press, 1990): 63–96.

20 Friedrich Nietzsche, *The Birth of Tragedy from the Spirit of Music* [1872], trans. Clifton P. Fadiman (New York: Dover, 1995): 59–60.

21 For Lacan and feminism, see Elizabeth Grosz, *Jacques Lacan: A Feminist Introduction* (London: Routledge, 1990) and Joan Copjec, *Imagine There's No Woman: Ethics and Sublimation* (Cambridge MA: MIT Press, 2002). See also Juliet Mitchell, *Psychoanalysis and Feminism* (New York: Pantheon Books, 1974); Terry Eagleton, *Literary Theory: An Introduction* (Oxford: Basil Blackwell, 1983); Toril Moi, *Sexual/Textual Politics: Feminist Literary Theory* (London: Methuen, 1985).

22 Jacques Derrida is another influential voice who assigns to the feminine the status of being outside discourse and representability. See Peggy Kamuf (ed.), *A Derrida Reader* (New York: Columbia University Press, 1991).

23 See Chapter 2, note 33. Also Sarah Kent and Jacqueline Morreau (eds), *Women's Images of Men* (London: Writers' and Readers' Publishing Cooperative Society, 1985).

24 For a discussion of the similarities and differences among Irigaray, Cixous, and Kristeva, the three "French feminist" thinkers most familiar to English-speaking audiences (who, as Kelly Oliver points out, are neither French nor feminist) see Kelly Oliver, *Reading Kristeva: Unraveling the Double-Bind* (Bloomington: Indiana University Press, 1993): Chapter 7; Elizabeth Grosz, *Sexual Subversions: Three French Feminists* (Sydney: Allen and Unwin, 1989).

25 Luce Irigaray, "Any Theory of the 'Subject' has always been Appropriated by the 'Masculine'" in *Speculum of the Other Woman* [1974], trans. Gillian C. Gill (Ithaca, NY: Cornell University Press, 1985): 133–46.

26 Luce Irigaray, *This Sex which is not One*, trans. Catherine Porter (Ithaca, NY: Cornell University Press, 1985): 159. Italics in original.

27 Elizabeth Grosz, "The Hetero and the Homo: The Sexual Ethics of Luce Irigaray" in Carolyn Burke, Naomi Schor, and Margaret Whitford (eds), *Engaging with Irigaray: Feminist Philosophy and Modern European Thought* (New York: Columbia University Press, 1994): 335–50.

28 Hilary Robinson, "The Morphology of the Mucous: Irigarayan Possibilities in the Material Practice of Art" in Penny Florence and Nicola Foster (eds), *Differential Aesthetics: Art Practice, Philosophy and Feminist Understandings* (Aldershot, UK: Ashgate, 2000): 261–77.

29 Luce Irigaray, *Je, Tu, Nous: Toward a Culture of Difference*, trans. Alison Martin (New York: Routledge, 1993): 53.

30 Naomi Schor, "This Essentialism which is not One" in Burke *et al.*, *Engaging with Irigaray*: 57–78.

31 Margaret Whitford pursues possible meanings of "female imaginary" in *Luce Irigaray: Philosophy in the Feminine* (London: Routledge, 1991): 89 ff.

32 Kant, *Critique of Judgment*: 215.

33 Whitford, *Luce Irigaray*: 52.

34 Joanna Frueh, *Erotic Faculties* (Berkeley and Los Angeles: University of California Press, 1996): 162. Most of the essays in this book are transcriptions or adaptations from Frueh's performances.

35 Kant, Critique of Judgment: 180.

36 William Ian Miller, The Anatomy of Disgust (Cambridge, MA: Harvard University Press, 1997): xii.

37 Ibid.

38 For a feminist treatment of bound feet and related physical beauties, see Eva Kit Wah Man, "Female Bodily Aesthetics, Politics and Feminine Ideals of Beauty in China" in Peg Zeglin Brand (ed.), Beauty Matters (Bloomington: Indiana University Press, 2001): 169–96.

39 For Chicago's Dinner Party, see Judy Chicago and Edward Lucie-Smith (eds), Women and Art: Contested Territory (New York: Watson-Guptill, 1999): 13, 44–5; for a variety of feminist treatments of the body, see Chapter 8, "Body as Battleground,": 126–47.

40 Desa Philippi, "Mona Hatoum: Some Any No Every Body" in M. Catherine de Zegher (ed.) Inside the Visible: An Elliptical Traverse of 20th-century Art in, of, and from the Feminine (Cambridge, MA: MIT Press, 1996): 363–69.

41 Helpful general studies of Kristeva are provided in Oliver, Reading Kristeva and John Lechte, Julia Kristeva (London: Routledge, 1990). Although Kristeva has influenced feminism, she herself rejects the label "feminist" because she views that politics as connoting women seeking male authority. See Oliver, Reading Kristeva: 2–3 and Chapter 7.

42 On language and sound in music, see the work of another French psychoanalytic theorist: Catherine Clément, Opera, or the Undoing of Women, trans. Betsy Wing (Minneapolis: University of Minnesota Press, 1988).

43 Elizabeth Gross, "The Body of Signification" in John Fletcher and Andrew Benjamin (eds), Abjection, Melancholia and Love: The Work of Julia Kristeva (London: Routledge, 1990): 87–8.

44 Kristeva connects the abject and the sublime in her treatment of aspects of the mother. See Oliver, Reading Kristeva: 61.

45 Sigmund Freud, Beyond the Pleasure Principle [1920], trans. James Strachey (New York: W. W. Norton, 1975).

46 Julia Kristeva, The Powers of Horror: An Essay on Abjection, trans. Leon S. Roudiez (New York: Columbia University Press, 1982): 1.

47 Barbara Creed, The Monstrous Feminine: Film, Feminism, Psychoanalysis (London: Routledge, 1993). For a cognitivist critique of psychoanalytic interpretations of horror, see Cynthia Freeland, "Woman and Bugs," Chapter 2 of The Naked and the Undead (New York: Westview, 1998).

48 We can see this in the monster of Dino de Laurentiis' Conan the Barbarian (1984), or the brain bug of Peter Verhoeven's science-fiction thriller Starship Troopers (1997). Both of these creatures actually display characteristics of both male and female genitalia that must be disabled before the monsters are subdued, though in both cases it is the female mouth that is harder to disable.

49 Although Cynthia Freeland argues that what she calls "realist horror" can be interpreted in ways that are critical of male violence. See "Realist Horror" in Carolyn Korsmeyer (ed.), Aesthetics: The Big Questions (Malden, MA: Blackwell, 1998): 283–93.

50 For an analysis of Sherman's work in terms of abjection, see Laura Mulvey, "Cosmetics and Abjection: Cindy Sherman 1977–87" in Fetishism and Curiosity (Bloomington: Indiana University Press, 1996): 65–76. Also see Rosalind Krauss, Bachelors: Essays on Nine Women "Bachelors" who Challenged Masculinist Aesthetics (Cambridge, MA: MIT Press, 1999): Chapter 5.

51 Such perspectives fan out to arts other than those discussed here. Elizabeth Grosz, for example, uses Irigaray and Kristeva to speculate about bodies, space, and architecture in Space, Time, and Perversion: Essays on the Politics of Bodies (New York: Routledge, 1995).

52 Adrienne Rich, "Diving into the Wreck" from Diving into the Wreck: Poems 1971–1972 (New York: W. W. Norton, 1973): 23.

BIBLIOGRAPHY

Agonito, Rosemary (ed.), *History of Ideas on Women*, New York: G. P. Putnam's Sons, 1977.

Agosin, Marjorie, *Scraps of Life: Chilean Arpilleras*, trans. Cola Franzen, Trenton, NJ: Red Sea Press, 1987.

Alberti, Leon Battista, *On Painting* [1435], trans. John R. Spencer, New Haven, CT: Yale University Press, 1966.

Allen, Prudence, RSM, *The Concept of Woman: The Aristotelian Revolution, 750 BC–AD 1250*, Montreal: Eden Press, 1985.

Anderson, Richard L., *Calliope's Sisters*, Upper Saddle River, NJ: Prentice-Hall, 1990.

Aristotle, *Poetics*, trans. D. W. Lucas, Oxford: Clarendon Press, 1968.

Augsberg, Tanya, "Orlan's Performative Transformations of Surgery" in Peggy Phelan and Jill Lane (eds), *The Ends of Performance*, New York: New York University Press, 1998: 285–314.

Banes, Sally, *Dancing Women: Female Bodies on Stage*, London: Routledge, 1998.

Bar On, Bat-Ami (ed.), *Engendering Origins: Critical Feminist Readings in Plato and Aristotle*, Albany: State University of New York Press, 1994.

— *Modern Engendering; Critical Feminist Readings in Modern Western Philosophy*, Albany: State University of New York Press, 1994.

Battersby, Christine, *Gender and Genius: Towards a Feminist Aesthetics*, Bloomington: Indiana University Press, 1989.

— "Stages on Kant's Way: Aesthetics, Morality, and the Gendered Sublime" in Peggy Zeglin Brand and Carolyn Korsmeyer (eds), *Feminism and Tradition in Aesthetics*, University Park, PA: Pennsylvania State University Press, 1995: 88–114.

— *The Phenomenal Woman: Feminist Metaphysics and the Patterns of Identity*, New York: Routledge, 1998.

Baumgarten, Alexander, *Reflections on Poetry* [1735], trans. Karl Aschenbrenner and William B. Holther, Berkeley and Los Angeles: University of California Press, 1954.

Beauvoir, Simone de, *The Second Sex* [1949], trans. H. M. Parshley, New York: Vintage Books, 1989.

Bell, Clive, *Art*, London: Chatto and Windus, 1914.

Berger, John, *Ways of Seeing*, New York: Penguin, 1972.

Bindman, David, *Ape to Apollo: Aesthetics and the Idea of Race in the 18th Century*, Ithaca, NY: Cornell University Press, 2002.

Bloom, Lisa (ed.), *With Other Eyes: Looking at Race and Gender in Visual Culture*, Minneapolis: University of Minnesota Press, 1999.

Bolt, Barb, "Shedding Light for the Matter," *Hypatia* 15:2 (Spring, 2000): 202–16.

Bordo, Susan, *Unbearable Weight: Feminism, Western Culture, and the Body*, Berkeley and Los Angeles: University of California Press, 1993.

— "The Feminist as Other" in Janet Kourany (ed.) *Philosophy in a Feminist Voice: Critiques and Reconstructions*, Princeton, NJ: Princeton University Press, 1998: 296–312.

Bourdieu, Pierre, *Distinction: A Social Critique of the Judgment of Taste* [1979], trans. Richard Nice, London: Routledge, 1994.

Bowers, Jane and Judith Tick (eds), *Women Making Music: The Western Art Tradition, 1150–1950*, Urbana: University of Illinois Press, 1986.

Brand, Peg Zeglin, "Revising the Aesthetic–Nonaesthetic Distinction: The Aesthetic Value of Activist Art" in Peggy Zeglin Brand and Carolyn Korsmeyer (eds), *Feminism and Tradition in Aesthetics*, University Park, PA: Pennsylvania State University Press, 1995: 245–72.

— "Disinterestedness and Political Art" in Carolyn Korsmeyer (ed.), *Aesthetics: The Big Questions*, Malden, MA: Blackwell, 1998: 155–71.

— *Beauty Matters*, Bloomington: Indiana University Press, 2000.

— "Glaring Omissions in Traditional Theories of Art" in Noël Carroll (ed.), *Theories of Art Today*, Madison: University of Wisconsin Press, 2000: 175–98.

— "The Virtual Body: Orlan and Morimura" in Annette W. Balkema and Henk Slager (eds), *Exploding Aesthetics*, L&B: Series of Philosophy of Art and Art Theory 16 (2001): 92–104.

Brand, Peggy Zeglin and Carolyn Korsmeyer (eds), *Feminism and Tradition in Aesthetics*, University Park, PA: Pennsylvania State University Press, 1995.

Brown, Wendy, "'Supposing Truth were a Woman . . . ': Plato's Subversion of Masculine Discourse" in Nancy Tuana (ed.), *Feminist Interpretations of Plato*, University Park, PA: Pennsylvania State University Press, 1994: 157–80.

Bryson, Norman, Michael Ann Holly and Keith Moxey (eds), *Visual Theory: Painting and Interpretation*, Cambridge: Polity Press, 1991.

Budd, Malcolm, *Music and the Emotions*, London: Routledge and Kegan Paul, 1985.

Burke, Edmund, *A Philosophical Enquiry into the Origin of our Ideas of the Sublime and Beautiful* [1757], ed. James T. Boulton, Notre Dame, IL: University of Notre Dame Press, 1968.

Butler, Judith, *Gender Trouble: Feminism and the Subversion of Identity*, New York: Routledge, 1990.

— *Bodies that Matter: On the Discursive Limits of "Sex,"* New York: Routledge, 1993.

Campbell, Sue, *Interpreting the Personal: Expression and the Formation of Feelings*, Ithaca, NY: Cornell University Press, 1997.

Carrier, David (ed.), *Danto and his Critics: Art History, Historiography and After the End of Art*, Middletown, CT: Wesleyan University Press, 1998.

Carroll, Noël, *The Philosophy of Horror: or Paradoxes of the Heart*, New York: Routledge, 1990.

176

— *A Philosophy of Mass Art*, Oxford: Clarendon Press, 1998.

— (ed.), *Theories of Art Today*, Madison: University of Wisconsin Press, 2000.

Chadwick, Whitney, *Women, Art, and Society*, London: Thames and Hudson, 1990.

Chicago, Judy and Edward Lucie-Smith (eds), *Women and Art: Contested Territory*, New York: Watson-Guptill, 1999.

Citron, Marcia J., *Gender and the Musical Canon*, Cambridge: Cambridge University Press, 1993.

Clark, Kenneth, *The Nude: A Study of Ideal Art*, London: John Murray, 1956.

Classen, Constance, *Worlds of Sense: Exploring the Senses in History and across Cultures*, London: Routledge, 1993.

Clément, Catherine, *Opera, or the Undoing of Women*, trans. Betsy Wing, Minneapolis: University of Minnesota Press, 1988.

Cohen, Ted, "Why Beauty is a Symbol of Morality" in Ted Cohen and Paul Guyer (eds), *Essays in Kant's Aesthetics*, Chicago: University of Chicago Press, 1982: 221–36.

Coldwell, Maria V., "*Jougleresses* and *Trobairitz*: Secular Musicians in Medieval France" in Jane Bowers and Judith Tick (eds), *Women Making Music*, Urbana: University of Illinois Press, 1986: 39–61.

Collingwood, R. G., *The Principles of Art*, Oxford: Clarendon Press, 1938.

Copjec, Joan, *Imagine There's No Woman: Ethics and Sublimation*, Cambridge MA: MIT Press.

Cousin, Victor, *Lectures on the True, the Beautiful, and the Good* [1818], trans. O. W. Wright, New York: D. Appleton and Co., 1870.

Creed, Barbara, *The Monstrous Feminine: Film, Feminism, Psychoanalysis*, London: Routledge, 1993.

Croce, Benedetto, *The Aesthetic as the Science of Expression and General Linguistic* [1902], trans. Douglas Ainslie, New York: Noonday Press, 1963.

Cunningham, Suzanne, *What is a Mind?* Indianapolis: Hackett, 2000.

Curran, Angela, "Feminism and the Narrative Structures of the Poetics" in Cynthia Freeland (ed.), *Feminist Interpretations of Aristotle*, University Park, PA: Pennsylvania State University Press, 1998: 289–326.

Danto, Arthur C., "The Artworld," *Journal of Philosophy* 61 (1964): 571–84.

— *The Transfiguration of the Commonplace: A Philosophy of Art*, Cambridge, MA: Harvard University Press, 1981.

— *The Philosophical Disenfranchisement of Art*, New York: Columbia University Press, 1986.

— *After the End of Art: Contemporary Art and the Pale of History*, Princeton, NJ: Princeton University Press, 1997.

— *The Body/Body Problem: Selected Essays*, Berkeley and Los Angeles: University of California Press, 1999.

— *Philosophizing Art: Selected Essays*, Berkeley and Los Angeles: University of California Press, 1999.

Davies, Stephen, *Definitions of Art*, Ithaca, NY: Cornell University Press, 1991.

— *Musical Meaning and Expression*, Ithaca, NY: Cornell University Press, 1994.

— "Non-Western Art and Art's Definition" in Noël Carroll (ed.), *Theories of Art Today*, Madison: University of Wisconsin Press, 2000: 199–216.

Devereaux, Mary, "Oppressive Texts, Resisting Readers, and the Gendered Spectator" in Peggy Zeglin Brand and Carolyn Korsmeyer (eds), *Feminism and Tradition in Aesthetics*, University Park, PA: Pennsylvania State University Press, 1995: 121–41.

— "Feminist Aesthetics" in Jerrold Levinson (ed.), *The Oxford Handbook of Aesthetics*, New York: Oxford University Press, 2003: 647–66.

DeWitt, Simeon, *The Elements of Perspective*, Albany: Southwick, 1813.

Dickie, George, *Art and the Aesthetic: An Institutional Analysis*, Ithaca, NY: Cornell University Press, 1974.

— *The Century of Taste: The Philosophical Odyssey of Taste in the Eighteenth Century*, New York: Oxford University Press, 1996.

— "The Institutional Theory of Art" in Noël Carroll (ed.), *Theories of Art Today*, Madison: University of Wisconsin Press, 2000: 93–108.

Doane, Mary Ann, *The Desire to Desire*, Bloomington: Indiana University Press, 1987.

— *Femmes Fatales: Feminism, Film Theory, Psychoanalysis*, New York: Routledge, 1991.

Dobie, Elizabeth Ann, "Interweaving Feminist Frameworks" in Peggy Zeglin Brand and Carolyn Korsmeyer (eds), *Feminism and Tradition in Aesthetics*, University Park, PA: Pennsylvania State University Press, 1995: 215–34.

Douglas, Mary, "Food as an Art Form" in *In the Active Voice*, London: Routledge and Kegan Paul, 1982: 105–13.

duBois, Page, "The Platonic Appropriation of Reproduction" in Nancy Tuana (ed.), *Feminist Interpretations of Plato*, University Park, PA: Pennsylvania State University Press, 1994: 139–56.

Duncan, Carol, "The MoMA's Hot Mamas" in Carolyn Korsmeyer (ed.), *Aesthetics: The Big Questions*, Malden, MA: Blackwell, 1998: 115–27.

Dutton, Denis, "But They don't Have our Concept of Art" in Noël Carroll (ed.), *Theories of Art Today*, Madison: University of Wisconsin Press, 2000: 217–38.

Eagleton, Terry, *Literary Theory: An Introduction*, Oxford: Basil Blackwell, 1983.

— *The Ideology of the Aesthetic*, Cambridge, MA: Blackwell, 1990.

Ecker, Gisela (ed.), *Feminist Aesthetics*, trans. Harriet Anderson, Boston: Beacon Press, 1986.

Elkins, James, *The Object Stares Back: On the Nature of Seeing*, San Diego, CA: Harcourt Brace, 1996.

Etcoff, Nancy, *Survival of the Prettiest: The Science of Beauty*, New York: Doubleday, 1999.

Fausto-Sterling, Anne, *Sexing the Body: Gender Politics and the Construction of Sexuality*, New York: Basic Books, 2000.

Feagin, Susan L., "Feminist Art History and de facto Significance" in Peggy Zeglin Brand and Carolyn Korsmeyer (eds), *Feminism and Tradition in Aesthetics*, University Park, PA: Pennsylvania State University Press, 1995: 305–25.

Feal, Rosemary Geisdorfer and Carlos Feal, *Painting on the Page: Interartistic Approaches to Modern Hispanic Texts*, Albany: State University of New York Press, 1995.

Felshin, Nina, *But is it Art? The Spirit of Art as Activism*, Seattle: Bay Press, 1995.

Felski, Rita, *Beyond Feminist Aesthetics: Feminist Literature and Social Change*, Cambridge, MA: Harvard University Press, 1989.

Ferry, Luc, *Homo Aestheticus: The Invention of Taste in the Democratic Age*, trans. Robert de Loaiza, Chicago: University of Chicago Press, 1993.

Florence, Penny and Nicola Foster (eds), *Differential Aesthetics: Art Practice, Philosophy, and Feminist Understandings*, Aldershot, UK: Ashgate, 2000.

Foster, Hal (ed.), *The Anti-Aesthetic: Essays on Postmodern Culture*, Port Townsend, WA: Bay Press, 1983.

Foucault, Michel, "What is an Author?" in Paul Rabinow (ed.), *The Foucault Reader*, New York: Pantheon Books, 1984.

Freeland, Cynthia, "Plot Imitates Action: Aesthetic Evaluation and Moral Realism in Aristotle's *Poetics*" in Amélie Rorty (ed.), *Essays on Aristotle's Poetics*, Princeton, NJ: Princeton University Press, 1992: 111–32.

— "Film Theory" in *A Companion to Feminist Philosophy*, Malden, MA: Blackwell, 1998: 353–60.

— *The Naked and the Undead*, New York: Westview, 1998.

— (ed.), *Feminist Interpretations of Aristotle*, University Park, PA: Pennsylvania State University Press, 1998.

— "Realist Horror" in Carolyn Korsmeyer (ed.), *Aesthetics: The Big Questions*, Malden, MA: Blackwell, 1998: 283–93.

— *But is it Art? An Introduction to Art Theory*, Oxford: Oxford University Press, 2001.

Freeman, Barbara Claire, *The Feminine Sublime: Gender and Excess in Women's Fiction*, Berkeley and Los Angeles: University of California Press, 1995.

— "Feminine Sublime" in Michael Kelly (ed.), *Encyclopedia of Aesthetics*, vol. 4, New York: Oxford University Press, 1998: 331–4.

Freud, Sigmund, *Beyond the Pleasure Principle* [1920], trans. James Strachey, New York: W. W. Norton, 1975.

Frueh, Joanna, *Erotic Faculties*, Berkeley and Los Angeles: University of California Press, 1996.

Fry, Roger, *Transformations: Critical and Speculative Essays on Art*, London: Chatto and Windus, 1926.

Frye, Marilyn, *The Politics of Reality: Essays in Feminist Theory*, Trumansburg, NY: The Crossing Press, 1983.

Garrard, Mary, *Artemisia Gentileschi: The Image of the Female Hero in Italian Baroque Art*, Princeton, NJ: Princeton University Press, 1989.

Gatens, Moira, *Feminism and Philosophy: Perspectives on Difference and Equality*, Bloomington: Indiana University Press, 1991.

— *Imaginary Bodies: Ethics, Power and Corporeality*, New York: Routledge, 1996.

Gatens, Moira and Genevieve Lloyd, *Collective Imaginings: Spinoza Past and Present*, London: Routledge, 1999.

Gilbert, Katharine Everett and Helmut Kuhn, *A History of Esthetics* [1939], New York: Dover Publications, 1972.

Gilbert-Rolfe, Jeremy, *Beauty and the Contemporary Sublime*, New York: Allworth Press, 1999.

Goody, Jack, *Cooking, Cuisine, and Class*, Cambridge: Cambridge University Press, 1982.

Gould, Timothy, "Intensity and its Audiences: Toward a Feminist Perspective on the Kantian Sublime" in Peggy Zeglin Brand and Carolyn Korsmeyer (eds), *Feminism* and Tradition in Aesthetics, University Park, PA: Pennsylvania State University Press, 1995: 66–87.

Gracyk, Theodore, I Wanna Be Me: Rock Music and the Politics of Identity, Philadelphia, PA: Temple University Press, 2001.

— Rhythm and Noise: An Aesthetics of Rock, Durham, NC: Duke University Press, 1996.

Greer, Germaine, The Obstacle Race: The Fortunes of Women Painters and their Work, New York: Farrar, Strauss, Giroux, 1979.

Gross, Elizabeth, "The Body of Signification" in John Fletcher and Andrew Benjamin (eds), Abjection, Melancholia, and Love: The Work of Julia Kristeva, London: Routledge, 1990: 80–103.

Grosz, Elizabeth, Sexual Subversions: Three French Feminists, Sydney: Allen and Unwin, 1989.

— Jacques Lacan: A Feminist Introduction, London: Routledge, 1990.

— "The Hetero and the Homo: The Sexual Ethics of Luce Irigaray" in Carolyn Burke, Naomi Schor, and Margaret Whitford (eds), Engaging with Irigaray: Feminist Philosophy and Modern European Thought, New York: Columbia University Press, 1994: 335–50.

— Volatile Bodies: Toward a Corporeal Feminism, Bloomington: Indiana University Press, 1994.

— Space, Time, and Perversion: Essays on the Politics of Bodies, New York: Routledge, 1995.

Hall, Kim, "Sensus Communis and Violence: A Feminist Reading of Kant's Critique of Judgment" in Robin May Schott (ed.), Feminist Interpretations of Immanuel Kant, University Park, PA: Pennsylvania State University Press, 1997: 257–72.

Hanslick, Eduard, On the Musically Beautiful, 8th edition [1891], trans. Geoffrey Payzant, Indianapolis: Indiana University Press, 1986.

Haraway, Donna, "Situated Knowledges: The Science Question in Feminism and the Privilege of Partial Perspective," Feminist Studies 14:3 (Fall, 1988): 575–96.

Hawthorne, Susan, "Diotima Speaks through the Body" in Bat-Ami Bar On (ed.), Engendering Origins: Critical Feminist Readings in Plato and Aristotle, Albany: State University of New York Press, 1994: 83–96.

Herndon, Marcia and Susanne Ziegler (eds), Music, Gender, and Culture, Wilhelmshaven: Florian Noetzel Verlag, 1990.

Higgonet, Anne, Berthe Morisot, New York: Harper and Row, 1990.

Hildegard of Bingen, Illuminations of Hildegard of Bingen, Santa Fe: Bear and Company, 1985.

Hogarth, William, The Analysis of Beauty [1753], ed. Ronald Paulson, New Haven, CT: Yale University Press, 1997.

Home, Henry, Lord Kames, Elements of Criticism [1762], Hildesheim, NY: Georg Olms Verlag, 1970.

hooks, bell, "The Oppositional Gaze," Black Looks, Boston: South End Press, 1992: 115–31.

Howe, Susan, My Emily Dickinson, Berkeley, CA: North Atlantic Books, 1985.

Howes, David (ed.), The Varieties of Sensory Experience, Toronto: University of Toronto Press, 1991.

Hume, David, "Of the Standard of Taste" [1757] in *Essays Moral, Political, and Literary*, ed. T. H. Green and T. H. Gross, two vols., London: Longmans, Green, 1898.

Hutcheson, Francis, *An Inquiry concerning Beauty, Order, Harmony, Design* [1725], ed. Peter Kivy, The Hague: Martinus Nijhoff, 1973.

Irigaray, Luce, *Speculum of the Other Woman* [1974], trans. Gillian C. Gill, Ithaca, NY: Cornell University Press, 1985.

— *This Sex which is not One*, trans. Catherine Porter, Ithaca, NY: Cornell University Press, 1985.

— *Marine Lover of Friedrich Nietzsche*, trans. Gillian C. Gill, New York: Columbia University Press, 1991.

— *An Ethics of Sexual Difference*, trans. Carolyn Burke and Gillian C. Gill, London: Athlone Press, 1993.

— *Je, Tu, Nous: Toward a Culture of Difference*, trans. Alison Martin, New York: Routledge, 1993.

— "Sorcerer Love: A Reading of Plato's *Symposium*, Diotima's Speech," trans. Eleanor H. Kuykendall, in Nancy Tuana (ed.), *Feminist Interpretations of Plato*, University Park, PA: Pennsylvania State University Press, 1994: 181–95.

Jacobson, Anne Jaap (ed.), *Feminist Interpretations of David Hume*, University Park, PA: Pennsylvania State University Press, 2000.

Janaway, Christopher, *Images of Excellence: Plato's Critique of the Arts*, Oxford: Clarendon Press, 1995.

Jay, Martin, *Downcast Eyes: The Denigration of Vision in Twentieth-century French Thought*, Berkeley and Los Angeles: University of California Press, 1993.

Kamuf, Peggy, (ed.), *A Derrida Reader*, New York: Columbia University Press, 1991.

Kandinsky, Wassily, *Concerning the Spiritual in Art, and Painting in Particular* [1912], trans. Michael Sadleir, amended Francis Golffing, New York: Wittenborn, Schultz, 1947.

Kant, Immanuel, *Observations on the Feeling of the Beautiful and Sublime* [1763], trans. John T. Goldthwaite, Berkeley and Los Angeles: University of California Press, 1960.

— *Grounding for the Metaphysics of Morals* [1785], trans. James W. Ellington, Indianapolis: Hackett, 1993.

— "Conjectural Beginning of Human History" [1786], trans. Emil L. Fackenheim, in *Kant on History*, ed. Lewis White Beck, Indianapolis: Hackett, 1963.

— *Critique of Judgment* [1790], trans. Werner S. Pluhar, Indianapolis: Hackett, 1987.

— *Anthropology from a Pragmatic Point of View* [1798], trans, Victor Lyle Dowdell, Carbondale: Southern Illinois University Press, 1978.

Kaplan, E. Ann (ed.), *Psychoanalysis and Cinema*, New York: Routledge, 1990.

Keller, Evelyn Fox, *Reflections on Gender and Science*, New Haven, CT: Yale University Press, 1984.

Keller, Evelyn Fox and Christine R. Grontkowski, "The Mind's Eye" in Sandra Harding and Merrill B. Hintikka (eds), *Discovering Reality: Feminist Perspectives on Epistemology, Metaphysics, Methodology, and Philosophy of Science*, Boston: D. Reidel, 1983: 207–24.

Kelly, Michael (ed.), *The Encyclopedia of Aesthetics*, four vols., New York: Oxford University Press, 1998.

Kennick, William, "Does Traditional Aesthetics Rest on a Mistake?" Mind 67 (1958), reprinted in John W. Bender and H. Gene Blocker (eds), Contemporary Philosophy of Art: Readings in Analytic Aesthetics, Englewood Cliffs, NJ: Prentice-Hall, 1993: 134–44.

Kent, Sarah and Jacqueline Morreau (eds), Women's Images of Men, London: Writers' and Readers' Publishing Cooperative Society, 1985.

Kivy, Peter, "Recent Scholarship and the British Tradition: A Logic of Taste—The First Fifty Years" in George Dickie and R. J. Sclafani (eds), Aesthetics: A Critical Anthology, New York: St Martin's Press, 1977: 626–42.

Klinger, Cornelia, "The Concepts of the Sublime and the Beautiful in Kant and Lyotard" in Robin May Schott (ed.), Feminist Interpretations of Immanuel Kant, University Park, PA: Pennsylvania State University Press, 1997: 191–211.

— "Aesthetics" in Alison M. Jaggar and Iris Marion Young (eds), A Companion to Feminist Philosophy, Malden, MA: Blackwell, 1998: 343–52.

Kneller, Jane, "Discipline and Silence: Women and Imagination in Kant's Theory of Taste" in Hilde Hein and Carolyn Korsmeyer (eds), Aesthetics in Feminist Perspective, Bloomington: Indiana University Press, 1993: 179–92.

— "The Aesthetic Dimension of Kantian Autonomy" in Robin May Schott (ed.), Feminist Interpretations of Immanuel Kant, University Park, PA: Pennsylvania State University Press, 1997: 173–89.

Korsmeyer, Carolyn (ed.), "Instruments of the Eye: Shortcuts to Perspective," Journal of Aesthetics and Art Criticism 47:2 (Spring, 1989): 139–46.

— "Gendered Concepts and Hume's Standard of Taste" in Peggy Zeglin Brand and Carolyn Korsmeyer (eds), Feminism and Tradition in Aesthetics, University Park, PA: Pennsylvania State University Press, 1995: 49–65.

— Aesthetics: The Big Questions, Malden, MA: Blackwell, 1998.

— "Perceptions, Pleasures, Arts: Considering Aesthetics" in Janet Kourany (ed.), Philosophy in a Feminist Voice: Critiques and Reconstructions, Princeton, NJ: Princeton University Press, 1998: 145–72.

— Making Sense of Taste: Food and Philosophy, Ithaca, NY: Cornell University Press, 1999.

Kourany, Janet (ed.), Philosophy in a Feminist Voice: Critiques and Reconstructions, Princeton, NJ: Princeton University Press, 1998.

Krauss, Rosalind, Bachelors: Essays on Nine Women "Bachelors" who Challenged Masculinist Aesthetics, Cambridge, MA: MIT Press, 1999.

Kris, Ernst and Otto Kurz, Legend, Myth, and Magic in the Image of the Artist [1934], trans. Alastair Laing, revised Lottie M. Newman, New Haven, CT: Yale University Press, 1979.

Kristeller, Paul Osker, "The Modern System of the Arts: A Study in the History of Aesthetics," Parts I and II, Journal of the History of Ideas 12 and 13 (1951, 1952) 496–527, 17–46. Also in Peter Kivy (ed.), Essays on the History of Aesthetics, Rochester, NY: University of Rochester Press, 1992: 3–64.

Kristeva, Julia, The Powers of Horror: An Essay on Abjection, trans. Leon S. Roudiez, New York: Columbia University Press, 1982.

Kuppers, Petra, "Living Dialectics, Aufhebung and Performance Art" in Penny Florence and Nicola Foster (eds), Differential Aesthetics: Art Practice, Philosophy, and Feminist Understandings, Aldershot, UK: Ashgate, 2000: 141–57.

Langer, Suzanne, *Feeling and Form: A Theory of Art*, London: Routledge and Kegan Paul, 1953.

Lechte, John, *Julia Kristeva*, London: Routledge, 1990.

LeDoeuff, Michelle, *The Philosophical Imaginary*, trans. Colin Gordon, London: Athlone Press, 1989.

Lévi-Strauss, Claude, *The Raw and the Cooked*, trans. John and Doreen Weightman, New York: Harper and Row, 1969.

Lind, Marcia, "Indians, Savages, Peasants and Women: Hume's Aesthetics" in Bat-Ami Bar On (ed.), *Modern Engendering: Critical Feminist Readings in Modern Western Philosophy*, Albany: State University of New York Press, 1994: 51–67.

Lippard, Lucy R., *From the Center: Essays on Women's Art*, New York: E. P. Dutton, 1976.

— *Get the Message? A Decade of Art for Social Change*, New York: E. P. Dutton, 1984.

— *The Pink Glass Swan: Selected Essays on Feminist Art*, New York: The New York Press, 1995.

Lipton, Eunice, *Alias Olympia: A Woman's Search for Manet's Notorious Model and Her Own Desire*, New York: Charles Scribner's Sons, 1992.

Lloyd, Genevieve, *The Man of Reason: "Male" and "Female" in Western Philosophy*, Minneapolis: University of Minnesota Press, 1984.

Locke, John, *Essay Concerning Human Understanding* [1690], Freeport, NY: Books for Libraries Press, 1969.

Lorraine, Tamsin, *Irigaray and Deleuze: Experiments in Visceral Philosophy*, Ithaca, NY: Cornell University Press, 1999.

Lyotard, Jean-François, "Presenting the Unpresentable: The Sublime," *Artforum* 20:8 (April, 1982): 64–9.

— *The Postmodern Condition*, trans. Geoff Bennington and Brian Masumi, Minneapolis: University of Minnesota Press, 1984.

— *Lessons on the Analytic of the Sublime*, trans. Elizabeth Rottenberg, Stanford, CA: Stanford University Press, 1994.

McCabe, Colin (ed.), *High Theory/Low Culture: Analyzing Popular Television and Film*, Manchester, UK: Manchester University Press, 1986.

McClary, Susan, *Feminine Endings: Music, Gender, and Sexuality*, Minneapolis: University of Minnesota Press, 1991.

MacColl, San, "A Woman on Paper" in Hilde Hein and Carolyn Korsmeyer (eds), *Aesthetics in Feminist Perspective*, Bloomington: Indiana University Press, 1993: 150–66.

Man, Eva Kit Wah, "Female Bodily Aesthetics, Politics and Feminine Ideals of Beauty in China" in Peg Zeglin Brand (ed.), *Beauty Matters*, Bloomington: Indiana University Press, 2000: 169–96.

Marcus, Greil, *Lipstick Traces: A Secret History of the Twentieth Century*, Cambridge, MA: Harvard University Press, 1989.

Mattick, Paul Jr. (ed.), *Eighteenth-century Aesthetics and the Reconstruction of Art*, Cambridge: Cambridge University Press, 1993.

— "Beautiful and Sublime: 'Gender Totemism' in the Constitution of Art" in Peggy Zeglin Brand and Carolyn Korsmeyer (eds), *Feminism and Tradition in Aesthetics*, University Park, PA: Pennsylvania State University Press, 1995: 27–48.

Mermin, Dorothy, *Godiva's Ride: Women of Letters in England, 1830–1880*, Bloomington: Indiana University Press, 1993.

Meyer, Ursula (ed.), *Conceptual Art*, New York: E. P. Dutton, 1972.

Meyers, Diana Tietjens, *Gender in the Mirror: Cultural Imagery and Women's Agency*, New York: Oxford University Press, 2002.

— (ed.), *Feminists Rethink the Self*, Boulder, CO: Westview Press, 1997.

Miller, Geoffrey, *The Mating Mind: How Sexual Choice Shaped the Evolution of Human Nature*, New York: Doubleday, 2000.

Miller, William, *The Anatomy of Disgust*, Cambridge, MA: Harvard University Press, 1997.

Mitchell, Juliet, *Psychoanalysis and Feminism*, New York: Pantheon Books, 1974.

Modleski, Tania, *Loving with a Vengeance: Mass-produced Fantasies for Women*, New York: Methuen, 1982.

Moen, Marcia, "Feminist Themes in Unlikely Places: Re-reading Kant's Critique of Judgment" in Robin May Schott (ed.), *Feminist Interpretations of Immanuel Kant*, University Park, PA: Pennsylvania State University Press, 1997: 213–55.

Moi, Toril, *Sexual/Textual Politics: Feminist Literary Theory*, London: Metheun, 1985.

Mortensen, Ellen, *The Feminine and Nihilism: Luce Irigaray with Nietzsche and Heidegger*, Oslo: Scandanavian University Press, 1994.

Motherwell, Robert, *The Dada Painters and Poets*, New York: Wittenborn, Schultz, 1951.

Mulvey, Laura, "Visual Pleasure and Narrative Cinema," *Screen* 16:3, Autumn, 1975: 6–18.

— *Visual and Other Pleasures*, London: Macmillan, 1989.

— *Fetishism and Curiosity*, Bloomington: Indiana University Press, 1996.

Nead, Lynda, *The Female Nude: Art, Obscenity and Sexuality*, London: Routledge, 1992.

Neuls-Bates, Carol (ed.), *Women in Music: An Anthology of Source Readings from the Middle Ages to the Present*, New York: Harper and Row, 1982.

New York Times, "Is it Art? Is it Good? And Who Says So?", "Arts and Leisure", October 12, 1997: 36.

Nietzsche, Friedrich, *The Birth of Tragedy from the Spirit of Music* [1872], trans. Clifton P. Fadiman, New York: Dover, 1995.

Nixon, Mignon, "The Gnaw and the Lick: Orality in Recent Feminist Art" in Helena Reckitt (ed.), *Art and Feminism*, London: Phaidon Press, 2001: 275–6.

Nochlin, Linda, "Why Have There Been No Great Women Artists?" *Women, Art, and Power and Other Essays*, New York: Harper and Row, 1988: 145–78.

— "Women, Art, and Power," *Women, Art, and Power and Other Essays*, New York: Harper and Row, 1988: 145–78.

Nye, Andrea, "Irigaray and Diotima at Plato's Symposium" in Nancy Tuana (ed.), *Feminist Interpretations of Plato*, University Park, PA: Pennsylvania State University Press, 1994: 197–215.

Oliver, Kelly, *Reading Kristeva: Unraveling the Double-Bind*, Bloomington: Indiana University Press, 1993.

O'Neill, Maggie (ed.), *Adorno, Culture, and Feminism*, London: Sage Press, 1999.

Orlan, "Intervention" in Peggy Phelan and Jill Lane (eds), *The Ends of Performance*, New York: New York University Press, 1998: 315–27.

Parker, Rozsika and Griselda Pollock, Old Mistresses: Women, Art and Ideology, New York: Pantheon Books, 1981.

— (eds), Framing Feminisms: Art and the Women's Movement 1970–1985, London: Pandora, 1987.

Penley, Constance (ed.), Feminism and Film Theory, New York: Routledge, 1988.

Phelan, Peggy, Unmarked: The Politics of Performance, London: Routledge, 1993.

— "Survey" in Helena Reckitt (ed.), Art and Feminism, London: Phaidon Press: 2001.

Phelan, Peggy, and Jill Lane (eds), The Ends of Performance, New York: New York University Press, 1998.

Philippi, Desa, "Mona Hatoum: Some Any No Every Body" in M. Catherine de Zegher (ed.), Inside the Visible: An Elliptical Traverse of 20th-century Art in, of, and from the Feminine, Cambridge, MA: MIT Press, 1996: 363–69.

Piper, Adrian M. S. "Monologues from 'Four Intruders Plus Alarm Systems' and 'Safe'" in Peggy Zeglin Brand and Carolyn Korsmeyer (eds), Feminism and Tradition in Aesthetics, University Park, PA: Pennsylvania State University Press, 1995: 235–44.

— "Xenophobia and Kantian Rationalism" in Robin May Schott (ed.), Feminist Interpretations of Immanuel Kant, University Park, PA: Pennsylvania State University Press, 1997: 21–73,

Plato, Phaedo, Republic, and Symposium in The Collected Dialogues of Plato, ed., Edith Hamilton and Huntington Cairns, New York: Pantheon, 1961.

Pliny the Elder, The Elder Pliny's Chapters on the History of Art, trans. K. Jex-Blake [1896], Chicago: Argonaut, 1968.

Pollock, Griselda, Vision and Difference: Femininity, Feminism and the Histories of Art, London: Routledge, 1988.

— "Inscriptions in the Feminine" in M. Catherine de Zegher (ed.), Inside the Visible: An Elliptical Traverse of 20th-century Art in, of, and from the Feminine, Cambridge, MA: MIT Press, 1996: 67–87.

Price, Janet and Margrit Shildrick (eds), Feminist Theory and the Body, Edinburgh, Edinburgh University Press, 1999.

Purdom, Judy, "Nancy Spero and Woman in Performance" in Penny Florence and Nicola Foster (eds), Differential Aesthetics: Art Practice, Philosophy, and Feminist Understandings, Aldershot, UK: Ashgate, 2000: 161–74.

Raven, Arlene (ed.), Art in the Public Interest, Ann Arbor, MI: UMI Research Press, 1989.

Reckitt, Helena (ed.), Art and Feminism, London: Phaidon Press, 2001.

Revel, Jean-François, Culture and Cuisine: A Journey through the History of Food, trans. Helen R. Lane, New York: Doubleday, 1982.

Rich, Adrienne, Diving into the Wreck: Poems 1971–1972, New York: W. W. Norton, 1973.

Rivière, Joan, "Womanliness as Masquerade," The International Journal of Psychoanalysis 10 (1929), reprinted in Victor Burgin, James Donald, and Cora Kaplan (eds), Formations of Fantasy, London: Methuen, 1986: 35–44.

Robinson, Hilary, "The Morphology of the Mucous: Irigarayan Possibilities in the Material Practice of Art" in Penny Florence and Nicola Foster (eds), Differential Aesthetics: Art Practice, Philosophy, and Feminist Understandings, Aldershot, UK: Ashgate, 2000: 261–77.

Roth, Moira (ed.), *The Amazing Decade: Women and Performance Art in America, 1970–1980*, Los Angeles: Astro Artz, 1983.

Sadie, Stanley (ed.), *The New Grove Dictionary of Music and Musicians*, second edition, London: Macmillan, 2001.

Santayana, George, *The Sense of Beauty: Being the Outline of Aesthetic Theory* [1896], New York: Dover, 1955.

Scheman, Naomi, "Thinking about Quality in Women's Visual Art," *Engenderings: Constructions of Knowledge, Authority, and Privilege*, New York: Routledge, 1993: 158–9.

Schiller, Friedrich, *On the Aesthetic Education of Man in a Series of Letters* [1793], trans. Elizabeth M. Wilkinson and L. A. Willoughby, Oxford: Clarendon Press, 1967.

Schneider, Rebecca, *The Explicit Body in Performance*, London: Routledge, 1997.

Schopenhauer, Arthur, *The World as Will and Representation*, [third edition, 1859], vol. I, trans. E. F. J. Payne, New York: Dover, 1969.

Schor, Naomi, "This Essentialism which is not One" in Carolyn Burke, Naomi Schor, and Margaret Whitford (eds), *Engaging with Irigaray: Feminist Philosophy and Modern European Thought*, New York: Columbia University Press, 1999: 57–78.

Schott, Robin May (ed.), *Feminist Interpretations of Immanuel Kant*, University Park, PA: Pennsylvania State University Press, 1997.

Sheets-Johnstone, Maxine, *The Roots of Power: Animate Form and Gendered Bodies*, Chicago: Open Court, 1994.

Shiner, Larry, *The Invention of Art: A Cultural History*, Chicago: University of Chicago Press, 2001.

Sibley, Frank, "Tastes, Smells, and Aesthetics" in John Benson, Betty Redfern, and Jeremy Roxbee-Cox (eds), *Approach to Aesthetics: Collected Papers on Philosophical Aesthetics*, Oxford: Clarendon Press, 2001: 207–55.

Silverman, Kaja, *Male Subjectivity at the Margins*, New York: Routledge, 1992.

Silvers, Anita, "Has Her(oine's) Time Now Come?" in Peggy Zeglin Brand and Carolyn Korsmeyer (eds), *Feminism and Tradition in Aesthetics*, University Park, PA: Pennsylvania State University Press, 1995: 279–304.

— "Feminism: An Overview" in Michael Kelly (ed.), *Encyclopedia of Aesthetics*, vol. 2, New York: Oxford University Press, 1998: 161–7.

Sinfield, Alan, *Cultural Politics—Queer Reading*, Philadelphia: University of Pennsylvania Press, 1994.

— *The Wilde Century: Effeminacy, Oscar Wilde, and the Queer Moment*, New York: Columbia University Press, 1994.

Sircello, Guy, *Mind and Art: An Essay on the Varieties of Expression*, Princeton, NJ: Princeton University Press, 1972.

Smith, John Rubens, *Juvenile Drawing Book No. 1*, New York, 1822.

Soussloff, Catherine M. *The Absolute Artist: The Historiography of a Concept*, Minneapolis: University of Minnesota Press, 1997.

Steiner, Wendy, *Venus in Exile: The Rejection of Beauty in Twentieth-century Art*, New York: The Free Press, 2001.

Stolnitz, Jerome, "On the Origin of 'Aesthetic Disinterestedness'," *Journal of Aesthetics and Art Criticism* (Winter, 1961): 131–43.

— *Aesthetics and the Philosophy of Art Criticism* [1960], excerpted in Philip Alperson (ed.), *The Philosophy of the Visual Arts*, New York: Oxford University Press, 1992: 7–14.

Tatarkiewicz, Władysław, *The History of Aesthetics* (3 vols), The Hague: Mouton, 1970.

— *A History of Six Ideas: An Essay in Aesthetics*, trans. Christopher Kasperek, Warsaw: Polish Scientific Publishers, 1980.

Telfer, Elizabeth, *Food for Thought: Philosophy and Food*, London: Routledge, 1996.

Tolstoy, Leo, *What is Art?* [1898], Trans. Aylmer Maude, New York: Liberal Arts Press, 1960.

Tompkins, Jane, *Sensational Designs: The Cultural Work of American Fiction 1790–1860*, New York: Oxford University Press, 1985.

Tormey, Alan, *The Concept of Expression*, Princeton, NJ: Princeton University Press, 1971.

Trippi, Laura, "Untitled Artists' Projects by Janine Antoni, Ben Kinmont, Rirkrit Tiravanija" in Ron Scapp and Brian Seitz (eds), *Eating Culture*, Albany: State University of New York Press, 1998: 132–60.

Tuana, Nancy (ed.), *Feminist Interpretations of Plato*, University Park, PA: Pennsylvania State University Press, 1994.

Turner, Maria, *The Young Ladies' Assistant in Drawing and Painting*, Cincinnati: Corey and Fairbank, 1833.

Vasseleu, Cathryn, *Textures of Light: Vision and Touch in Irigaray, Levinas, and Merleau-Ponty*, London: Routledge, 1998.

Weitz, Morris, "The Role of Theory in Aesthetics," *Journal of Aesthetics and Art Criticism* 15 (1956), reprinted in John W. Bender and H. Gene Blocker (eds), *Contemporary Philosophy of Art: Readings in Analytic Aesthetics*, Englewood Cliffs, NJ: Prentice-Hall, 1993: 191–8.

Whitford, Margaret, *Luce Irigaray: Philosophy in the Feminine*, London: Routledge, 1991.

Wiseman, Mary Bittner, "Beautiful Exiles" in Hilde Hein and Carolyn Korsmeyer (eds), *Aesthetics in Feminist Perspective*, Bloomington: Indiana University Press, 1993: 169–78.

Wollheim, Richard, *Art and Its Objects*, second edition, Cambridge: Cambridge University Press, 1980.

Woodmansee, Martha, *The Author, Art, and the Market: Rereading the History of Aesthetics*, New York: Columbia University Press, 1994.

Woolf, Virginia, *A Room of One's Own* [1929], New York: Harcourt, Brace, Jovanovich, 1981.

Yaeger, Patricia, "Toward a Female Sublime" in Linda Kauffman (ed.), *Gender and Theory*, Oxford: Basil Blackwell, 1989.

Zegher, M. Catherine de (ed.), *Inside the Visible: An Elliptical Traverse of 20th-century Art in, of, and from the Feminine*, Cambridge, MA: MIT Press, 1996.

Zeitlin, Froma I., "Playing the Other: Theater, Theatricality, and the Feminine in Greek Drama" in John J. Winkler and Froma I. Zeitlin (eds), *Nothing to Do with Dionysos? Athenian Drama in Its Social Context*, Princeton, NJ: Princeton University Press, 1990: 63–96.

INDEX

Note: page numbers in *italics* refer to illustrations

eBooks – at www.eBookstore.tandf.co.uk

A library at your fingertips!

eBooks are electronic versions of printed books. You can store them on your PC/laptop or browse them online.

They have advantages for anyone needing rapid access to a wide variety of published, copyright information.

eBooks can help your research by enabling you to bookmark chapters, annotate text and use instant searches to find specific words or phrases. Several eBook files would fit on even a small laptop or PDA.

NEW: Save money by eSubscribing: cheap, online access to any eBook for as long as you need it.

Annual subscription packages

We now offer special low-cost bulk subscriptions to packages of eBooks in certain subject areas. These are available to libraries or to individuals.

For more information please contact webmaster.ebooks@tandf.co.uk

We're continually developing the eBook concept, so keep up to date by visiting the website.

www.eBookstore.tandf.co.uk